NOW WHAT?

The Irreverent Memoirs of a Daydreamer, Counterspy, Prosecutor, Defense Attorney, and Adventurer

What reviewers have said about Steinhouse's other books:

.

[*Wily Fox*] is a moment in the annals of Holocaust history that bears constant retelling, and Steinhouse has brought it to remarkable life." **Abraham I. Foxman,** *National director of the Anti-Defamation League*

"The writing is compelling. The reader gains a sense of the desperation of the Jews, the compassion of Sugihara and Zwartendijk, the determination of the murderers and the indifference of so many. It is a chilling story made all the more real, all the more vivid by Steinhouse's account." **Dr Michael Berenbaum,** *noted Holocaust scholar and author and former Director of the United States Holocaust Research Institute at the U.S. Holocaust Memorial Museum*

Sugihara's exceptional kindness certainly deserves a wider audience that this book will provide, [blending] scholarship and information to provide an uplifting and profoundly true story of kindness. **Rabbi Marvin Tokayer,** *Author of the "Fugu Plan"*

"A carefully researched historical novel that combines fascination with a powerful message." **Paul Simon,** *late and former United States Senator from Illinois; professor at Southern Illinois*

NOW WHAT?

The Irreverent Memoirs of a Daydreamer, Counterspy, Prosecutor, Defense Attorney, and Adventurer

By

Carl L. Steinhouse

authorHOUSE®

AuthorHouse™
1663 Liberty Drive
Bloomington, IN 47403
www.authorhouse.com
Phone: 1-800-839-8640

Published by AuthorHouse 5/28/2013

ISBN: 978-1-4817-5538-2 (sc)
ISBN: 978-1-4817-5537-5 (e)

Library of Congress Control Number: 2013909018

Dedicated to my wife, Diana, and my children, Sam, Jane
and Lani, co-travelers on this exciting journey through
life

NOW WHAT?

CARL L. STEINHOUSE

I. THE EARLY YEARS

The Tomato and Onion with Mayo on Wonder Bread Catastrophe—Circa 1937

My father had three brothers and oodles of sisters. I say oodles because some died before I was born, so I'm really not sure of the numbers. Anyway, my father and his brothers were in business together, running four Florsheim Shoe stores, which reminds me of an incident that happened at the 125th Street store, in the heart of Harlem. It's not part of the story I am going to tell you, but it's a quickie and since I was only six or seven when it occurred and I remember it so vividly, the event, obviously, made a deep impression on me.

I had just come back from Miami Beach after spending the winter there with my mother. I have sort of an olive tint to my skin to begin with so the three months in the sun gave me a very dark complexion. Anyway, during my visit one Saturday to the Harlem shoe store, my father and Uncle Irving intended to take me out to eat at Frank's Steakhouse, a block away. I was holding my father's newspaper under my arm. Being my usual daydreaming self, I lagged behind by a half a block and by the time I reached the restaurant my father and uncle were already seated. As I entered, a strong, black hand gripped my shoulder. "Whatta you want in here, BOY. You can't sell newspapers here so get your black ass out." Five minutes later, it must have dawned on my father that I was missing. He found me sitting at the curb bawling. He carried me into the restaurant to the accompanying apologies of the bouncer.

On to my story. My Uncle Irving Steinhouse and his wife, Aunt Florence, were childless. Since we lived in the same apartment house in the Bronx, 1530 Sheridan Avenue, the proximity caused him to dote more on me than his other nephews and nieces. It wasn't so bad;

3

certainly better that my Uncle Abe (another of my father's brothers) who lived farther away and thus saw me less often. Uncle Abe thought dispensing affection meant giving my cheek a good, hard pinch. If he didn't have his own two girls to dote on, I have no doubt that he could have altered my facial anatomy.

But, again, I am straying from the story, which is about Uncle Irving and Aunt Florence. Irving didn't know this but I still remembered the unfulfilled promise he made, when I was five or six, to get me a Boston bulldog for my birthday. Conveniently for him, my birthday fell in July so I was away in the Catskills for the summer at the Rainbow Lodge in Livingston Manor, New York. Out of sight, out of mind. I never made an issue of it because I think the truth is that my mother leaned on him to forget all about bringing a dog into HER household. But I never forgot that broken promise, even when I was eight years old. That was the year my mother and father went on a rare vacation without me.

Florence and Irving offered, rashly it turned out, to take care of me for the week. They'd never done this before—they'd never taken care of anything except each other—not a dog, not a cat, not a canary, not a gerbil. My visit started out innocently enough. Monday they saw me off to school. In those days in the Bronx there was no such thing as a school bus. I walked to PS70, which was about eight blocks from their house. It was no big deal; I'd been doing it since kindergarten. That's how safe the streets of the South Bronx were back then! But when I came home from school that day, I burned with a fever. Now things were getting dicey for this childless couple—they hadn't figured on this! In a panic, they called our family doctor, Dr. Herman Frimmel. Frimmel calmed them down—he was great at that (I remember that about 15 years later my wife and were trying to have a child and we went to see him and … but that's a story for a later chapter).

4

NOW WHAT?

I keep straying. Sorry about that. Anyway, Frimmel assured my uncle that it was only a mild flu that had been going around and he would come by to check me out. Remember when doctors used to make house calls? By Wednesday, Frimmel's magic had begun working and I was feeling better. That evening I was starving and had this insane desire for a tomato and onion sandwich with lots of mayonnaise. My mother, of course, had she been there, would have started me out on a more modest menu like chicken soup or tea and crackers with jam. But my childless caretakers were delighted I wanted to eat, so out came the tomato and onion sandwich on Wonder Bread, brimming over with Hellmann's Mayonnaise.

Now you have to understand one thing about Florence. She was a compulsive neatnik. Oh, she had a great sense of humor and used to tell dirty stories at family gathering, even in front of the kids. But cleanliness next to Godliness was her mantra. Anyway, I devoured about half the sandwich before the concoction turned on me and without any warning I puked on the floor, right at my Aunt's feet. She took one look at the mess and screamed and then added her upchuck to the brew. My Uncle, hearing her scream came rushing in. "What's the ..."

He never finished the sentence, promptly vomiting into the rancid pile as he took in the horrible scene.

Needless to say, Florence was not a happy camper, having to clean up a tripartite mess beyond her wildest imagination. She might as well have been facing a horrible protoplasm alien. She took it out on poor Uncle Irving. After all, she scolded him, "Carl comes from YOUR side of the family."

The end result is that I ruined it for my other uncles and aunts who had hoped that at last, a successful experience with me would lead Florence and Irving to take care of other nephews and nieces while their parents vacationed. Forget about it!

What Makes Freddie Run?

My mother's brother, my Uncle Fred, had to be one of the sweetest men alive. My affection for Fred started when I still slept in a crib in my parents' bedroom. When the double glass doors of the bedroom were open, I could see across the hall into Fred's room and watch with fascination while he stretched out on his bed. I can't remember a lot of things from that tender age, but I could remember Fred living with my parents until he married Faye.

While he lived at home, he would shower me with attention and I loved him. I became traumatized when he married Faye and moved out. He was handsome and she was gorgeous. That they made a beautiful couple hardly mattered to me.

Faye and Fred just married

But the trauma did not last long because beautiful Faye was just as kind to me as my uncle had been. I was never a good eater as a child and my mother would literally have to force-feed me. But when my Aunt Faye came over to take care of me, which was quite often, she too fed me, but in the most fun ways. I loathed scrambled eggs and with Mom, it was always a battle royal. Faye would take those eggs on a fork and pretend she was a plane zooming around the sky by running around the room, eventually landing, where else? In my mouth, of course. Faye became my good friend and confidant and when I needed help she was there, such as the time, much later, when I desperately needed a date for a fraternity prom. Like my uncle, I was very shy, especially around girls. She not only found me a date, but a date that eventually became my wife. But that story is covered in another chapter.

Fred had great talent as an artist. After graduating Cooper Union College, he obtained a job as a cartoonist with King Features. But he was shy and lacked self-confidence. He'd always do a great job of filling in for other artists—so well that no one ever knew when he drew the comic strip and when the original artist did. He stepped in and drew such strips as Prince Valiant, a very detailed strip requiring a great deal of artistic talent and patience; Blondie; Hi and Lois; They'll Do It Every

Time; among others. He also did the hand printing for the dialog in these strips. He became an important cog in the King Features comic strip machinery.

Fred at work at a summer bungalow in Rockaway

He felt safe in what he was doing and turned down all offers of promotion by King Features. He made an adequate living but certainly didn't acquire the wealth of the more famous fellow cartoonists he drew for.

At family events he always did appropriate caricatures of the honorees.

CARL L. STEINHOUSE

Fred's caricature for the author's 70th Birthday

Let's fast forward to his putative retirement years when, in his late eighties, he was still commuting from his Yonkers apartment to downtown Manhattan to the King Features offices where he continued to draw strips. We wondered what kept him making that hour-and-a-half commute; they certainly didn't pay him that much. Perhaps he was lonely now that his life-long companion, Faye, had died—or maybe he just liked work so much. Those may have been some of the reasons but the real motive became apparent on the day his niece Allyne picked him up from work in front of the King Features offices. He exited the office building with two young beautiful women, one on each arm, who escorted him to the automobile.

"We just love Fred" the buxom blonde cooed.

"He soooo cute," the redheaded beauty gushed.

10

NOW WHAT?

Each planted a kiss on his cheek before bundling him into the car. And the secret of his longevity was finally out.

CARL L. STEINHOUSE

If the Shoe Fits

Let's back up a little to before I was born. My natural father, Sam, owned a shoe store. Eventually he'd have many stores. Two years after Sam married Sophia, he let her mind his lone shoe store in the Bronx while he was out doing whatever shoe store owners do to replenish their stock. This was her chance to show her husband how capable she was--she'd sell a couple of pairs of shoes and make him proud. She greeted the two potential customers with a big smile. "And what can I show you two fine gentlemen?"

"Lady, you can show us the inside of your cash register."

Obviously, they were not gentlemen, especially when both drew guns and pointed all this firepower at Sophia. She accommodated her customers, who took the money and locked her in the store room in the back of the store.

I first had a copy of the original New York Times newspaper report of the robbery, dated August 1, 1929 set forth in these pages, but sigh, for this very short three paragraph 86 year-old article, the newspaper wanted an obscene amount of money. Very greedy, indeed!

In any event, it was reported that the bandits were caught in a car chase in the Bronx after they robbed the shoe store of Sam Steinhouse on East Burnside Avenue. But that did not discourage Sam.

NOW WHAT?

He invested in and owned several Florsheim shoe stores in partnership with his brothers. That's him in the photo, second from left, with his brothers left to right, Abe, Bob, and Irving.

My father ran the 125th Street store in Harlem, one of the highest grossing Florsheim shoe stores in the country. So Florsheim let him design shoes especially for his customers whose tastes were more on the side of daring than the usual staid Florsheim shoe. He built up the shoe business for all his brothers. It was a good living for all of them. But for my father and his family, that ended abruptly in 1940.

But let me back up, once again. My father had been ill for many years, first with a bad ulcer and then with leukemia. He spent much of his summers convalescing in the Catskills at a resort called Rainbow Lodge. Every summer, Mom and I would join him up there for a week or two. It was no Grossinger's or Concord—just a modest place with a cracked swimming pool and a weed-infested clay tennis court. But Teddy Golub, the owner, kept it clean and the food was passable. No big name entertainers either. Solly Alper, a friend of my father's, in ladies hats, used to sing there in the evenings for his room and board. But for me, compared to the Bronx heat with no air conditioning back then, this was the height of luxury. I could romp in the fields, swim in the pool, and most important, be with my dad.

Author with father and mother at Rainbow Lodge, circa 1933

We were Rainbow Lodge owners' best customers and were treated like family. I even called the proprietor and proprietress Uncle Teddy and Aunt Bess. My father would take me for automobile rides at the breathtaking speed of fifty miles per hour on those country roads around Rainbow Lodge.

* * *

My uncles and older cousins told me they loved my father who, they said, had a great sense of humor and was generous to everyone in the family. That's why, in hindsight, I am bothered by what happened.

The year was 1940, not a good year for my mother. Her mother, in 1939, had died a painful death from brain cancer and her father, a chronic cigarette smoker, was slowly dying from lung cancer. My father was very ill with leukemia and everyone knew he was dying but him. It is strange that the partnership had an agreement to exclude the heirs of any deceased partner from inheriting any part of the business.

My father, in healthier times

My father died, we had little money and I don't think she got any from the shoe business. My mother had to go to work to support her and me. She'd always loved my father's family, with whom she was generous to a fault, and refused to think ill of them. I think they could have done a lot more to help her back then.

Getting back to 1940, I developed a guilt trip of my own. My father lay dying in the Royal Hospital in the Bronx. I would come to the hospital on occasion and it was always more fun to visit and play in the children's ward than to spend time in my father's dreary hospital room. I disappeared from his room the day he was dying, and by the time my mother had found me, he'd passed away. My mother didn't throw it up to me but at nine years old I fully realized that I had squandered an opportunity for my father to say one last goodbye to me. I was inconsolable for weeks.

But that wasn't the end of our traumatic year of 1940. My mother's father, my Poppy (grandfather), died at the same time I was stricken with an appendicitis attack. For all her grief, my mother had to rush me to the hospital before my appendix burst. It was a close call.

By now, my mother had given up our large apartment and moved into one room in the Concourse

Plaza Hotel. I came through the operation without incident and the doctor had placed a large bandage with plenty of tape on my belly, covering the incision. When the nurse removed the bandages days later, she ripped them off on the theory it was less painful if done quickly. She was wrong. The top layer of my belly skin came off with the bandage, I let out a bloodcurdling scream, and the doctor had a fit. But the damage was done. The doctor instructed my mother to give me a warm bath and let me soak.

That evening, mother prepared a *hot* bath for me and put me in it—but not for long. The pain was excruciating and I let out a howl that could be heard throughout the hotel and with the pain-induced adrenaline, I bolted out of the tub bowling over my mother. No amount of coaxing could get me anywhere near that tub.

My mother survived 1940 and she supported me for four years working in a dentist's office before she finally remarried. The same four years his brothers thrived in a business that had grown in large part through my father's initiative and design.

NOW WHAT?

Breaking the Ice

This may come as a surprise to my children and grandchildren, but my mother never drove me to get from one place to another in the city. She never chauffeured me to play ball, to after-school activities, to the dentist, or most anywhere. We were perfectly capable of making our own way to such places. Unless we were visiting someone outside the city, we just didn't use the car. As a matter of fact, I can't recall that my friends' parents had cars.

My friends and I got around the city very nicely, thank you, without the aid of our parents or their cars. The preferred mode of transportation, if going someplace locally in the Bronx, was the city bus; anywhere outside the borough, we used our magic carpet, the New York subway system. For a nickel, the world, at least as far as it extended to the city boundaries, lay at our feet: Manhattan west to the Hudson River and south to Bowling Green, east to Queens to the Long Island counties and to Brooklyn and Canarsie, and west to Staten Island to the New Jersey shore. That was our domain. It was no big deal to take a ride to Coney Island, forty miles away. Going down to Times Square was a snap. Hop the D train express to Forty-Second Street, about a twenty-five minute ride, and we were a block away from the Great White Way. We feasted on Neddick's hot dogs and orange drinks or had hamburgers and chocolate egg creams at some corner candy store where we could ogle the posters of the beautiful girls in bathing suits (one piece of course, this was pre-bikini) entered in the Miss Rheingold contest. It was safe enough in those days that our parents did not worry about us until dinnertime. Cinderella had her magic midnight curfew; we had our six in the evening one. That was the

17

witching hour to start the parents worrying and in our family, at least, all hell broke loose if I wasn't home at that hour. The fact that my friend Lewis and I bicycled up to Mount Vernon in Westchester County for thirty miles in heavy traffic to visit his cousin (whom I didn't even like—but it was an adventure) did not evince the concern that being late for dinner did, even though the excursion was a lot more dangerous. On one such trip I was sideswiped by a hit and run driver that sent me flying off my bike, fortunately onto a grassy area. Bruised and scraped of flesh, and dented of bike, we continued on to our destination, unfazed. Of course, I never told my parents about that incident. That would have ended those adventures *tout suite*.

Saturdays weren't usually a problem of worry since my close friends, Lewis, Harry and Mike, had a standing date to go to the Earl Theater on 161st Street and Jerome Avenue to see not only a double feature (for those too young to understand, that's two movies for the price of one admission of twenty-five cents, usually the main feature and what they call a grade B movie). But that was not all. The movie house threw in a serial adventure, to be continued each week, a fifteen minute exciting episode invariably ending with the hero or heroine facing inescapable death, such as being in a car that just gone off a thousand-foot cliff. Of course the next week, they backed up the story a smidgen and showed the hero or heroine leaping out of the car just before it went over the cliff. But it kept us coming back, week after week to see Captain Midnight, Superman, Terry and the Pirates, Dick Tracy, and the like. Further inducements were the give-a-ways. The movie house would give away dishes, glasses and sometimes, a nice red bicycle (only one speed, they didn't know from 10-speed, or even 3-speed bikes back then) to the lucky holder of the ticket stub with the winning number; you never, ever threw away the stub until you left the theater.

NOW WHAT?

Around the winter holidays, we'd occasionally venture to Radio City Music Hall in Rockefeller Center to see a *first run* movie (one that didn't show up at the Earl theater in the Bronx until a month or two later) and the special Christmas show with the Rockettes. The line for tickets usually stretched from Sixth Avenue (it didn't have such a complicated name back then like "Avenue of the Americas") all the way to Fifth Avenue, past the Rockefeller skating rink with its huge sentinel Christmas tree, overlooking and keeping an eye on the skaters. But Radio City Music Hall was huge, and it was usually able to seat everyone in that line, to the surprise of many of those in the back of the line.

One cold winter day, with the temperature hovering just above freezing, Lewis and I headed uptown from the Broadway Theater District (I cannot recall if we took in the show at Radio City Music Hall that day) to Central Park, about fourteen blocks away. We slogged through the snow in the park to one of the lakes. The lake was frozen over—at least that's what we all thought—so we gingerly slid around the western edge of the lake, having snowball fights and generally cavorting around in the snow (you didn't want to do that on the streets of New York where if not cleared, the snow soon turned a disgusting brown, punctuated by yellow streaks, courtesy of the city's dogs—that was another thing— there were no curb-your-dog signs or laws in those days so the streets became a constant obstacle course of dog droppings, requiring your full-time attention; and a light covering of snow just compounded the problem).

CARL L. STEINHOUSE

Lewis, right, and author on the Grand Concourse, circa 1944

Lewis and I were having a grand time that mid-afternoon when we heard the scream. Looking toward the middle of the lake from which the cry of distress seemed to emanate, we saw a young boy, may be six or seven (we were twelve-year-old big shots by then) struggling in the icy water where he fell through on an undetected soft spot in the ice. As he struggled, he kept breaking off more ice at the edges of the hole. We raced (more like slid) across the ice to where he was. Approaching the break in the ice we got down on our stomachs and inched toward the boy. I suppose the theory is that by spreading your weight over your entire body you did not put as much pressure on the ice as you would standing up with all your weigh concentrated on the small area of your feet. Well, it worked for a while. We reached the edge of the broken ice and I grabbed the hand of the struggling boy while Lewis hung on to my foot. Then it happened. As I pulled the boy up our combined weigh broke the ice under me sending both of us into the frigid water. Trying to pull both of us out of the water, Lewis hung on to my foot, so he ended up in the water as well.

The park personnel, "Parkies," as we called them, had always been the bane of us young boys, chasing us off the grass (particularly in Joyce Kilmer Park in the Bronx where we played football on the grass until interrupted by a Parkie), or moving us out of the park if we were particularly loud or boisterous. But we certainly welcomed this Parkie who came out onto the ice and managed to pull all three of us out of the drink and to safety.

"Go on, get home and changed before you guys catch pneumonia," he groused. But this time we didn't mind him chasing us out of the park.

"My Aunt Ann and Uncle Pat live close to the park," Lewis advised in a chattering voice, "let's go there."

As cold as I was, I didn't need a second invitation. We crossed Central Park South and ran down the street to Lewis' relatives' apartment building. The doorman recognized Lewis, saw our condition, and immediately escorted us up to our destination.

His Aunt Ann opened the door. By now our lips had turned blue. "My God, Lewis, Carl," she exclaimed, "what in the world happened to you both?"

As an aside, if she had been my mother, I would have been dressed down and punished but good for coming home soaking wet in the middle of winter. Mother would have shrugged off my story as just a bad excuse. (Later, in high school, I tried out for the swim team and when I came home from *one* practice with a wet head, again in the middle of winter, she abruptly pulled the plug on my athletic career.)

But God bless Lewis' Aunt Ann and Uncle Pat. They treated us royally. "My heroes," she gushed.

"We're so proud of you," he waxed eloquently.

The hot chocolates and the change of clothes didn't hurt either.

Long after, in our adult years, when his aunt and uncle were in the twilight of their lives, Ann still had that twinkle in her eye when she greeted me, leading me to believe that Lewis and I were still her heroes when we broke the ice.

CARL L. STEINHOUSE

The Sock-It-To-Em Championship—
1944

At thirteen-years-old, five-foot-three, and 110 pounds, I neither had the height to be a basketball star, the weight to be a football star, nor the strength to be the school bully. In other words, I was your average schlub student, possessing no self-confidence socially, academically, or physically.

But I did have one outstanding attribute. I was a daydreamer without peer. Walter Mitty had nothing on me. I hit home runs to the cheers of a packed Yankee Stadium, caught game-saving passes in the end-zone to bring the football championship to the New York Giants; I sank the game winning two-hand set shot to give William Howard Taft the Madison Square Garden high school championship.

But I did more than daydream. In my bedroom, not terribly large to begin with, I set up my own basketball court. My cousin Alfred, in Europe fighting the Nazis in World War Two, had sent me a German helmet, with the dirt and blood still in it. Much to my chagrin, my mother immediately took that monstrosity and cleaned it out thoroughly, over my violent (or least loud and whining) protests. What daydreams that could have evoked! But that's another story.

Anyway, I perched the German helmet high up on the top bookshelf above my bed, took out a pair of rolled up socks from my dresser, and *viola*, I had myself a ready-made basketball court. I became the high school star player, driving to the basket, hitting long jumpers and always scoring in the double digits. And the crowds cheered. Rah, rah—mimicking the approving roar of the crowd as I stepped onto the court.

NOW WHAT?

My bedroom with my friend Mike Oldstone, right. Bookshelf behind us held my "basket," the German helmet

Every night, I took the floor to the cheering throng, and every night I did not disappoint them. Somehow that last minute shot with the game on the line always fell on me, and like a true-blue trooper, I always came through.

Over the season, I became amazingly accurate in dropping that pair of rolled up socks into the cleansed German helmet. It seems that unwittingly, I had developed my hand-eye coordination to a high degree. Now things started to happen. First, I noticed that in PT (that's what they called gym time, "PT") I had developed a very consistent basketball shot both in the backcourt and under the basket. So much so that whereas before I was always last chosen when sides were picked, now I was one of the first taken. Eventually, the coach took notice of me and asked me to try out for the team. Me, unathletic Carl Steinhouse, asked to try out.

Anyway, to make a long story short, I made the basketball team. The team made it to the intercity finals, which were being played in Madison Square Garden. We won the championship thanks to my stellar shooting. In a ceremony after the game I was awarded the game ball. I held the ball proudly, examining it carefully, noting the brown argyle pattern on the pair of socks as I put them back in the drawer. Another daydreaming championship season completed in my bedroom. It was time to move on to the baseball season. The Yankees were anxiously awaiting my hot bat.

NOW WHAT?

Temporary Release from Bondage

I'm an expert on braces. No, I'm not an orthodontist but my claim to fame is just as impressive as their eight years of training; I wore braces for *twelve years* and survived three orthodontists. My bite was so bad, a plaster cast of it is displayed in the Bronx Orthodontia Museum, at least it was fifty years ago. By the time the braces came off, my upper front teeth were loose because the constant pressure for all those years absorbed much of the root structure. Every night I wore this contraption right out of dungeons of the Inquisition, a strapped helmet looking much like what you could buy in a torture shop, if there was such a store. From the helmet, attached with heavy rubber bands, protruded two narrow metal bars that hooked onto the braces of my upper teeth, kind of like a horse with a bit in his mouth. The ravages of orthodontia did not stop there. Every two weeks the orthodontist tightened my braces by twisting the wires that were connected to both the bands, cemented to my teeth, and to the braces: one turn, just like the medieval torture rack to inflict pain. For a week my teeth were too sore to eat anything but mush. For the next week, they'd feel normal, and then the one turn would be applied again.

So now you can understand what I am about to tell you. The corner candy store in my neighborhood on Sheridan Avenue sold these wax whistles. All the candy stores did because it was the rage at the time. You could whistle a tune with it and when you were tired of whistling, you could bite into the wax and release the delicious candy syrup. Well, I bought one of these confections and whistled with it for a while. Then I bit hard into the wax and when I opened my mouth, lo and

25

behold, my upper and lower braces, bands and all, were out of my mouth and embedded in the wax.

Author, pre-braces, 1938

Post-braces, 1952

I didn't mean for it to happen but since it did, I reveled in it. Unless you've had braces, you can't understand the feeling of releasing your teeth from bondage. It felt wonderful--slimy, yes--I hadn't felt the enamel of my teeth for years--but nevertheless wonderful. For three days I avoided smiling in front of my parents and only confessed when facing my next orthodontia appointment. There was hell to pay but it was worth it-- especially the look on my orthodontist's face when I brought in the full set of bands and braces firmly ensconced in that wax whistle.

NOW WHAT?

The Bar Mitzvah That Disappeared—1945

For my bar mitzvah, the biggest day of my then young life, only three meager mementos remain--but I'll get to those later when I explain how my bar mitzvah disappeared.

My growth spurt hadn't started yet so that at the time of my bar mitzvah, my head barely cleared the bema (the lectern used by the rabbi for the services, sitting up in front of the Ark that contained the Torah scrolls). Thus, when I sang my portion of the Torah reading, to most of the congregants, I represented merely a disembodied, if somewhat squeaky voice, nothing like the booming deliveries the rabbi and cantor emitted, but after all, they go through years and years of training to be able to project and boom out their sermons and liturgies.

Literally, bar mitzvah means "son of the commandment." One doesn't get *bar mitzvahed,"* one becomes a bar mitzvah. Under Jewish law, a boy becomes a man, a bar mitzvah, by the mere fact of reaching his thirteenth birthday. He can still be an immature, whiny, sniveling brat, but in theory at least, the bar mitzvah is now capable of filling the central tenets of Jewish law as an adult.

Okay, we've cleared up the technical stuff, so let's get down to *my* bar mitzvah. The bar mitzvah is an important milestone in a Jewish boy's life. I can't speak for other boys at age thirteen, but for me it meant the end of my tedious daily grind of after-school training in Hebrew chanting (called davening) and Bible history; the end of being harassed as I left Hebrew school by the boys from All Hollows, a Catholic parochial school across the street from our synagogue that let out the same time as we did; and most important, the catered party that would be thrown for me (with presents), the likes of which I would not get to see again until I got married. Finally, I

27

had to endure the limelight for my one half hour on the bema. I say "endure" because anticipating that half hour frightened the hell out of me for weeks prior to the event; so much so that after the bar mitzvah, I studiously avoided every public speaking course in college. But it's funny how life is. I embarked upon a career as a criminal trial lawyer that demanded the ability to speak publicly. Forcing me to confront my bugaboo, I discovered from the experience that it was no big deal and after a while I actually began to enjoy public speaking. It certainly gave me greater insight into that famous line from Franklin Delano Roosevelt's first inaugural speech in March 1933, "The only thing we have to fear is fear itself."

I received my Hebrew training at Young Israel of the Concourse, as did my friends. I don't know why the synagogue had that name because it was located not on the Grand Concourse but on Walton Avenue. Much later, it moved to a larger building, actually on the Concourse, I suppose to fulfill its destiny.

The old synagogue on Walton Avenue was so small that when the High Holidays came around, services had to be held in the grand ballroom of the Concourse Plaza Hotel to accommodate the majority of the members called the High Holiday Jews, as it was the only time they attended other than for the occasional relative's or friend's bar mitzvah. During the holiday services our parents would lay on the guilt so that my friends and I spent at least half the time at the services. For the other half, notwithstanding our now-achieved adult status, we cavorted around--like kids--in our suits, white shirts, ties, and dress oxford shoes (sneakers if your parents were very religious) on the lower level rest area out of earshot of our parents doing some serious praying and repentance upstairs in the grand ballroom. On Yom Kippur, once I became a bar mitzvah, my parents permitted me to fast for the day. It began as a big deal, a challenge we tried to meet with great heroics. But as the day wore on, we would torture each other with talk of juicy hamburgers, hot fudge sundaes, jelly apples, and the like. I even recall once declaring, late into the fast, that if someone served them to me, I would gladly eat soft-boiled eggs (which I hated) or lima beans (which I really loathed).

Other than it was held in some hotel downtown, I don't remember much about my catered bar mitzvah affair. I'll tell you why. Forty years after the event, the Wicked Witch obliterated almost all traces of my bar mitzvah. Let me explain. After my mother died in 1973, my stepfather, whom I loved as dearly as any natural father, and who was very close to my wife and three children, remarried a woman, whom I'll call the Wicked Witch of the West. Wicked made us feel unwelcome whenever we visited my stepfather. My stepfather had a summer cottage in the beach community of Long Beach, New York, and we had been always invited to spend the summer there--but not once since he married Wicked.

Stepfather and author, circa 1943

My mother and stepfather had kept the photo album of my bar mitzvah and many other important mementos and milestones in my life and I thought nothing of it, even after mother died in 1973. In 1985, stepfather, in his mid-eighties and still working full time in his own accounting and law firm, quietly slipped away in the elevator of his apartment building, his heart giving out. After the funeral, we sat Shiva (like a wake) at my late stepfather's and Wicked's apartment. I politely asked Wicked for my bar mitzvah album and any other mementoes that my stepfather's saved for us, things that certainly would be of no interest to her. That last expressed thought turned out to be a gross understatement. Nonchalantly, and with not the slightest tinges of regret, guilt, or apology in her tone, she shrugged and told me she threw out "all that junk" when they'd moved from the Bronx to the new apartment in midtown Manhattan. The "junk', in Wicked's eyes, included my bar mitzvah album, the invitations, and the bar mitzvah cards (yes, they even have cards for that occasion) of well-wishers.

Being a criminal lawyer, I had to weigh the pros and cons of murdering Wicked right on the spot. After careful consideration, I had to reject the temptation of such a course of conduct. It was a practical, not a moral decision and I'll tell you why. While the act I considered totally deserving, I faced the punishment of the exes. I could have been *ex*ecuted—fried in Old Sparky—for the crime (the appeals process was much shorter in those days), and I could have been *ex*communicated for slaying someone sitting *Shiva* for the dead. In our religion, it's a no-no and just not done.

The only things I have left from my bar mitzvah, beside some fragmentary memories, are those items that never left my possession, namely, one non-functioning, inscribed gold Benrus watch (without strap), one official photo of the bar mitzvah boy, and one prayer tallis (prayer shawl) I wore at the bar mitzvah ceremony.

Benrus watch gift

Bar Mitzvah Photo Portrait

I'm sure I must have received several fountain pens (ball points not yet invented) long since lost and war bonds (World War II still raging then) long since cashed.

CARL L. STEINHOUSE

How My Worst Nightmare Came True—1945

My worst dreams were those where I was stuck in a public place in only my undershorts. I never dreamt I was nude--being my underwear was sufficiently devastating.

I was fourteen, impressionable, and thoroughly intimidated by my first few days as a freshman in William Howard Taft High School in The Bronx. I don't know why they call it "The Bronx"--they don't say The Brooklyn, or The Manhattan. Anyway, that day I witnessed a full-blown riot in the school. The coaches of the sports teams had gone on strike--why I don't remember--but the entire sports program was closed down. The student body was large, as New York City high schools tended to be. Since we weren't allowed to lunch outside the school during the noon hour, the entire student body of several thousand assembled in cafeteria. The older students began the ruckus first by chanting their support for the coaches and then by marching around the room, knocking over tables and chairs. From then on, things got out of hand, dishes were smashed, silverware thrown, and several students got hurt. I ended up with the white shard of a plate in my sandwich. The police were called to restore order. It was exciting, although personally, I took no part in the melee, But I did take it all in.

I know, people will say, "What did you expect, being from the South Bronx." Well, it wasn't like that back then. The South Bronx was an attractive middle class community with wide, tree-lined boulevards and narrower streets packed with six to ten story apartment houses and populated by friendly, active neighbors. The streets reverberated with the shouts of the tradesmen plying their wares from horse-drawn carts and trucks--the "high cash clothes" man (that's what he sung as he rung his bell), the knife and scissors sharpener, the vegetable peddler, and the ice man.

My friends Harry, Lew, and Mike and I walked home from school that day down the Grand Concourse, chatting excitedly about the riot. We bought charlotte rouses--sponge cake with lots of whipped cream on top sitting in a white cups the shape of a king's crown--from a vendor who fished them out of his ice-filled cart. Then we stopped at the corner luncheonette for a greasy hamburger smothered with grilled onions and washed down with a chocolate egg cream. Finally, we bought chocolate ice cream pops on a stick from either The Good Humor Man or Bungalow Bar trucks. I licked the stick clean to see if I had the lucky stick--which meant a free pop the next time. Looking back, it's no wonder that, fifty years later, I'm on Lipitor for high cholesterol.

That evening, I went about my usual routine—dinner, homework, maybe watching Uncle Miltie [Berle] or Molly Goldberg on TV, and playing basketball into my German helmet, sitting high on the bookshelf above my bed.

I went to bed before my parents returned from the movies. By routine, I locked the windows and placed obstacles in front of the bed. I sleepwalked and had this fear that I would walk out of the window—not unreasonable since we were eight stories up.

I dreamed about the riot. Slamming my fist into my palm, I got out of bed and spit on the floor. I stormed out of the apartment, muttering, "I can strike, too." As the apartment door clicked shut and locked behind me, I woke finding myself in the hall, locked out and in my underwear. No one was home to let me back in. My embarrassment was extreme. I sneaked down the stairs to the lobby. I didn't dare take the elevator. I opened the door to the lobby a crack, trying to get the doorman's attention, hoping he had a key.

When I finally caught his attention, his first question was "Whatcha doin' in the lobby at this time of night in your underwear?" Apparently, if it had not been "this time of the night", it would be okay to be in my underwear. The doorman rang up my parents. It was useless because they weren't home. To my surprise, I heard my mother's voice on the intercom. She had gone up the elevator while I came down the stairs.

"What do you mean Carl is in the lobby in his underwear? Ridiculous! He's asleep, in his bed."

A moment's silence. "He's missing," she yelled into the intercom. I didn't hear the rest of the frantic conversation because I was racing up the stairs, two steps at a time.

She opened the door for me. Mother posed the same question as the doorman, but this time I was prepared.

"I was taking the garbage out to the incinerator and the door closed behind me."

She gave me the fish eye. She knew I had been sleeping walking again, and hustled me off to bed. But only after I first cleaned off the bottoms of my feet. Then I climbed into to bed, knowing I had survived living my worst nightmare.

NOW WHAT?

Summer Camp Years-Circa 1941-1950

Green Mountain Camp

The Great Story Teller

In my younger years at Green Mountain Camp, one counselor, an elderly gentleman and great story teller named Lloyd Samilow, enthralled us and sometimes, scared the living wits out of our impressionable, young minds, when he dealt up a horror story while we sat around the weekly campfire before going to bed. According to Samilow, he was a former outfielder for the New York Giants, which then, I took as gospel. Now that I think of it, however, considering his tall tale-telling abilities, I just wonder.

For us young campers, it was a love-hate relationship with those horror stories as we sat around that crackling fire: we'd love the excitement of the horror tales, but hated going to bed after hearing them. But don't get me wrong. He told mostly wonderful, heart-warming stories, including a serial one about aerialists in a traveling circus, which he'd continue from week to week (I'm sure he made them up on the spot as he was talking). I can't remember the aerialist stories, however enchanting I found them, but I sure as hell never forgot some of the horror stories; they made an impression (I'm sure he contributed to some of my sleepwalking episodes in my teens). I vividly recall one such story told some seventy years ago when I was twelve: the story of a man who had a strange affliction that, when it hit him, he appeared to be dead; his breathing so shallow and heart beat so faint, it was not readily detectable with a stethoscope.

John got on the train and settled into his Pullman seat. He fingered his necklace that stated,

THIS MAN IS AFFLICTED WITH A RARE DISEASE THAT MAY MAKE HIM APPEAR DEAD. HE IS NOT. TAKE HIM TO A HOSPITAL FOR FURTHER TESTS. DO NOT BURY HIM.

Normally, he hung out with his friends and relatives who were well aware of his problem. But pressing business required him to travel alone from New York to Chicago. Now he was returning home with no untoward incidents--so far. At eleven that evening the Pullman porter came through converting the seats into Pullman beds. He climbed up into bed, stretched out, and closed the curtain for privacy.

He awoke in the middle of the night. It was hot and stuffy. Trying to sit up he banged his head against hard metal. He reached up--hard, smooth metal; he raised his foot--hard, smooth metal. Now he started to panic. He tried to extend his arm to the right--the same; behind him--the same; he squiggled down to the foot of the bed, his toes touching hard metal. Then he knew. He was buried alive!

He began scream and pound on the lid of the coffin.

The curtain pulled back and the porter stuck his head in. "Are you ill? Is everything okay?"

Sweat-drenched, he could at first only smile. He'd forgotten he took the windowless and somewhat confining upper berth! And he'd never thought to reach out to his left, where he would have found not hard, smooth metal, but a flimsy curtain. Finally finding his voice, he assured the porter he was fine and apologized for his bad dream. He got up, showered in the shower

room, got into another pair of pajamas, and returned to his berth.

He awoke in the middle of the night. It was hot and stuffy. Trying to sit up he banged his head against hard metal. He reached up--hard, smooth metal; he raised his foot--hard, smooth metal. Now he started to panic. He tried to extend his arm to the right--the same; behind him--the same; he squiggled down to the foot of the bed, his toes touching hard metal. Frantically he reached for his warning necklace. It wasn't there! He'd taken off in the shower and forgot it. Stupid, stupid, stupid! Then he remembered where he was and smiled. THIS TIME he extended his arm to the LEFT to find the curtain. But it was only smooth, hard metal that he touched.

So you can see the type of story that made the lasting impression on me. Certainly not the delightful aerialists; but being buried alive, that stayed with me for over these seventy years. To this day I won't sleep on my back with my hands folded across my chest!

Eternal Loyalty?

I spent seven hard-earned years of my life at summer camp at Green Mountain Camp (well, I consider the teen years as hard-earned years, especially in my case like the 97 pound weakling famous for getting sand kicked in his face in the Charles Atlas body-building ads —actually, I was 110 pounds, but the results were not dissimilar). In truth, if anything was hard earned, it was my parent's money that sent me there.

Actually, when I started going to summer camp at age ten, I weighed a lot less than 110 pounds. We had a sister camp for girls, called Camp Birchwood. Every weekend we would trade visits with Birchwood, the highlight being the evening's square dance, mostly participated in by the older campers and the counselors. That year at Camp Birchwood, the future Miss America was a counselor and let me tell you, she was one gorgeous woman at five-ten and well endowed. I had a crush on her. Anyway, this future Miss America took a shine to the cute skinny kid, me, and when they paired off for square dancing, she came over and picked me! I was less than five-foot and maybe 70 or 80 pounds soaking wet. The music began and she'd pick me up bodily and carry me through the steps of the entire square dance without my feet touching the floor, planting a kiss on my forehead when the dance concluded. It was the highlight of my young life, at least up to then! [Fifty years later, I happened to sit next to this Miss America at a charity dinner. If I was very impressed with the square dance experience, even fifty years later, Miss America was not. She brushed off my mention of it and turned away to hold a conversation with the diner on her other side.]

I was a shy kid and it didn't take much to embarrass me. Some of the counselors had mean streaks and they enjoyed taunting us eleven-year-olds, like the time I was sitting peacefully on the toilet and began to unroll the toilet paper. I was used to using a lot of toilet paper and the counselor just outside the stall could hear me unraveling it from the roll. He burst in, grabbed the toilet paper out of my hand, screaming at me, "Don't you know there's a war on? Is THAT how you conserve paper for our boys overseas dying to protect you?" Simply bursting in on me in such a delicate position was embarrassing enough, but to load the guilt of our boys dying on the front was almost too much to bear. That, however, was not the end of it. At the nightly flag lowering before dinner in front or the entire camp, this counselor unrolled the wad to show how Steinhouse wasted paper. I'm in my eighties now and I still remember that incident. To this day I carefully limit the amount of toilet paper I use.

But don't get the wrong impression. On the whole, I enjoyed summer camp, except for the last two weeks when the camp declared COLOR WAR! For color war, the camp was divided evenly between the Green team and the Gray team. I hated it because competition was stoked to a fever pitch by the counselors--not ordinary counselors, mind you, but those recruited each year from the Columbia football and basketball teams (those years when they had good teams).

Camp counselor, a varsity basketball player for Columbia U.

Picture Columbia quarterback, Don Kaspersak leading the Greens and Bruce Ghercke, Columbia's right offensive end, leading the Grays. You would think Columbia was playing Army for the national title. Fight songs were written based on such tunes as Schubert's *Military March* ("Stop, look and listen as Gray team goes marching by"). For us young ones the pressure was just too much and not something to look forward to. You could lose the entire color war if you struck out at the plate. Actually, one color war spared me that ignominy. I was catching on the Gray baseball team and on the first pitch of the first game, the batter fouled a pitch off my right thumb, driving the entire digit a few inches up my hand. When I showed my thumb to the scowling coach, who had little use for malingerers or crybabies, he promptly threw up. As the nurse walked me down to the infirmary, my thumb slid neatly back into place and that got to me—I swooned. But I was happy. A dislocated thumb was a small price to pay for being excused from the competitive pressures of color war.

Color war football game

During the camp season, we sang songs of undying loyalty to Green Mountain Camp to melodies such as *Finlandia,* with lyrics such as "you are to us a symbol 'ere to rally round, a refuge, a true love and a home." But the true love apparently ran in only one direction. When I was too old to be a senior camper, the owners of Green Mountain Camp "permitted" me to be a "junior" counselor, for which toils I did not earn a red cent, but my parents had the privilege of paying "only" three-quarters of what the regular camper fees were. For that fee, I was permitted to assist the riding master, which really meant I got to sweep the manure out of the stables and brush down the sweaty horses after all the fun rides by the full-paying campers.

CARL L. STEINHOUSE

Mol-Jo-Ha —Rah, Rah

Despite the seven years of rallying around its flag and giving my true love, Green Mountain Camp did not turn out to be the refuge of the song. As soon as I applied for a counselor's position the next year, I was turned down flat. I wasn't on the Columbia University football team. What did they want with a skinny accounting major from NYU? The owners had a French last name (Dubois), so what could you expect? Gratitude?

I did find a job as a counselor at Camp MOL-JO-HA. My neighborhood friend Mike, also bounced by Green Mountain Camp, joined me on the staff of MOL-JO-HA. I'd like to say that the name was derived from sacred American Indian tribes such as:
MOL =**M**ohawks, **O**tos, **L**umbees
JO = **J**icarillas, **O**neidas
HA = **H**urons, **A**rapahos
The truth is far less exciting--to the point of embarrassment. The owners' names were Molly, and her brothers, Joe and Harry Resnick, hence, MOL-JO-HA.

But that didn't stop the campers from singing robust camp songs like:
MOL-JO-HA, hats off to thee,
To thy colors, hardily we ever sing,
Loyal and true forever are we,
MOL-JO-HA, HA, MOL-JO-HA, HA,
Rah, rah for MOL-JO-HA!
I always wondered why the biblical pronouns constantly showed up in summer camp songs. Maybe "thee" is easier to rhyme than "you." But can you imagine? Professing to be loyal and true forever to Molly, Joe, and Harry? It's a good thing summer camp only lasted eight weeks; otherwise parents might never get their kids loyalty back. Such undying professions to Molly, Joe and Harry were one thing, but what teenager

would ever afford the same sentiments to his own mom and dad? Unthinkable!

But the MOL-JO-HA summer season didn't last eight weeks. About the third week of camp, one of the campers in my bunk became deathly ill. He was taken out on a stretcher.

The campers in my bunk and I, their counselor, were immediately sent to the camp infirmary where we were examined not only by the camp doctor, but a whole slew of strange doctors and nurses.

I was scared. "What's going on, Doc?"

"A camper has polio."

The camper was the boy they carried out of my bunk on a stretcher.

Polio! He might as well have said the bubonic plague. Polio was the scourge of the forties and fifties-- no vaccines, no known cure, no effective treatments, and highly contagious. If you didn't die, you stood an excellent chance of being paralyzed for life. After all, didn't the March of Dimes show small children in Iron Lungs? And the stricken camper was in my bunk, no less!

Panicky parents rushed up to camp to rescue their little darlings; to hell with being loyal and true. My parents kept their heads, but only because they were unaware, taking advantage of my eight weeks away with a trip to Argentina, Chile and heaven knows where else.

My Uncle Abe came to the rescue, picking up both my friend Mike and me. My uncle deposited us at our respective homes. My parent's housekeeper Martha was there to administer to me since my family physician, Dr. Frimmel, had ordered me to bed for a two-week quarantine period. Frimmel didn't take any guff from his patients and certainly not from me. My strenuous objections to quarantine and restrictions were of no avail.

I never did check if Molly, Joe, and Harry had ever recovered from that disastrous season, undying loyalty notwithstanding.

The next season I spent as a counselor at a summer camp owned by my Aunt Sophie and Uncle Oscar.

Sophie and Oscar with their sons at camp

My parents weren't taking any more chances. I could just as well profess my undying love to Tunis Lake Camp, as anywhere else. Tunis Lake Camp? It certainly didn't roll off the tongue in song like MOL-JO-HA!

The Sheridan Avenue Gang—1945-1949

We lived in the South Bronx, and the only crimes locally would usually be kids swiping things off the counters in the Five and Ten. "Five and Ten," that's what we called the big general stores of Woolworth, Kress, and Kresge. In theory only, most items were supposed to cost five or ten cents. Those stores went the way of that wonderful gourmet institution, the Automat, a cafeteria where the change maker could immediately toss you a bunch of nickels for your dollar bill without seemingly counting them--and always correctly. Armed with your 20 nickels (buffalo heads at that time), you approached a wall with hundreds of little windows framed in brass, like miniature crypts, and you look salivatingly at the tempting dishes inside, dishes such as macaroni and cheese, baked beans, among dozens of other selections. See what you like? You put your two or three nickels in the slot, turn the gold knob and, lo and behold, the little glass door opened and you could remove your delectable selection. My favorites were spaghetti with tomato sauce, creamed spinach, hot beets in a sugary sauce, a roll with butter, and topped off with a hot chocolate, poured from the mouth of a brass lion spigot, after, of course, you fed it your nickel.

Automat

Later, you could always find a delectable dessert out on the street from one the pushcart vendors plying their trade of sweets. My favorite, as I said earlier, was the charlotte rouse; others preferred "shoe leather", a concoction of apricots beaten into long strips looking like, well, shoe leather.

My closest friends were Lewis, Harry, and Michael who never succumbed to the macho desire to smoke cigarettes, so under no peer pressure, I never adopted the filthy habit (though later in life I did yield to temptation and smoked cigars for years). Thank you guys! Our aging never outgrew our friendship and we still keep in regular contact with each other and our families, though spread throughout the United States. The one exception is dear friend Harry, who, afflicted with a virulent cancer, died in his mid-thirties. A brilliant electrical engineer and a wonderful person, his death was a great loss to his friends, family, and society.

Left to right: Author, Diana and Harry enjoying a respite from winter in Miami Beach

My friends and I, all living within a three-block area, usually congregated on Sheridan Avenue after walking back the mile from the high school, also on Sheridan Avenue, but further uptown. Sheridan Avenue was our ball field for playing stickball, which only required a sawed-off broomstick, a Spaulding (a pink rubber ball) and of course the field for city kids--Sheridan Avenue. You may wonder how a narrow city street may work as a ball field. The sewer manhole cover in the middle of the street acted as home plate, the front tires of the cars parked at the curbs were first and third base respectively and the manhole cover further down the street became second base. The game was fairly simple. There was no pitching. You simply threw the ball in the air or bounced it and swung from the heels at the ball with the broomstick. The absence of pitching leveled the playing field (so to speak) for those of us who couldn't hit a pitched ball if our lives depended on it. Strange, New York's Finest had a thing about stickball, like it was a crime ranked just ahead of bank robbery. Whenever the cops caught us playing stickball, they'd confiscate our broomsticks and order us off the streets. Of course, as soon as they turned the corner, another broomstick was produced and the game continued. I guess in a way you could call us scofflaws. Our mothers were always puzzled about their disappearing brooms.

Anyway, I, Harry, Lewis, Mike, Pete, Hank, Tubby and a few transients formed our own gang--well, really a club--with a name designed to strike abject fear into the hearts of our opponents--the Penguins! Yes, that fearsome waddler in a tuxedo brought guffaws from our competitors. What where we thinking? But we were committed after putting out hard-earned parent's cash for the blue and red club jackets emblazoned on back with PENGUINS.

As a team we weren't very good, and in football, often as not, we got our asses kicked good. Most of our team, weighing in at 115 pounds and under, faced players 150 pounds and over. We had one big player, Tubby. He wasn't an athlete by any standard, but he weighed in at 250 pounds, so we'd give him the ball and he'd drag tacklers for yards before going down. It wasn't state-of-the-art football, but at least Tubby kept us somewhat competitive on the offense. In one of these sandlot football games, I, a mighty Penguin, got my face stepped on by a 150 pounder in a pileup at the line of scrimmage, breaking my nose. Mother, a tough, no-nonsense coach, ended my budding sandlot football career. [I did not play football again until I joined a fraternity in college and had my just-fixed-by-the-orthodontist teeth knocked out in an inter-fraternity touch football game, but that's a story for later.]

If my friends weren't athletic, they were as smart as hell. The doomed Harry was one of the smartest and the nicest, becoming a leader in the field of electrical engineering.

Mike was always the mad scientist in our circle of friends (later becoming renowned in medical researcher for the Scripps Institute), and the political idealist of the group, proclaiming his intention to go to China to join the fight against Generalissimo Chiang Kai-shek. What he had against the guy, I don't know. He never even met him! And Mike was not above some hell raising either. Mike did a lot of extracurricular work in Mr. Dragoon's high school biology lab and was not above taking chemicals out of the lab for various nefarious purposes. At the end of one school year, Mike and I headed to Green Mountain Camp together. Mike had a real crotchety and nasty neighbor in an apartment across the hall from where he and his mother lived. An elderly gent with a mean temper and a cane; and he was not above swinging it when he was unhappy with my friend. Well, Mike had purloined some chemicals from the bio lab and mixed them so that when the concoction dried into a powder it would explode on contact—not dangerous but damn loud. As we left for camp, he sprinkled this powder on the hall floor next to Mr. Crotchety's apartment so that the old grouch's cane would set off these mini blasts. It worked, we found out later, but it was Mike's mom, Mona, that took the brunt of the anger of Mr. Crotchety, that is, until Mike got home from camp. Mona was never reticent about punishing Mike. Lord knows he often needed it.

NOW WHAT?

Lewis, another brain in our group, eventually became a pioneer in educational programming. His parents were something else. Oh, they were real good, sweet people, for whom I had a great deal of affection, but they had some real weird notions about diet. They were on a health food kick long before it was a fad, with things like wheat germ, soy, and other foods that were esoteric at that time in our lives. Poor Lewis, he wasn't allowed to drink milk or eat ordinary cookies. When he was over our house—which was quite often—my mother felt he didn't have proper nutrition so she stuffed him full of milk and Mallowmars (that Nabisco treat with shortbread and marshmallow, covered with luscious dark chocolate). He devoured all she gave him.

Once, when my parents went to Lakewood, New Jersey, for a holiday weekend, I stayed with Lewis and his family. While there, I became ill, throwing up and running a low fever. It was then I discovered his mother's tried and true home remedy for most illnesses— the enema! This was not a simple Fleet enema—they didn't have them back then. This process involved a large red bag filled with some form of liquid with a transparent tube ending in a lubricated tip. His mother set up the ironing board, hooked the enema bag up high, and hefted me up and aimed that lubricated tip you know where and opened the valve. I had objected strenuously. After all, I was already a teenager and to be given an enema by someone else's mother was almost more than I could bear. To no avail—my protests notwithstanding, I received the special cure. I hate to admit it, but I did feel better afterwards.

CARL L. STEINHOUSE

The Monroe Avenue Gang

Friendships can be complicated; I'd be the first to admit it. But this was more complicated than usual. But let me go back to the beginning.

Allyne and I had a common aunt though we ourselves were not related. My mother's brother, my Uncle Fred, married Faye, Allyne's aunt (her mother and Faye were sisters). I spent a lot of time with Fred and Faye and that led naturally to becoming acquainted with Allyne and her friends, a wholly separate group from the neighborhood friends of my Sheridan Avenue Gang. See, already it's complicated.

I got to know a lot of people outside of my Sheridan Avenue orbit because Allyne's father, Charlie, a watchmaker, was a magnet for attracting people (including myself) from all over his neighborhood, centered on the one-block street of Monroe Avenue in the Bronx. It's perhaps a ten-block walk from my neighborhood to Monroe Avenue, so getting there was no problem. Why was he a magnet? Because Charlie had something most people did not possess, and that thing could draw crowds. He acquired a rhesus monkey that he kept in a cage in the kitchen. Not many people in the Bronx had monkeys in their apartments. But I forgot to mention, Charlie didn't have an apartment. He was one of the few in the South Bronx to live in his own house. Hence, another reason there were so many people around—unlike an apartment in which most of us mortals lived, his house was easily accessible from the street.

NOW WHAT?

On left: Aunt Faye and Uncle Fred. Standing: Allyne's father, Charlie, the watchmaker, and mother. That's Allyne up front with the bow. Circa late thirties

The monkey in the kitchen was not a good idea, at least in my mind. When the primate got cantankerous, he'd toss his feces out of the cage, usually at the people sitting around the kitchen table having a snack or drinking coffee, or both. I was a great nosher, but I didn't do that much at Allyne's house. But it wasn't the monkey and his crap that really attracted the people; it was the brand new, only-one-on-the-block TV set he bought in 1945 that really packed them in. Since Charlie loved people, the crowds didn't bother him one bit. I'm not sure Allyne's mother appreciated it but I never really discussed it with her. I was too busy watching the new-fangled invention, the TV, a console with a black and white ten-inch tube and ghosts galore; a TV that would be pathetic by today's standards but a big, big hit back then. So big that Charlie had to restrict entrance to the inside of the house only to friends and relatives (happily, I was among that privileged group).

What about the rest of the people? Charlie wouldn't think of shooing them away, so they'd congregate on his front porch and watch TV through the picture window in the living room. Good eyes were a requisite, because the porch was at least forty feet from the TV and don't forget, we're talking about a ten-inch screen and poor reception. Well, one evening, during the popular college basketball playoffs at Madison Square Garden, neighbors, apartment dwellers all, with no concept of the structural integrity of a house, crammed onto that porch jumping up and down, screaming for their favorite teams. One jump too many and the porch came crashing down with all its occupants. Since it was the ground floor, the porch people came away only with bruises and scrapes, but the porch was a total loss. No problem for Charlie. After all, if he could disassemble, repair, and put back together the most expensive and complicated Swiss timepieces, rebuilding the porch would be no problem.

It's a long way around of explaining how I happened to become friendly with the Monroe Avenue gang, but I thought Charlie's house of attractions was interesting.

I got to know and hang out with Allyne's friends, Mary, Diana, Freddie, Irving, Jackie, Archie and others. Diana? Yeh, it's the same girl I married twelve years later, so you can see something good came out of it. But at that time, believe me, it was the last thing in my mind. Then, I kind of had a crush on Allyne. Also, at that time, Diana was taller than all of us, which was a turn-off for us macho boys.

The eleven-year-olds, Diana, Allyne and Mary, circa 1943

NOW WHAT?

An interesting aside: Earlier I told you about how the New York subway system was our own magic carpet, freeing us from having our parents carting us around (or more accurately, freeing them from having to do it). Charlie the watchmaker, who also dealt in precious jewelry, thought nothing of giving Allyne, when she was no more than ten or eleven, a case full of watches and jewels worth several thousand dollars, and having her deliver it downtown to Midtown to the Jewelry District, and then pick up stuff for the trip home. She'd take the subway, usually with her friend Diana, to make the delivery. This one day they stopped for some chocolate malt soft ice cream at the five and ten cent store (there were plenty of them back then) and after they finished, headed for the subway back to the Bronx. Starting down the steps, they looked at one another. Neither of them had the jewelry case! They raced back to the store, Allyne way ahead. (Digressing, I want to mention that Allyne could outrun any of her friends and was a demon on roller skates—you know the ones with four metal wheels where you slipped your shoe into the skate and tightened the toe clamp with a skate key. Skate key? Go ask someone who was a kid in the forties or fifties, they'll tell you what it is. Monroe Avenue ran downhill from 175th Street to 174th. The sidewalk at one point was composed of squares of what appeared to be cracked blue slate with not insignificant gaps between the squares making it almost impossible to navigate the hill on roller skates without going down on your butt or your head. I said *almost* impossible because Allyne could negotiate that hill and that sidewalk at top speed without losing her balance. An ego-buster for us guys.)

Anyway, getting back to the story, the case was gone when they got back to the five and ten, never to be recovered. But that never stopped Charlie from using his favorite courier.

When we grew up, Allyne forsook me for Freddie, but I snared her beautiful friend Diana whom, by now, I was several inches taller, and we two couples became lifelong friends.

Allyne, Fred and their first child

Freddie was an incurable practical joker. Once, walking through Macy's with my cousin Diane, he suddenly stopped her.

"This is the glass department. You have to be very careful where you walk. Otherwise, you could go smack into the hanging glass panels, face first."

That had poor Diane walking very gingerly down the aisles, her arms outstretched in front of her, feeling for the potential glass panels. When everyone on the floor began staring at her she turned beet red.

We went on several vacations with Allyne and Freddie. On the first one, we were in Boothbay Harbor, Maine, on the Atlantic Ocean. We stayed at the Outlook Inn, which had its own dock. Fred and I decided to take out the rowboat tied up there. Fred hopped in the boat and I released the lines—I should have known better. Just as I began to step into the boat he gave a hard shove from the dock propelling the boat away from me and into the water I stepped. Now I don't know if you've ever been in the water off the Maine coast but I can tell you it's as cold as it can be without freezing over. I hit that water in pure agony. You know, I can take a joke as well as the next man but when it came to Freddie, it was vendetta time. Gritting my teeth I surfaced and smiled. "The water's great," I yelled, and began swimming around like a racer. He thought I was having fun. I was just trying to keep warm.

As he dove in the water, I scrambled up into the boat and wrapped a towel around myself. Freddie screamed bloody murder. He couldn't get back into the boat fast enough. He had diarrhea for two days after that.

Outlook Inn was an interesting place. There were no rooms available in town and the AAA suggested trying the inn, which they said was closed, but heard it was accepting some guests. We really lucked out. Not only did we obtain rooms, there was no charge for them—only whatever you cared to donate. There was no help. You had to clean your own room, or not, as you wished. We found the inn only in desperation and found only desperation at the inn. It seems the proprietor's wife had just left him. He became despondent and he just wanted company to drink and eat with until all the provisions of the Inn were gone; then he'd close the place. The drinks were free—you could donate some change into the kitty if you desired. He took the guests out on his yacht, then anchored in Boothbay Harbor by an uninhabited island and served an all-you-can-eat Maine lobster dinner. That was a nice time in our lives for that to happen since neither Freddie nor I had much money between us to afford either the Outlook Inn or Maine lobster dinner on yachts.

The second joint vacation I want to talk about occurred much later, as a matter of fact, almost forty years later, when we went on a long, long train ride, starting in Beijing, going up through Outer Mongolia, then switching trains to traverse the Trans Siberian railroad tracks in rail cars supplied by the Orient Express, all the way to Moscow.

At one of the stops in Siberia, after a tour of the area, we boarded the train. That night, I crawled into the sack, only to smash my foot on what looked like an iron anvil placed under the covers at the foot of bed. Somehow, Freddie had found this very heavy piece of iron, got it onto the train and into my bed. Freddie is no dummy; he's a brilliant entrepreneur who developed his father's small fur manufacturing and wholesale business into a multimillion-dollar enterprise in New York, becoming a celebrity in his own right by starring in his own ads blanketing New York City as "Fred the Furrier."

Fred and Allyne on the Trans-Siberian railroad tour

As I said, he's no dummy, so he was on full alert for any retribution, and I knew it. I racked my brain. He'd be ready for anything. Then an idea hit me.

The next night, after we turned in, there was a knock on my door. It was Freddie, holding up a large rock, a triumphant look on his face. "I discovered this under my pillow *before* I got into bed. Too bad, Carl, your ploy didn't work."

I shrugged, muttered "damn," and turned over. He went back to his cabin. Two minutes later I heard the scream in the next compartment. I smiled and went to sleep, happy with the thought that the diversion worked and Freddie had never thought to look for the unidentifiable metal rod, knobbed at both ends, I found alongside the tracks and had placed at the *bottom* of his bed.

NOW WHAT?

Fred, still smiling, found this in his bed

Don't think I always got the best of Freddie; not by a long shot--but since this is my book, I get to choose the incidents to write about.

CARL L. STEINHOUSE

A Cinderella Story

Forget that stuff about Cinderella. I got on famously with my stepfather and stepsister, Marion. I lived with Marion, a few years older that I was, when she attended college at NYU and I was still in high school. She was attractive and very popular with the boys. That's why it was strange how she had a total lapse of judgment when she became engaged to Stan R.

Marion and author, circa 1946

Stan R., to use a Yiddish expression, was a *nebbish*. He had sinus problems, and as far as allergies are concerned, you name it, he had it. And it wasn't that Marion was bowled over by his masculine physique or good looks, because he had neither. My stepfather was beside himself, but when a girl Marion's age wants to do what she wants to do, it is very difficult to dissuade her. As I said, Stan R. wasn't athletic, he didn't have as sense of humor that I could discern, and he certainly did not have the gift of gab.

Stepfather and his doctor friend, Leo, had conspired to save Marion for Leo's nephew, Stanley B. Though Stanley B. adored Marion and hoped she'd wait, he was too busy getting through medical school to seriously consider marriage. It was too bad, because he was everything the other Stan wasn't.

NOW WHAT?

Author, Marion and a boyfriend

We needn't have worried. Stanley B. was patient. Marion went through Stan R., then Harry with the bad heart, and then Burt and a few others by the time Stanley B. graduated from medical school. This time the Cinderella story held true. Stanley B. found his princess and married her. Oh yes, they lived happily ever after. And why not? It isn't hard when you live in Hawaii surrounded by all your children, grand children and great grand children.

A postscript. Diana and I had maintained a close relationship with Marion and Dr. Stanley. Though they live in Hawaii and we in Naples, Florida, once a year we met halfway--in Charleston, South Carolina, for the Spoleto Festival and to gouge ourselves on oysters on the half shell at AW Shucks. (They thought it was halfway, so I never told them.)

Visiting them in Hawaii after we all retired. L to R, Author, Marion, Stan & Diana

NOW WHAT?

A Fantasy--If You Only Knew--1946

"Oh, if I only knew then what I know now." Ever say that to yourself? I'm sure you did. I know we can't turn back the clock but nothing prevents us from fantasizing about it. Did you ever do that? Well, I did and here's what happened.

I picked up a newspaper. It was dated June 25, 1946. Then I spotted him--I mean me. I walked up to him.

"Hey kid, got a minute?"

The skinny fifteen-year-old kid looked at me suspiciously. "Do I know you?"

I smiled. "You might say so?"

"What does that mean?"

"I'm you!"

He furrowed his brow. "When did they let you out, mister?"

"Look, I know it sounds impossible, and I can't explain it except to say it's a onetime chance, so neither of us should pass it up."

The skinny kid looked at my potbelly. "I'll never end up looking like that! How do I know you're not jerking me around? Maybe you're a pervert!"

I ignored the last remark and moved on. "Your Uncle Abe calls you 'snake-hips' and your classmates tease you by calling you 'Steinmouse' or 'Steinlouse'. Remember when you were six or seven? You wanted to grow up to be a garbage man. And the day you got a good conk on the head from a rock thrown by one of the Brookies, the gang from Brooks Avenue in the Bronx that used to come up and harass you guys, the same guys that chased you and Lew through Claremont Park?"

He blushed. "How'd you know all that?"

I smiled. "And Dad, when he was alive, used to tease you and your friend Lewis, by calling you 'Carol' and 'Louise'. It made you so angry, didn't it?"

His eyes widened. I was getting to him. So I bored in. "Remember when you were about six and had just came back from a few months in Florida, and your Uncle Irving pulled down your pants in front of the family to show off your tan?"

"Don't remind me, I never forgave him for that-- or for the Boston bulldog he promised me but never delivered on. Come on, how'd you know? I've never spoken about that to anyone, not even to my best friends, Lew, Mike, Harry, or Freddie."

"I told you kid, I'm you and I have the same memories, even if mine are somewhat dimmer."

"This is weird beyond belief. If you're an older version me, as you claim, tell me what sport I play in my bedroom?"

"That's easy. You take a rolled up sock and try to toss it into that German helmet sitting on your bookshelf, making believe you're playing on the NYU basketball team alongside Sid Tannenbaum."

"Holy shit, no one knows that."

"And that German helmet was sent to you by your cousin Alfred from Europe during World War II? Well, your mom cleaned out all the blood and dirt, over your strenuous objections. And your orthodontist? He's Dr. Al Smith on 188th Street and the Grand Concourse. Remember how angry he was when you bit into a wax whistle that removed all your braces and caps?"

"Yeah, I sure felt nice. I didn't tell Mom for two days."

"See? My memories are your memories."

"Okay, okay, I believe you. What do you want from me?"

"Just to talk, kid. And maybe give you some insights."

He looked at me. "Just how old are you?"

"Never mind that kid, I'm old enough."

"You look older than Mom and Uncle Dan."

I frowned. "Hey, that hurt kid."

He shrugged. "How come you didn't lose your hair like my uncles and Cousin Alfred?"

"Just lucky, I guess."

He rubbed his chin. "What should I call you?"

"Carl will be fine. And it does not start with a 'K', right?"

He laughed. "Right! Put 'er there!" He extended his hand.

"Gimme five!" I responded, raising my right hand, palm out.

He looked at me funny.

I felt foolish. "That's what they'll be doing in about forty years," I said sheepishly. I lowered my hand and shook his.

Young Carl looked me over. "So Carl, tell me everything about the future."

I shook my head. "Can't do that kid 'cause it's liable to change that future, then where would I--or for that matter you--be? But maybe I can give you some guidance."

"Such as?"

"Such as overcoming your shyness with girls. Just because Beth wouldn't go out with you, doesn't mean all girls will reject you."

"It took all my courage just to ask her--and she just shot me down."

I looked sympathetically. "I know, I know. That's one memory that hasn't dimmed."

Young Carl brightened. ""You remember Aunt Faye's niece, Allyne?"

"I sure do."

"I kinda like her, and she's pretty--and can run and skate faster and better than most of the guys. I go

63

over to her house a few times a week because her Dad has the only television set in the neighborhood."

I patted him on the back. "Well, I'll only tell you that she'll hook up with one of your best friends, but hang in there anyway, because you just may make it with one of her best friends."

His eyes widened. "Which one? The Irish Catholic Mary or that tall, gawky one that's a head taller than me, Diana?"

I smiled. "You'll just have to see. Believe me, things will change. Your perceptions will be much different in a few years. And you'll overcome your shyness."

His face brightened. "I can start now by wearing by my pegged pants, long key chain, and blue suede shoes!"

I shuddered at the image of the in clothes of the forties, but decided not to put a damper on his enthusiasm. "That's cool."

He looked at me questioningly. "Actually, the pants are wool and they're pretty warm when I wear them."

I forgot that the word was taken literally in those days. I let it slide so as not to confuse him any more than necessary.

He locked into my gaze, hazel eyes to hazel eyes. "Will I make it through high school?" he said, almost in a whisper. "I have such lousy grades."

"Don't sweat it, kid. You'll graduate and go on to college, survive the army and be first in your class in graduate school."

"Graduate school? Go on! What kind of graduate school?"

I shook my finger. "You're getting sneaky. That's for you to find out."

"At least tell me--will I make a good living?"

I nodded. "It'll be tough at first, but eventually you'll do just fine. More than that I'm not at liberty to say."

Young Carl's face lit up. "Hey, you want to come home with me? You can maybe shoot some socks into the German helmet and hear my Perry Como collection."

"What, no rock and roll?"

He screwed up his face. "Rock and who?"

I shrugged. "Never mind, I keep forgetting the time line. Listen, kid, I'd love to come home with you and shoot some baskets, but I don't think it's a good idea for Mom and Stepdad to see me. Their hearts aren't as strong as yours, you know."

He frowned. I could see he was disappointed.

"But you can do me a favor, young Carl. Give them kisses for me. I miss them very much."

He looked at me strangely for a moment, and then he nodded. He understood.

"Mum's the word on our meeting, kid," struggling for forties' vernacular.

I took out a handkerchief and blew my nose.

Young Carl frowned. "I can see that sinus problem didn't go away."

I shrugged.

He waved goodbye as his friends, Mike, Harry, and Lew came running up with a broomstick and Freddie waved the pink Spaulding ball. How I would have loved to play strikeout against the wall of my old apartment building and try, futilely, to hit one of Freddie's damn curve balls--just one more time.

II. COLLEGE YEARS 1949-1952

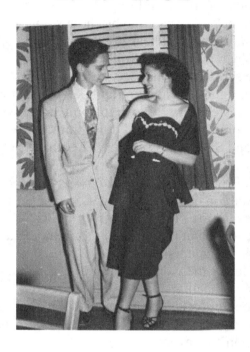

My First Love: 1949

"What do you mean, Pledge, that you can't get a date? If you want admittance into this fraternity, you damn well better get one for our Eastern Regional Conclave," the Pledge Master said.

I dreaded the damn Conclave, a two-night affair, the first night at a Manhattan nightclub, the second, a formal dance at an exclusive downtown hotel. I was 18 and painfully shy. I might as well strip in Macy's window at high noon as call a girl for a date.

My Aunt Faye to the rescue! She knew Diana, niece Allyne's friend, who was a year and a half younger than I. Aunt Faye felt Diana would make a perfect date. With the formal dance a week away, she took it upon herself to ask Diana on my behalf. Of course, which was worse for my self-esteem? I'm not sure: having to call a girl for a date myself, or having my aunt call for me? Diana, who really liked my Aunt Faye, said yes, as a favor to her, even though she only had a few days to scrounge up a formal dress. What a nerd I am, I thought. I shuttered at what Diana must have thought of me.

The first night of the conclave was at the China Doll nightclub and the second night was the formal affair at the Belmont Hotel.

I picked her up at 7 o'clock on the first night. It was December 27, 1949. Puffing my way up to the fifth floor walkup apartment, I rang the bell. An older woman answered the door--it had to be her mother--please God. It was her mother. Standing behind her, was an absolute vision: That can't be my date, it had to be her sister, I thought. She looked in her twenties.

It was Diana. I hadn't seen her for five years. Never in all my fantasies had I dated such a beauty--I may have been a nerd but it did not stop me from being an incurable daydreamer. It was just like the movies--I walked on air and my heart felt like bursting. The name Diana fit my date perfectly. If I knew then how to sigh, I would have--but I wasn't that sophisticated at the time.

Diana

I did not have my driver's license yet so we took the subway downtown to 50th Street and Broadway. For the first time it was I that saw the looks of envy on other guys in the subway car.

And she was so easy to talk to. I could not believe the conversation I was having with a girl-- absolutely inspired. Just like I was talking to one of the guys.

We arrived at the China Doll and let me tell you, heads turned. I could hear the whispers--"Who is *that* with pledge Carl?" We danced. I was not a good dancer, but she made me feel light on my feet. Holding Diana around her beautiful waist, dancing cheek to cheek--if that wasn't heaven to a college freshman, I don't know what was. Much later, Diana told me, that several of the fraternity brothers tried to date her--that night. So much for fraternity brotherhood and all the high-sounding garbage.

My first date with Diana, at the China Doll Nightclub

I got home around one in the morning. I couldn't sleep. All I could think about was Diana--an angel, the moon goddess. I fantasized making passionate love to her--I didn't tell her this, of course. I was totally, unequivocally and madly in love--I didn't tell her that either. I suppose any pretty girl who gave me a tumble might affect me the same way. But Diana was not just any female--and not some imaginary figment on gossamer wings. She was a breathing, lovely and beautiful girl. (Later in life, I would have to change that word to politically correct, "woman".) But right now she was my girl--at least in so far as we had a date for tomorrow night's formal.

After the dreaded--but now wonderful--Eastern Regional Conclave was concluded, I came face to face with reality, namely, that Diana was very popular and it was damn difficult getting a date with her. I tried hard. I pined for her company. My love was so overwhelming that I did my own telephoning--really! She went out with me a few times that spring. Up to now, I thought my Bar Mitzvah was the crowning event of my life. It was nothing compared to a date with Diana.

By fall, Diana was going out with me with more frequency, so I mustn't have been such a nerd, after all. I was a fraternity brother now, very proud of my fraternity pin and my power to lord it over the new crop of pledges.

By spring, I could wait no longer. I drove (I had gotten my driver's license) with Diana up to one of my favorite spots, Sleepy Hollow, New York. We sat on a large boulder on the shore of the Hudson River. It was a bucolic scene. Heart in my mouth, I screwed up my nerve and popped the question.

"Will you go steady with me?" I blurted out, offering her my fraternity pin.

"Oh Carl," she said, "I do like you a lot, but you're such a little boy. I'm not sure what I want to do at this point, so you keep your pin and we'll see what happens in the future." Actually, as she told me much later, she always intended to marry me after I grew up. So, after all, it seems I chased after her until she caught me!

But for that moment at Sleepy Hollow, she might as well have stretched me out on a rack in a medieval dungeon chamber, and turned the big wheel. To be rejected by my only true love was bad enough, but to be called "a little boy"--that was almost too much to bear. Sleepy Hollow was no longer bucolic. I felt more like the headless horseman's domain and me, like Ichabod Crane, head in hand.

Eventually, she accepted my fraternity pin. Naturally, I was delighted, but I'm not sure it was the best thing for me physically, and I'll tell you why. By now I had been a full-fledged brother in Alpha Epsilon Pi and played on the fraternity touch football team. See, I told you we'd get back to football eventually. Anyway, we were playing Tau Epsilon Pi (TEP) and it just so happened one of her ardent suitors that I beat out for Diana's hand belonged to that fraternity. Now this was only touch football and seemed relative safe. But the TEP guys ran every play over my position until eventually I absorbed a hard shot to the mouth knocking out my front teeth. Diana claims that her ex-boyfriend

70

had nothing to do with my injury; that he wasn't even athletic. That may be so, but I'm sure he passed the word to his fraternity brothers to work me over and nothing she says has disabused me of that belief.

The injury was particularly galling to my parents, who had invested thirteen years and tens of thousands of dollars in my orthodontia work. I had a particularly bad bite and had just had completed my orthodontia treatment. I had had my braces off for only two weeks before I received that blow to the mouth. I had never seen my stepfather cry, or my orthodontist, for that matter.

I know that TEP guy's name that dated Diana and so far, I've never run into to him, but he'd still better watch out, because sixty years is not too long to hold a grudge.

CARL L. STEINHOUSE

Skiing, Bow Legs, and Broken Bones

For a while I was down on skiing after my
excursion to Bear Mountain in the late fifties with my
Monroe Avenue buddy, Fred, and my law school pal,
Frank. We were beginners and young Turks, willing to
try anything. Clearly, this constituted a bad mixture for
healthy skiing, borne out by what happened by the end of
the day. I'd taken a bad fall trying to avoid a skier
crossing the slopes on foot, and nipped some cartilage in
my right knee. Frank had twisted his ankle, could hardly
walk on it, and Fred lacerated his shin. The three of us,
walking though the parking lot looked like that famous
Homer Winslow painting of the three minute men in the
fife and drum corps, limping back from the wars.

By day's end I had my right knee in a cast and
walked on crutches. That presented a serious problem
because I worked in my stepfather's CPA office as a
junior accountant and it was tax season. He warned me--
no, ordered me would be more accurate--not to go skiing
and risk being out injured during his busiest season. But
at that age I felt invincible and snuck off anyway one
Sunday for some fun (sometimes we actually got Sundays
off in the tax season). Of course, I could forget taking a
few days off as the doctor had ordered. It took a hell of a
lot of planning on my part to arrange my schedule so as to
avoid my crutches and me meeting face to face with
stepfather that week. The office, after all, wasn't that big.
All my machinations went for naught when my mother
spilled the beans. But since I did not miss a day of work,
the boss could only grumble "I told you so."

You would think that, having experienced the
pitfalls of skiing, I would protect myself and, more
importantly, my children, from such a dangerous sport.
Not so. First of all, in the lessons-not-learned
department, I took up skiing again and so did Diana--

72

well, Diana, not really. She never graduated from snow plowing on the beginner's slope. We visited friends in Aspen with a home in Starwood, not far from John Denver's place. They took us skiing on Aspen Mountain. Diana, ever the snowplower, stayed down on the beginner's slope with hostess Paula while the host Bill and I took the ski lift up to the top of the mountain for lunch and then the five-mile ski down. While lunching, we watched the skiers unloading from the ski lift. Two women, trying to get off the ski lift chair became entangled in each other, ending up sprawled in the snow. We laughed until we recognized them--it was Diana and Paula!

Bewildered, I stammered, "What the hell are they doing up here?"

"More important," Bill added, "How the hell are we going to get Diana down the mountain?"

Paula had talked Diana into going to the top to see the glorious scenery.

It took us several hours but I have to hand it to Diana, she snowplowed down the entire five-mile course without falling. I fell dozens of times. We'd ski and wait for her, ski and wait for her. When we finally got to the bottom and Diana relaxed and found she couldn't move her legs. She walked like a bow-legged cowboy back to the car.

* * *

The big mistake of my life was taking Sam and Jane skiing. Sam, about eleven, was scheduled to go to ski camp over the Christmas holidays, so I took him to a small local ski area to practice. Skiing down a not too challenging slope, Sam fell. It didn't even look serious.

"Are you okay?" I yelled.

"No."

I skied over to him. He was crying and in a great deal of pain. I released his bindings and called for the ski patrol, which took him down the slope in a sled and put a temporary splint on his left leg, permitting me to transport him to our local Warrensville Hospital. He had a spiral fracture of his left leg.

Now I had a problem. I had promised Jane a ski trip to Holiday Valley, New York, while Sam was supposed to be away (of course, he never made it to ski camp). I figured, what the hell, lightening can't strike twice. Wrong. I shouldn't rely on clichés in making life's important decisions.

Like a bad recurring nightmare, on one of the simple runs, Jane fell and broke her leg. Once again, bundled in the car by the ski patrol, I drove her to the nearest hospital in Erie, Pennsylvania, screaming bloody murder all the way there. The intern advised that the doctor would be in the next morning to set her leg. It did not sound to me like such a good idea to wait so long so I called my doctor at home who said to give her Demerol and take her to the Warrensville Hospital in Cleveland, where he'd meet me. The Demerol worked. All the way home Jane rhapsodized about how now that she had a broken leg she could get the attention plus have everyone sign *her* cast, too.

Sam and Jane after their skiing mishaps. Sam signs Jane's cast. He is still on crutches

NOW WHAT?

After being treated at the Warrensville Hospital, I took Jane home. Carrying her from the garage to the side entrance of our house, I tried to kick the door shut and managed to catch my index finger in the doorjamb, cracking open my fingernail. Back to Warrensville Hospital I went. By now they were viewing me with a great deal of suspicion.

But it did not end there. The next evening, sitting on a high bar stool at our kitchen counter eating dinner, Lani fell off the stool, breaking her wrist. Back to Warrensville Hospital I went. Lani's treatment completed, the nurse gave me the evil eye. "Is your wife next? She's the only one left. What are you going to do, break her arm?"

I'm sure she was only half kidding.

III. YOU'RE IN THE ARMY NOW! 1953-1954

NOW WHAT?

Desperate Times, Desperate Measures

The time was February 1953, the Korean War was at its height, and I was taking infantry basic training at Fort Dix, New Jersey in the dead of winter. Definitely not a good scenario. Basically, I'd never left home until I was drafted in the army. Even in my college life I was a commuter student.

The first weeks of basic training were wake-up call for me. First of all, the training cadre did not treat me nicely. They called me all sorts of vile names, assigned me, who never even had cleaned my own room, to the KP garbage detail, cleaning out the grease pits in the company kitchen; sometimes they put me on the midnight weapons cleaning detail cleaning and greasing heavy and light machine guns, B.A.R.s, bazookas, mortars, and similar instruments of mayhem; and this after a hard day in the field and probably a harder one the following day with only three hours of sleep.

Author on garbage detail at Fort Dix, March 1953

One night the first sergeant assigned me to stoke the furnace in the barracks. This meant I had to get up every two hours and make sure the fires were properly banked, kept lit, and fed with coal. I lived in an

77

apartment house all my life. So who ever stoked a
furnace? Who knew about banking a furnace? As sure
as the sun rises in the morning, the fire in the furnace,
under my care, died out in the middle of the night and
everyone, including the first sergeant, woke up at reveille
freezing their asses off. I did not earn brownie points
from either my fellow draftees or the first sergeant for
that goof. It was traumatic, no doubt about it. So I began
sleepwalking again--not a wise thing to do in an army
barracks full of disgruntled trainees. Anyway, after one
such nocturnal stroll, I climbed back into my upper bunk,
except it wasn't my bunk! It belonged to a huge
redheaded farmer from Watertown, New York, not
known for his tolerance of gay people. He woke up
bellowing he'd kill the fag who tried to crawl in bed with
him. That alerted me instantly, and before he could
regain his all his senses, I was down from his cozy nest
and up into my own bunk in one bound. Thank heavens
it was dark. He never found out the identity of the person
he thought was attempting loving overtures.

Now we were in our eighth week of basic training
and I had applied to go to Army finance school; logical,
since I had graduated NYU with an accounting degree.
The entire C Company assembled in the battalion
headquarters building. It was here that the Army would
announce who would be going for special training.
Those whose names were not called out were cannon
fodder or, in other words, infantrymen, bound ultimately
for the war in Korea.

They called out the names for finance school,
officers' candidate school, special services (entertainment
of the troops), *etc*. I didn't hear my name called. It was
painfully obvious that I had failed in my bid to get into
finance school--and not incidentally, resulted in my
designation as cannon fodder.

Then the commanding officer rose to address the
company. "Any of you see errors on your personnel
records?"

NOW WHAT?

My absolute last chance, I figured. I raised my hand. "Sir, I believe the birth date is wrong on my records."

I was instructed to see a Captain--we'll call him Benson--in room 103. I knocked on the door. "Come on in," a disembodied voice shouted through the closed door. I turned the knob and entered with no specific plan in mind. *Now what, Einstein?* I thought.

My future brother-in-law, Larry, drafted a year before I was, managed to get into the CIC, that's the U.S. Army Counter Intelligence Corps. He had suggested I apply. I had forgotten about it until now.

"What can I do for you, Private?"

It just came out of my mouth without much thought. "I'm a college graduate and was told to see you about applying for CIC School, Sir."

He looked at me quizzically. "CIC School? I've never taken applications for that."

I shrugged. "They told me to come to you, Sir."

Fortunately, Captain Benson did not press me on whom the amorphous "they" were. "Okay, write down your name, rank, serial number, and unit on this piece of paper."

I did, and he dismissed me. *Well, that was a big waste of time,* I concluded dejectedly.

*   *   *

We were now in our fifteenth week of infantry basic training. I had learned in no particular order, how to shoot someone in the head from 100 yards away, how to bayonet an enemy who was bearing down on me in hand-to-hand combat, how to crawl under barbed wire with live ammo coming in over my head, and how to cut a sentry's throat noiselessly--things every soldier should be prepared for on return to civilian life. They turned me into a "fighting machine." But I was a very unhappy

79

fighting machine--and I was also a very muddy fighting machine. We were on bivouac for the week. Bivouac is a fancy name for camping out in a foxhole or tent-- "camping out" is perhaps not the phrase--more like living in dirt, slime, and slit trenches (for those who don't know what a slit trench is, it would make using an outhouse feel like the height of luxury). This time we were in muddy foxholes and I was one cold and miserable soldier. The army did an excellent job of emulating winter conditions on the Korean Peninsula.

I had just opened a can of K rations: a chocolate bar, some fouling tasting cracker with strawberry jelly and two cigarettes. This was before the reign of Surgeon General Koop. I had just given the cigarettes to the guy sharing my foxhole, when an Army sedan bearing the one star flag of a brigadier general drove into the camp. Needless to say our commanding officer, the C.O., snapped to attention. All eyes were focused on the civilian that emerged from the driver's side of the sedan. He conferred with the C.O. The C.O. nodded his head. He turned and shouted, "Private Steinhouse, front and center, pronto!"

"Holy shit," I exclaimed to my foxhole mate, "what kind of trouble am I in?"

He shrugged. He had a hard enough time bearing up in the mud and cold without taking on my troubles.

I slipped and slid out of the foxhole. Covered with mud from head to toe, I ran up to the C.O. and saluted.

"In the car, Steinhouse."

"Excuse me, Sir?"

"You deaf, Steinhouse? Get the hell in the car."

"Yes, *Sir*."

They scared up on old army blanket that was put on the seat to catch my mud.

The Army sedan with the one star general's flag took off, with me in it.

NOW WHAT?

We drove in silence for about two miles when the civilian driver pulled over. He flashed his credentials. "Captain F., CIC."

It didn't click. I thought I was in deep trouble, though I couldn't imagine why. It was true that I once sneaked out of a weapons cleaning detail in the thirteenth week of basic training. But I couldn't believe that would bring down the wrath of the Counter Intelligence Corps-- after all, they were counter-spies, not the Military Police.

I looked blankly at him.

I'm here to interview you for CIC School.

"Huh?"

"Well, you applied didn't you?"

The light in my brain finally lit up. "Oh, yes, Sir, Captain F., I sure did."

He spoke to me for about a half hour, alternately asking me questions and simply engaging in pleasant conversation--the first civil one I've had with an officer since I was drafted into the Army. He seemed preoccupied with the Abraham Lincoln Brigade. He asked me if I was or had been a member of the Brigade and whether I ever attended any of its meetings. I never even heard of the organization before he mentioned it. Apparently, it was the number one enemy in the Cold War--one of the domestic Communist subversive organizations--and with such a heroic name.

He drove me back to the bivouac area. Before I got out of the car, Captain F. turned to me and said, "Our conversation and your application to the CIC is confidential and not to be discussed with anyone. Understood, Private?"

He must be kidding, I thought. "Y-yes, Sir, Captain."

I got out of the car. The C.O. came up to me. "Steinhouse, what was that all about?"

The shit's really going to hit the fan, if I don't tell him something.

"Sir, the General's a friend of my father and he just wanted to check up on me."

The C.O. looked at me suspiciously. "What did you tell him?"

"Everything was fine and I was enjoying my basic training, Sir."

The C.O. frowned. "Yeah, I'll just bet, Steinhouse. If it gets back to me that you complained, your ass will be mine. Now get the hell back to your foxhole."

"Yes, *Sir!*"

* * *

The last week of basic training came and went with no word from the CIC. My orders were to report to the Embarkation Center for transportation to Korea. I received a week's leave, said the tearful good-byes to my family, friends, and fiancée Diana, and reported to the train station for the trip to a waiting troopship on the West Coast. Sitting around the station with my buddies, the loudspeaker on the train platform blared out, "Private Carl Steinhouse, report to the stationmaster's office immediately."

I turned to my buddy. "Now what did I do?"

He shrugged. He was introspective trying to deal with his own problems of having to face the war and the danger of death on the Korean Peninsula.

An MP directed me to the Stationmaster's Office.

"Private Steinhouse reporting as directed." He was a civilian, so I didn't say "Sir."

The Stationmaster spun the combination and opened the safe. He pulled out an envelope and handed it to me. I started to open it.

"Not in here, Private, don't you see the SECRET stamp on the envelope?"

NOW WHAT?

"Sorry, Sir." He was so authoritative, that I automatically said "Sir."

I raced to the men's room, closed the stall door, sat on the toilet and ripped open the envelope. I had new orders. I was to report back to Fort Dix until further notice. That was it. I shook the envelope to make sure there weren't any other orders in it. It was empty. Well, I certainly wasn't going to look the gift horse in the mouth. Anything was better than going to Korea--even if it meant going back to that hell hole, Fort Dix.

CARL L. STEINHOUSE

The Unlikely and Overweight Counterspy

After spending three weeks at Fort Dix as training cadre, I was given further "secret" orders. I was to report to Fort Holabird in Baltimore. That was the CIC School!

I came home for a long weekend, like a returning war hero without having actually gone to war. My fiancée and my parents were deliriously happy with this unexpected turn of events. I left Fort Dix with my personnel file, now marked "SECRET," securely under my arm. I spent the weekend at home and caught a Sunday afternoon train to Baltimore. I reported to the duty officer at Fort Holabird. He stuck out his hand. I put out mine to shake his.

He frowned and shook his head, making it clear he wasn't trying to be friendly. "Your secret personnel papers, please."

Holy shit, I thought, *I left them at home in the Bronx*. My career at the CIC was ending before it began, given that they were fanatics about secrecy. Back to being cannon fodder again.

I thought fast. "Sir, I left them in a locker at the train station while I took in a bit of Dundalk." Fort Holabird was located in Dundalk, an area of Baltimore then known for its strip joints. I winked.

"Private, those papers were secret; they shouldn't have left your possession."

"I know they were secret, Sir, that's why I locked them safely in a locker."

"Private, get your ass downtown, toot sweet, and get those papers, or you're out of CIC School."

"Yes, Sir." I snapped off a spiffy salute and retreated out of the office.

I ran to the telephone.

"Diana? Can you bring my personnel papers down to Baltimore by the next train?"

"What?"

"They're on my dresser. It's that or Korea."

Diana's train arrived at 11:50 at night. She got off the train, handed me my "SECRET" personnel file, and we raced to get her on the midnight train back to New York City.

I arrived at the Duty Officer's office at about twelve-thirty in the morning.

"What the hell happened to you, Private?"

"Took in a little more of Dundalk, Sir. But don't worry; I left the papers locked up at the train station until I was ready to come back."

The Duty Officer shook his head. "That's what happens when we let draftees into the CIC."

* * *

Halfway through the three month training to become an intelligence analyst, the CIC handed each of my class a form to check off the geographic areas of the world in which we preferred to do our service. Hawaii? Japan? Caribbean? Not me--nothing in the Pacific--too close to Korea. Not the Caribbean either because everyone would select that. I selected the most improbable theater of operations I could find, called "TRUST." It stood for "Trieste United States Troops."

I did a smart thing, for once. Everyone received orders for Korea, except classmate Bob Leyden and me. We were the only ones to select TRUST--and there were two openings.

In four weeks, I would be leaving for Trieste. Because dependents were allowed to join their spouse soldiers there, I called Diana and proposed marriage. She said yes.

My mother always had been a "can do" woman. Having only four weeks before I arrived home on the way overseas, she managed to get the Starlight Room of the St. Moritz Hotel on Central Park West, send out invitations, hire an orchestra, and arrange for a caterer. (Actually, my Uncle Oscar was a lawyer, a caterer, and an insurance agent, which qualified him to work on the "Mission Impossible" team.)

Starlight Room atop the St. Moritz Hotel looking south from Central Park

Oh yes, Mother also managed to scare up a wedding dress. The veil had been borrowed from opera star Roberta Peters. My friend Kenneth's parents knew Peters' parents and arranged the loan. To look at Diana, you'd have thought everything had been custom-made for her (at least that was *my* opinion).

The wedding went off without a hitch, and I left for Trieste with Diana awaiting word when she could join me. Well, not quite without a hitch. We spent our wedding night in a suite at the St. Moritz. Finally alone, we anxiously started shedding tux and wedding gown. After all, I had spent the last sixteen weeks in basic training and the some more weeks in Fort Holabird with hundreds of guys and no gals. We'd just got into bed when there was a persistent rapping on our door.

"What in damnation?" I exclaimed.

"Who the hell's there," I shouted through the door angrily.

"Don't you dare curse at me," was the response, just as angry.

"Mother?"

"Who do you think it is?" she said impatiently. The fact that I was a mature adult and a soldier ready to die for his country held no sway for Mother. She'd treat me just as she always has.

"What do you want?"

"I need Roberta Peters' head piece. I promised Kenneth's mother I would return it immediately."

"At two in the morning?"

"Just give it to me so I can leave."

I opened the door a crack and slipped the wedding veil out, immediately slamming the door before Mother got any other ideas.

Author's mother, circa 1950s

* * *

If you know me today and then looked at my wedding pictures, you would have never recognized me. Back then I weighed 119 pounds. My nickname was "snake hips." Remember that.

Anyway, I arrived in Trieste and everything hit the fan--big time. The United Nations, in its wisdom, partitioned the "Free Territory of Trieste." Strange, it was called "Free" even though it had been and still was occupied (since before the end of World War II) by the Americans and British. In other words the territory was under military government. The agricultural countryside, the UN decided, would go to Yugoslavia and the port city of Trieste would go to Italy. No one was happy. The Italian Fascists and the Yugoslav Communists rioted in the City and we were put on riot duty. All dependents were ordered out of Trieste and none were permitted to come back in.

After several months, things were quiet again and the Commanding General had sneaked his wife back into the Territory. I knew about it because the CIC was one of the organizations responsible for his security. Dependents were now permitted to visit Trieste, but not live there.

In April 1954, Diana and my parents were scheduled to come to Paris. I arranged to meet them there. I sent a memo to the General requesting permission to bring my wife into the Territory to live. Request denied. Another memo reminded the General that he had his wife living covertly in Trieste. A big mistake! You don't screw around with generals.

Major Black, my commanding officer, called me into his office.

"Steinhouse, I don't know what you said to the General, and I don't want to know. But I have been told that I would be relieved of my command and demoted, and I quote directly from General, 'if Steinhouse does not stop harassing me.' Now I can't fathom how you managed to harass a general, but whatever you're doing or did, I order you to stop it. Now that is a direct order. Do you understand?"

I sighed. "Yes, Sir." It wasn't fair, but then, that's the army for you.

Life in the CIC wasn't all that bad--for Army life, that is. Our CIC unit had our own villa in downtown Trieste. It used to be Gestapo headquarters, and the

Nazis, to set an example, had lynched several Tito communist partisans by dropping them out of my bedroom window with nooses around their necks. Anyway, every year on the anniversary of their deaths, the Communists would have a ceremony in CIC anti-Communist headquarters commemorating the martyrdom of their comrades--and in my bedroom, no less! It would be like Alger Hiss having Thanksgiving dinner at the White House with President and Mrs. Richard Nixon.

Remember how I'd gotten in trouble sleepwalking? It came to haunt me whenever it was my turn to be responsible for security of our premises for the twenty-four hour period. Anyway, it required me to be armed, a snub-nosed thirty-eight revolver on my hip. I didn't mind that, I'd be armed often during my army career. What bothered me was night time and sleeping in the OD room while armed. What if I shot up the place, or worse, shot myself, in my sleep? I solved it by sleeping with the weapon, but first unloading it and putting the cartridges on the other side of the room. I wasn't a great guard, I'll grant you that, but I was a well-rested one. But shhh, keep quiet about this, will you? My commanding officer never found out about it.

Author, left, on security duty, armed and dangerous.
Friend Agent Fred Tranfo on the right.

Our CIC unit had no mess hall so we were given $2.63 a day to eat out on the Trieste market. Believe it or not, we couldn't spend all of it. Dinner at the finest restaurant cost less than one dollar. So we pooled part of our allowances and hired a cleaning woman/cook. She cleaned and made our beds and cooked pasta for breakfast and prepared huge hero sandwiches for lunch. For dinner, we usually ate a ten-course meal at Dante's, the best restaurant in town--antipasto, soup, pasta, main course, salad (served after the main course--typically European), rich dessert, and cappuccino.

You will recall I told you that I weighed 119 pounds when I left for Trieste. I now tipped the scales at 186 pounds--that's what I said, 186 pounds. I arrived in Paris to meet Diana and my parents who were flying in from New York City. I got to the hotel an hour before they arrived. I was standing in the lobby of the hotel, when my wife and parents entered the lobby through the revolving door. I just stood there. They walked right by me without any recognition or acknowledgment. I turned around, facing their retreating backs and called out, "You'd think the three people in the world most likely to recognize you are your mother, father, and wife."

They stopped in their tracks, turned around and stared.

"Carl?" my mother asked.

I smiled. "In the flesh!"

Everyone started screaming at once.

"What's happened to you?" my mother cried.

"You should be happy; you were always trying to stuff food down me so that I'd gain weight."

Diana flew into my arms and that stopped all the discussion about my weight.

* * *

After eight months apart, Diana and I had things on our mind other than passport control. We were on the night train from Paris to Lucerne. We hit the Swiss border at midnight and were as snug as bugs in a rug in our sleeping compartment. While we were lovey-dovey, the Swiss passport officials burst into the room.

90

NOW WHAT?

"Passports please!" Wrapping the blankets and sheets around our bodies, we complied. I'm sure the Swiss officials did it this way on purpose for whatever voyeuristic thrills it gave them.

Author and wife in Europe in 1954

After meeting my parents for a week in Nice, we reached the last leg of our trip, Trieste. I showed Diana around my home city on the Adriatic. As I said earlier, the Free Territory of Trieste was, in fact, occupied by a military government. The local police were called VGs. During the war, many Triestinas turned to prostitution to feed themselves and their families. And many of them continued the profession after the Nazis were driven out. The British (bless their hearts) instituted a curfew and strict regulations. Any woman out alone after ten o'clock at night was to be taken into to custody, automatically to be tested for venereal disease. If she was clean, she was given a dated certificate. If she wasn't, she was arrested and treated. A form of socialized medicine, I suppose. The law was enforced by the local VGs.

Diana, one of my CIC buddies, Fred Tranfo, and I were strolling in the old city of Trieste late one night. Diana was wide-eyed, taking in the cobblestone streets, the San Guisto castle and the nineteenth century homes and stores. Tranfo and I had dropped about a half a block behind Diana, when a VG policeman approached Diana, and tried to question her. We remained back to see what would happen. Diana didn't speak Italian and the VG didn't speak English. It was quite a scene. Diana yelled "Chich Americano" (Italian pronunciation of CIC). When the VG attempted to take her into custody, we intervened, flashing our CIC credentials. The VG was very apologetic and quickly retreated.

Three buddies on a stroll in Trieste

"What was that all about?" Diana asked.

"Oh, nothing much," I said nonchalantly, "he just wanted to take you in and have you tested for venereal disease."

"What? And you let him go on like that?"

Fred Tranfo looked the other way. I shrugged. I experienced the first cold shoulder of our short marriage-- a real cold one.

NOW WHAT?

The Boras of Trieste

When you walk the wide boulevards of Trieste in the glorious days of summer, you may wonder why, every few feet at the curbs, there are white and red metal stanchions, about three feet high, each one graced on top with a large metal loop. To the strictly summer vacationer these silent metal guardians may well remain a mystery. But the veterans of Trieste winters know; for more than one has been saved from a cold watery death by these stalwart protectors. This introduces you to the Boras, the cold, robust, hurricane-force winds that, for a period of two weeks every year, gather speed in the funnel-shaped Austrian Alps and roar down unmercifully through the streets of Trieste city on the way out to the Adriatic Sea.

At the beginning of winter, prior to the arrival of these devil winds, the city fathers, tiring of seeing many of their good citizens blown into the Adriatic, string heavy rope through the loops of these poles, thereby permitting its denizens, to navigate the streets to do their daily chores, proceeding, hand over fist, hanging onto these ropes for dear life.

Anyway, this is a roundabout way of introducing you to a Captain of the Army Counter Intelligence Corps, a new arrival I'll call Carson. He'd come in mid-winter, his beloved and trusty six-year-old Buick Roadmaster in tow. Like most officers, draftees were considered lower than dirt and they couldn't tell Carson a thing. He knew it all.

The first time he left the agency compound, I flagged him down. I stood in front of his car, blocking the exit. That was the only reason he bothered at all to roll down the window to hear what I had to say. I moved over to the Buick window and leaned in. "Captain Carson, Sir, if you're going for gas, I respectfully suggest that do not to check your oil. Let the motor pool guys do it when you get back."

Author in CIC motor pool compound in Trieste

"I always check the oil personally when I get gas," he huffed. "It's the only way to keep the car in tip-top shape."

"B-but..."

By mid-sentence, he'd already rolled up his window and drove off, tires squealing. He was not about to take advice from a lowly corporal.

I shook my head, a wicked smile forming on my lips. Don't look at me that way! It wasn't as if I didn't try. My conscience is clear.

Pulling into a Fina gas station on Piazza d'Unita, right smack on the shores of the Adriatic, while the attendant pumped the gas, our intrepid captain released the catch on his engine hood, the attendant's warning shout lost in the howling winds of the Boras, lifted the hood, and before he could say, "Oh, shit," the Buick Roadmaster hood with its distinctive four-hole ports, sailed a hundred feet up into the air before slowly settling on the water about a mile out, floating briefly before sinking forever into the depths of the Adriatic.

Needless to say, there's no way in hell he'd ever find another hood for a six-year-old Buick Roadmaster in Europe.

That kind of retired his Buick until summer. No matter, he was assigned a small nondescript Fiat for his work. It was about one quarter the size of his Buick Roadmaster but what the hell, it would get him around. At least that's what we plebian NCOs thought. I don't know about today, but back in the Fifties the Fiat was one strange little car. On the gearshift lever, reverse was where first gear normally was on most European cars. Our agency Fiats were backed into parking spaces next to a canal. You had to be careful because there was nothing to prevent you from backing into the canal--no curb, no fence, no nothing--well, you get the idea. We led him to his Fiat in its assigned canal parking spot.

He looked the little car over, shaking his head. He was not a small man. He shrugged and poured himself into the Fiat.

Captain, Sir" I said, "that there shift is real tricky and. . ."

Once again, he cut me off in mid-sentence, barking angrily, "I know how to drive goddamn a shift car, Corporal." Peevishly, he rolled up his window.

"Yes *Sir*, Captain, *Sir*," I said and saluted smartly as he promptly put the car into reverse, gunned the engine, let up on the clutch, and backed into the canal. The Adriatic, it seems, became Carson's personal garage--one engine hood and an entire Fiat, parked under water, courtesy of the good, but unheeding, Captain.

Water, it seems, depending on the season, brought out the worst--and best--in the captains assigned to our counterintelligence outfit.

95

This time, it was summer, and our unit was celebrating a beautiful Sunday with a picnic at the soldiers' beach at Udine, a suburb north of Trieste. As stiff and unbending as Carson was, another captain in our unit, I'll call him Luigi, was just the opposite--relaxed with the men he commanded--he could find humor in any situation.

Luigi, you see, had a huge potbelly; I mean it was Jelly Mountain. He looked gross in swimsuit, not that it bothered him one bit! Despite his girth, he had fantastic muscle control. Whenever young beauties in skimpy bathing suits approached, he took a real deep breath and moved his copious belly right up into his chest, making him look like Hercules. He enjoyed, of course, this impressive, but fleeting, fame. All he could do is hold his breath and smile. If he engaged in any conversation at all, his Schwarzenegger-like chest would immediately drop into a Fat Albert-like belly.

The captain at the beach: He expands his chest as the girls stroll by

NOW WHAT?

The Trieste Yankees

During the summer of 1954, our CIC unit sponsored an Italian baseball team called the Trieste Yankees; I became involved as first base coach because of my friendship with two members of our unit, George Kostelac, who had played briefly for the then New York Giants, and Emile Singel, a Brooklyn Dodger prospect (remember, I said this was back in 1954 when the Giants and the Dodgers were in New York and Brooklyn respectively!). The team played in the Italian version of the major leagues. Each team was permitted to have no more than two American players. Our unit supplied the two American ballplayers to the Trieste Yankees: Kostelac, who was the player-manager and outfielder, and Singel, who played shortstop.

Singel crossing the plate after a home run

For one season, I was first base coach, all decked out in my baseball uniform and spikes. For me, it was like fantasy baseball. The players were recruited from the local citizenry and were not paid. All the other teams were professional and paid their players. When we came in fourth in an eight-team league, we were quite proud of our boys.

Team celebrating end of season. Author, center, in suit jacket and tie. On Author's right is American star player, George Kostelac

It seemed arguing was as much a part of the sport as the actual playing of baseball. I recall our pitcher throwing a very high pitch, out of the reach of the opposing batter, who nevertheless swung at it and missed.

"Ball one," the umpire bellowed.

I raced out of the dugout screaming, "How can you call it a ball? He swung at it!"

Undaunted, the ump stood cheek to jowl with me and in Italian explained, "Since the pitch was out of the batter's reach (the pitch indeed had sailed to the backstop, too high for the catcher to stop it), it didn't matter whether or not he swung. Therefore," the ump concluded, "it was a ball."

Logical, yes; abiding by the rules, no. Well I kicked dirt on home plate, screamed, yelled and added a few uncomplimentary obscenities, making an utter nuisance of myself until he finally yelled the Italian equivalent of "You're out of the ballgame."

I stood there, hands on my hips, not backing down an inch. "I won't go," I shot back.

A dilemma ensued, because I don't think at that time, there was really a mechanism for kicking anyone out of the game. The umps conferred and then called me over.

"You could argue all you want," the plate umpire said, "and if you promise not to curse, you may stay in the game."

I promised and the crisis was resolved, though the pitch remained called a ball.

Author returning to the Trieste Yankee dugout after dispute with umpire

Back then, Italian baseball was played on the weekends. We hosted teams from other Italian cities and we traveled to those cities. The away games were always an event, particularly if we won. We'd have to beat a quick exit to escape the fury of the local fans. In Milan, in a hotly contested game, we actually needed a police escort to get safely out of the ballpark.

Author in Milan after ballgame

Of course then, I was a boisterous 23-year-old, who had found a trattoria in the train station and went blotto on white Chianti.

I got up from the table, barely able to walk and left my teammates sitting there while I wandered off. They assumed I left to go to the men's room. In fact, I staggered out of the station and later they searched frantically for me because if I missed the train, my weekend pass would have expired and I would have been considered AWOL. They found me several blocks from the station, hustled me back, barely catching the last train out of Milan to Trieste on Sunday night.

A happy ending to an indiscretion? Hell, no. I sat in the third class compartment like a zombie, facing a prim and proper elderly lady who looked on me with obvious distain--and well she should have! Because about a half hour into the trip back to Trieste, I up-chucked right into her lap. Mercifully, I was too out of it to be embarrassed as my friends hung my head out the window for the remainder of the trip.

George, my baseball friend, got discharged from the army two months ahead of me. On his way home, he stopped in New York and visited my wife in my parents' summer home in Long Beach. Anyway, the story I got was that George and Diana went to the beach and while

playing a friendly game of soccer on the sand, Diana
accidentally kicked George in the shins and broke her toe.
Now I ask you, would you buy a story like that?

Bombs Away on Our Friends and It's a Small, Small World

I was still in Trieste. Trieste bordered Yugoslavia, which at that time in the Cold War, was still an "Iron Curtain" country under the influence of Stalin and the Soviets. That kept our agency busy trying to keep track of the agents sneaking into Trieste from the Communist country. Dusan, a former prominent member of the Loyalist Party in Yugoslavia, opposing the Communist leader, Tito, escaped that country with his life after hiding out in a bunker for several years.

Dusan was hired by our intelligence unit as a Serbo-Croatian interpreter since at least one third of the population of Trieste spoke that language, as did the agents Tito was sending into Trieste for nefarious purposes. Dusan, as intelligent and educated as any of us in the Corps had completed four years of law school in Yugoslavia and had only to take the bar exam, when the Soviets occupied the country and sought to wipe out all opposition to Tito. Dusan, the son of one of the loyalist leaders opposing Tito, was never able to take the bar exam for his law license.

We worked with Dusan as our Serbian-Croatian interpreter and I became friends both with him and his wife, Marsha. On being invited to dinner by Marsha, I queried a Yugoslav auto mechanic in our unit as to an appropriate gift to bring to dinner.

Author, left, and Dusan

"They would really appreciate rabbit. It's a most favored gift among the Serbs."

"A rabbit?" I asked in a highly dubious tone.

He tapped my shoulder. "Take my word for it, you can't go wrong."

That evening, I found a butcher shop open that carried rabbit. I carried my unusual package--a rabbit wrapped in brown paper, except for its ears, which were tied together to form a handle by which I could carry the beast. I tried to act nonchalant as I walked down the street with my gift, but in truth, I was grossed out, feeling there would be disapproving eyes on me for carting a dead bunny, by its ears no less. "But the cute bunny was already dead when I bought him," I felt like shouting to the passing citizens, though no one seemed particularly interested in me or my burden. Martha was a good hostess and gushed appreciatively about my gift. I still had my doubts.

During the dinner, Dusan expressed his desire to emigrate to America and I encouraged him. Once I returned home, I told him, I would be glad to be one of his sponsors and in fact, several years later, I did sponsor Dusan and Marsha as part of their visa approval process. On their arrival in New York, we met them. She was about six or seven months pregnant.

Diana took one look at Marsha and knew the young woman was in serious trouble. She was terribly swollen, beyond the normal blossoming of pregnancy.

Diana took me aside. "Marsha has what I had with our first baby, edema. I almost lost our son as a result. She's in the end stages of it and I think both she and her baby are in deep trouble."

We bundled Marsha into our car and rushed her to the nearest hospital where doctors worked feverishly to save her life. They did, but she lost the baby.

Dusan did not have his law certificate and the bar associations in the United States would not recognize his law school degree from Yugoslavia. But he never became a dole on the public. I put him in touch with my friend Lewis who graciously employed Dusan and later got him a job in banking. That was enough for Dusan to get on his feet. He went back to school at night and obtained a master's and doctorate degrees in library science, which he parleyed into a position with the law library of NYU Law School, eventually becoming, for many years, its head librarian.

One summer, I invited Dusan and Marsha out to my parents' summer home in Long Beach. My stepbrother Bernard lived in Long Beach and I brought Dusan over to meet him. Bernard had flown in B-24 Liberators in the Fifteenth Air Force out of Foggia, Italy in World War II, flying fifty missions bombing targets in German, Romania and Yugoslavia. Bernard had kept high-altitude reconnaissance photos of the before and after results of his missions.

In the small world department, Dusan picked up one particular photo and looked at its date. He looked up at Bernard. "I recognize that site! I was there on the ground when you bombed it," pointing to the photo. "There were no Germans there, only Loyalist partisans fighting Germans. We lost a lot of men in that raid. I was wounded."

Bernard shook his head. "Oh my God, I honestly thought we were bombing the Germans, based on coordinates given to us by Tito's forces. I'm so sorry"

Dusan smiled. "No need to apologize, I know it's not your fault because Tito was fighting us at the same time we were fighting the Germans and he frequently called in American air strikes on our positions, claiming they were concentrations of German forces."

Author's stepbrother Bernard in Long Beach on return from Europe

After I left New York permanently, I lost track of Dusan and Marsha. Much later, I made inquiries of the NYU Law Library. It seems he had retired and he and Marsha had moved to a farm in West Virginia. I was given an address but my mail came back undelivered with the stamp, "no such addressee." It's too bad. I really would have liked to resume a relationship that was an important part of my history.

IV. GOODBYE ACCOUNTING, HELLO LAW

NOW WHAT?

The Education Of A Deadbeat

On leaving the army I began working as an accountant--bad career choice. I hated it. But I had a wife to support, so I contemplated going to night law school and working as--ugh--an accountant during the day. But I had this fear of failure. I'll tell you why.

In high school, I was a bad student--no, not behaviorally, but academically; simply stated, I stunk. I graduated high school with the lowest grade point average you can have and still get a diploma. College was a given in our family and for that matter in my community of friends and relatives. All my friends, cousins, stepsister and stepbrother went, were going, or planned to go. My parents expected it of me. That was true even though my natural father, my mother, and my uncles and aunts never went for a higher education. There was only one problem--my grades--so low that I even had trouble getting into NYU's School of Commerce, which, at that time, took almost everyone. My stepfather, an alumnus of the School of Commerce, helped me get in.

For a kid that barely graduated high school and had just above average grades in college, going to law school wasn't as bad as a feared. I managed pretty well. But I'm being modest. I did graduate first in my night class in law school. You see, I had an incentive I never had before in my schooling--I just had to get out of the accounting business because I found it boring beyond belief. On graduation from Brooklyn Law School; I was awarded the grand prize. What trauma! But I'll get to that later.

Actually, I turned the corner in my education quest while in college at NYU's School of Commerce, when I obtained my first "A" grade ever-- in a summer course in Geology I. The only thing I remember about

107

that class was the instructor's quite graphic description of a functioning wheat silo. As the wheat grain poured out of the silo into receptacles for conversion to flour, the professor explained, men with paddles on a platform at the bottom of the silo would swat out the falling rats. Ever the inquisitive one, I asked what happens if the paddler happens to miss. I shouldn't have asked because I received the unwanted answer: "If you ever see a hair in your bread, that's one of them." I told this story to my girl friend and she never forgave me for imparting that bit of liberal arts knowledge, thereby requiring her from then on, obsessively to examine every piece of bread she was about to consume. (She's my wife now, notwithstanding my abortive attempt to share my education.) Well, now you've read this too, and all I can say is--SORRY!

Going summers to college to save a year turned out to be supremely stupid--I just didn't think it through. The Korean War was in full swing and I managed, by going summers, to make up a whole year, so when I graduated in the summer of 1952, the army appeared with open arms to embrace me. I could have had another year of safety as an undergraduate. I frantically applied to NYU Law School, obtained an acceptance, and filed for a deferment with my local draft board. Now the draft boards were generally made up of men too old to fight in World War II and the Korean War and too young to have fought in World War I. Having lucked out, they became tigers at sending everyone else's sons to war. Anyway, it was September 1952, and I attended my first night school class at NYU Law. I remember my first assignment vividly—to read and digest the 400-page tome, *Studying Law,* by Arthur Vanderbilt. The book had to be read by the next week. The next week! Is the professor crazy, or what? After class I took the subway home to the Bronx-- I lived in the shadow of the Yankee Stadium. I removed the day's mail from my box. There was a postcard from the draft board (called the Selective Service System or the SSS--I called it the Sadly Sadistic System). There was not even the suspense of an envelope to rip open. There in boldface staring mockingly at me were the words **REQUEST FOR DEFERMENT DENIED.** Well, at least I did not have to read that damn Vanderbilt book! Incidentally, when I got out of the army, I remembered that assignment, so I enrolled in Brooklyn Law School instead. It wasn't any easier, but at least it did not have Arthur Vanderbilt's tome in the curriculum.

As a matter of fact, law school was extremely difficult for night students, particularly those with full-time day jobs. That was certainly true for me. I worked all day as a junior accountant and went to school at night. My study time was limited to when I got home from school, usually starting at ten or eleven o'clock at night, and on the weekends. My wife called herself a "law school widow." The accounting job was excruciatingly boring, which made the day seem all the longer.

Samuel Aaron and the Cookie Monster

1957: The year federal troops enforced desegregation in a Little Rock public school; the Soviets launched the first earth-orbiting satellite, Sputnik; Leonard Bernstein's *West Side Story* opened on Broadway; *The Bridge on the River Kwai* premiered in movie theaters; *Leave It to Beaver* series began on the TV screens; and Humphrey Bogart, Joe McCarthy, and Arturo Toscanini died.

The year before, I'd begun law school; we'd been married three years; and several our friends already were enjoying (or so I thought) their first born, so Diana and I decided it was time to have a child. Having been thoroughly indoctrinated on the dangers of pregnancy by having premarital sex, I figured all we had to do was, well, do it without the usual protection, and presto, Diana would become pregnant. It didn't work out that way.

Three months went by and still no results. We decided to visit my family physician, the good Dr. Frimmel, a no-nonsense general practitioner with fine healing skills.

"Doc," I began, sitting in his examination room holding Diana's hand, "we've been trying and trying to have a baby without success. Is there anything you can give us?"

NOW WHAT?

Doc Frimmel rubbed his chin. "How long have you been trying? One year? Two years?"

Simply by his questions, I knew we'd made a mistake coming in. "Three months," I said softly.

"Three months?" he bellowed. "Get the hell out of here and stop wasting my time. For crying out loud, three months! It takes my cat that long to become pregnant. Just go home and keep doing what you're doing and it'll happen."

He paused and looked at us. "Just to make sure-- you are having sex, aren't you?"

Sheepishly, we both nodded.

"Good. Go on, go home and have fun. There'll be no charge for my advice."

Sure enough, he was right. The next month, Diana became pregnant.

Diana's obstetrician worked out of New York Hospital, which was very convenient for Diana, since she had been working on research on psychosomatic illnesses as a lab technician in the renowned Payne Whitney Psychiatric Clinic at Cornell Medical School. Her job, she said, was quite interesting, having the opportunity to work with some of the leading research doctors in the field.

Diana in the research lab

She had some unusual patients to minister to. One young man, in a bad accident destroying his abdominal cavity, was hired by Diana's lab as a kind of a human guinea pig. His stomach was covered with a flap of skin that acted as sort of an access door so that the researchers could put him under stress and immediately check the effect on his stomach by opening his door and looking in or taking samples. Well, at least it was a living for someone who was too disabled to hold down a regular job. Some of the psychosomatic patients were famous movie stars who'd checked into the Payne Whitney. As side benefit, she and I developed a friendship with a Chinese researcher at the lab who introduced us to the intricacies and glories of feasting on the Chinese New Year.

Tuesday night and Diana was well into her eighth month, and getting pretty big. We discussed when she should quit working. We struggled with the idea of having to live solely on my salary as a junior accountant.

Diana, late into her first pregnancy

"I'm getting pretty tired," she said.

"Can you work one more week?" I asked hopefully.

"Tomorrow's Wednesday, I think I can make it to the end of the week."

* * *

Wednesday started out like any other day in the lab, with Diana conducting various experiments and checking up on the man with the door on his abdomen.

About three in the afternoon, she turned to a fellow lab technician, Maureen. "Uh-oh, I'm having contractions and they're pretty severe."

"What can I do to help?" Maureen asked, hovering over Diana.

"Nothing, really, I'll just walk over to the hospital's maternity ward."

And she did.

After fourteen or fifteen hours of tough labor, Diana gave birth on Thursday, January 31, 1957, to an eight-pound nine-ounce boy we named Samuel Aaron, after my natural father.

* * *

We'd hired a nurse for when we brought the baby home from the hospital. I won't bore you with the trials and tribulations faced by most parents with a newborn, particularly a first new born, except to tell you about our nurse. I've blocked her name out of mind with surprising permanence so I'll simply call her Nurse Nazi. It didn't help that she had a German accent.

Nurse with Sam

Nurse Nazi totally took over our household--and the baby. She did everything for the baby and while Nurse Nazi's efforts were welcome for the first few days it soon became extremely grating when we could see the baby, hold the baby, and feed the baby only at times dictated by her, usually when she took time off for personal reasons. My relationship with Nurse Nazi came to head one gorgeous Sunday winter morning that was unseasonably warm with the sun shining bright.

"Dress the baby warmly," I instructed Nurse Nazi, "I'm going to take Sam in his carriage for a walk in Franz Sigel Park." I couldn't wait for this opportunity to show off my son.

"*Nein*," she remonstrated, "I vill take him for a valk and make sure he gets his sleep."

That was it. I sent Nurse Nazi packing, dressed Sam, took him out in his carriage, and crossed Walton Avenue for one glorious walk in the park--the first with my new son in his new gleaming blue and black perambulator.

* * *

By the time Sam was a year and a half old, we had discovered he had starch intolerance. When he ate any flour-based products he'd get a severe case of the runs that were highly acidic, and since he was still in diapers, he'd end up with blisters and rashes on his butt that would make a grown man cry. So we were very, very careful to limit his diet. The poor kid didn't know what a cookie was until the day of the incident.

Sam was walking now, well, more like waddling. We'd take him to the park with his big Sam button pinned on to him and he was extremely cute, if I must say so myself.

Baby Sam in the Park with his SAM button

Sam was gregarious and warmly approached all the old folks sitting on the park benches. No one could resist him, including this one elderly gentleman who, with all good intentions, handed Sam a cookie. I was sitting on a park bench about twenty feet away watching Sam exam this morsel when my brain finally kicked in and realized what was about to happen. I leaped off the bench screaming to Sam not to eat the cookie. But he was simply too fascinated with the delectable tidbit and opened his mouth just as I reached him and slapped the cookie out of his hand.

Startled, Sam began to wail. If the angry old man had been agile enough, I bet he would have walloped me with his cane. All the old people on nearby benches rose up as one to condemn the cruel father.

"How can you deny your son the pleasure of one delicious cookie," the old man yelled at me. "Poor baby, to have a father like you." Sentiments echoed by those in the vicinity.

I decided it was too complicated to explain and beat a hasty retreat.

Well, at least I didn't suffer the further humiliation of picking up the offending cookie and eating it myself.

NOW WHAT?

Barefoot In the Park

As I said earlier, I hated working in my chosen profession and my college major--accounting. Why? Can you imagine sitting in the stuffy office of the sweater maker client's bookkeeper checking that 240 15/16 dozen at $34.5674 had been extended correctly (that's why it's called "checking extensions"), and then doing that for the month's 10,000 invoices, each containing dozens of extensions? That's what junior accountants did in those days. There was one way out to avoid a nervous breakdown--get out of accounting by going to law school.

But there were support issues. I had a child on the way and there was no way I could go to day law school, so, also as I told you before, I eschewed NYU and enrolled in Brooklyn Law School's evening program for a law degree. I'll tell you, law school at night is tough, especially when my day job was accounting.

A coven of us formed a study group (well, *I* studied and then they sucked me dry every weekend--but it was a good way for me to learn, as well). The highlight of my tough week became our study group's touch football game over lunch on Saturday and Sunday. Depending on whose house we were studying at, we'd either play in the street or in the park.

Frank, a classmate of mine, and a neighbor in the South Bronx on Walton Avenue near 161st Street, met for the first time in our first class in law school and have become fast friends--and we still are, more than fifty years later.

Every weekday night, Frank and I would ride home from Brooklyn to the Bronx on the subway. Getting off at 161st Street, it was a three-block walk south down Walton Avenue, with apartment buildings on our right and across the street on the left ran Franz Sigel Park.

Even in those days, you didn't cut through the park at night.

One night, as Frank and I walked briskly home, discussing the evening's classes, we heard a woman scream. It came from the basement entrance of the apartment house we'd just passed. Without second thought, we flew down the basement steps, slammed open the door to find this young hoodlum on top of a middle-aged lady who was kicking and screaming. We grabbed him by the scruff of his neck and yanked him off the lady. When we turned our attention to the frightened woman, the hoodlum picked up a metal garage can lid and tried to bring it down on my head. I saw him out of the corner of my eye and managed to deflect it with my forearm. Frank jumped him and knocked him to the ground. The hoodlum leaped up and took off like a jackrabbit out of the building and into the dark park. We didn't give chase but tended to the woman and walked her up to her apartment.

Normally, when I get home from class, I greet my wife, who is about to go to bed, and then study at the kitchen table (who had dens in those days?) for another three hours to prepare for the next evening's classes. This one night in December, with temperature hovering around 20 degrees Fahrenheit, I sat at the kitchen table in my trousers and underwear top, with no shoes, no socks. I heard blood-curling screams out in the hall. I raced out of my apartment and determined that the screams emanated from the lobby, four flights down. Taking the steps two at a time, I reached the lobby to see two men trying to grab this old lady's purse. By this time other apartment doors were opening.

Our apartment house lobby has two entrances at opposite ends. One leads to Walton Avenue and the other to Gerard Avenue. The two accosters took off in opposite directions. I chose to pursue the one leaving through the Walton Avenue door and when I say "through," I mean it literally. He was so excited he crashed right through the large glass of the lobby door without a pause. I ran after him in my undershirt, slacks, and bare feet on this cold winter's night, slowly gaining on him. Suddenly, he stopped, turned, and brandishing a large knife, yelling, "I'm going to carve you up, motherf___!"

He began running at me, whereupon I reversed course and started running away from him. He stopped; I stopped, always keeping about a quarter of a city block distance between us. This back and forth went on for about five minutes until he heard a siren; then he ducked into a basement entrance. I did not go in after him but stood across the street in the park until the police came. He wasn't hard to find, leaving a blood trail from his encounter with the lobby glass door. The police took him out handcuffed and bloody. And me? In all the excitement, I hadn't noticed that I was barefoot on a winter's night. Now I hurt. You think Neil Simon's character was the first to go "barefoot in the park?"

Be-Bop Spoken Here

Another member of our study group in law school was Bob, the New York City patrolman. He'd turned down promotion to detective so he wouldn't have to work evenings and miss school. His beat was in the south Bronx and he was tough but likable. One evening, after Bob and his wife, Mary, and Diana and I, took in a movie at the Earl Theater, we stopped for some coffee at the Jerome Cafeteria at River Avenue and 161st Street, under the Lexington Avenue Subway el.

Four toughs entered the cafeteria and sat down next to us. One loud mouth was particularly obscene.

"I'm not going to stand for this," Bob growled and began to get up.

"Relax, Bob" I said, "it's nothing all of us haven't heard many times before."

Bob shook his head. "No, it's just not right. They see we're here with our wives. They have no license to act like that."

He got up and approached the four guys. He tried the polite approach. "I'd appreciate it if you'd watch your language. We are here with our wives and it makes them uncomfortable."

"Oh yeah, and just what the fuck are you going to do about it, you panty-waist?" said the tough who had been mouthing off earlier.

"I'm truly sorry you feel that way," Bob said in a calm voice. He extracted a blackjack from his back pocket and without any seeming effort, bopped the tough between the eyes. First his eyes glazed and then he slid down in the chair.

Bob looked at the rest of them. "Now, is there anything else any of you gentleman wish to add?"

Three heads shook vigorously.

"Excellent." Bob returned the blackjack to his pocket. "Now, if you will excuse me, I will rejoin my friends."

"Gosh, Bob, you hardly tapped him," I said. "Yet his lights really went out."

Bob smiled. "Just have to know the right spot to hit to disable him without any lasting damage. You learn that on the job as a New York patrolman."

Law school pals and wives. L to R: Bob the cop, Diana, Bob's wife Mary, Author, Ann and Frank, also our neighbors

The Night My Child Was Almost Motherless

Midway through law school, we moved up to Yonkers, a northern suburb of New York City. With help from my stepfather (I was making $100 a week back then), we invested the huge sum of $3,000 (well, it was huge for the year 1958) in a co-op two-bedroom apartment. The move tripled my commute time from night school in Brooklyn, but with one child and other on the way, we needed the room and this is what was available.

One night I arrived home from law school and was not surprised to find Diana out. I paid off the babysitter and settled down to prepare my assignment for tomorrow's night law school classes. That was my routine.

I knew Diana had gone to the Metropolitan Opera with my stepfather and would be driving home from my parent's home in the Bronx, in our relatively new Renault Dauphine, a small car about the size of a VW Bug. Concerned about winter driving, I had earlier taken the Renault in to be fitted with snow tires. I was assured these tires would be perfect for the car. It turns out that the snow tires actually raised the rear end of the Renault a few inches. To you, that may not sound like a big deal, but it was enough to make the car highly unstable at high speeds.

Diana, pregnant with our second child, started home driving alone in our snow-tire-equipped Renault, heading north on the Major Deagan/New York State Thruway at sixty miles an hour. As she passed under the Yonkers Raceway, her rear tires barely touching the roadway, and the underpass a natural wind tunnel, a cross wind buffeted her and literally lifted up the rear-end of the car off the road and pushed it sideways, spinning it into a concrete abutment at a high speed. The abutment

122

sheared off the rear half the car from the back edge of the front seat. The remainder of the car flipped on its top and back into the right driving lane of the Thruway. Fortunately, the car was a piece of junk. She hit the dashboard and the light plastic collapsed; she slammed against the windshield and it immediately popped out. It was sheer luck that traffic on the Thruway was able to avoid remnants of the Renault straddling the lane.

Diana crawled out of the car through the collapsed windshield. Some Good Samaritan stopped to check on her, advising her to crawl back in and turn off the ignition so she doesn't have a fire. I guess he didn't notice that the entire back half of the vehicle, including the gas tank had sheared off. In any event Diana declined to crawl back in, suggesting he might want to do it if he was so inclined.

In the meantime, I was busy studying at our kitchen table when the phone rang. "Mr. Steinhouse? This is the State Police. Your wife was in an accident on the Thruway and she's here at the Cross County Hospital. She is not seriously hurt."

Yeah sure, I thought. They always say that so you don't panic, even when the victim is dying. Well, it didn't work, I panicked. How can you be in an accident on the high speed Thruway and not be hurt--or dead? Dragooning my neighbor to babysit, I raced to the hospital in our other car, my stepfather's old 98 Oldsmobile, about as opposite from a Renault as you can get. I put the pedal to the metal and almost bought it for myself, just missing a bus at a busy intersection.

Well, it turned out the policeman was not giving me a line; in fact, Diana was shaken, but otherwise unhurt, the biggest casualty being her ripped stockings. Relying on the old canard of getting back up on a horse immediately if you fall off, the next day, I convinced

Diana to drive the Oldsmobile. We went to see the wreck.

I'm glad I didn't see the Renault before I saw Diana. No way would I have believed she had survived.

I never did find out what opera Diana had seen that evening.

I Can Explain, Officer

1959: The year Castro came to power in Cuba, Alaska and Hawaii became the forty- ninth and fiftieth states to join the Union, "Ben Hur" and "North By Northwest" premiered in the movie theaters, and movie mogul Cecil B. DeMille, architect Frank Lloyd Wright, and comedian Lou Costello died.

Two and a half years after Sam was born, we were living in the co-op apartment in Yonkers, New York, but we returned to New York Hospital in Manhattan where Diana, having survived her Thruway crash, gave birth to a girl, again after a difficult labor. The baby had a tough time and the obstetrician had to pull her out with a forceps. She looked quite homely with her head temporarily misshapen from the trauma and black hair all over her face. But she was ours and we loved her no less. The problem was a name. We had been toying with the esoteric (at least for back them) name of Melinda or Melissa, but decided, the way the baby looked, to give her a plain name--Jane Wendy. We needn't have worried. Once the bruising and swelling subsided she turned out to be a beautiful baby.

Jane Wendy

There was, however, a problem with one foot. For some inexplicable reason, it was turned in. The pediatrician noticed it first and suggested a brace that would act, over time, to turn her foot out to the correct angle. It was a simple device. An aluminum bar to which two shoes were attached at an angle designed to correct the problem.

Poor Jane Wendy was thoroughly miserable with the brace on her feet. It made crawling difficult and learning to walk, impossible. But then Jane discovered wonderful new fun way to use her brace. She found she could wield her brace with lethal efficiency to chop up her crib, and when not in bed, to go after the furniture. We went through several cribs, whose narrow slat sides were no match for her aluminum blade. With her feet in the attached shoes, Jane learned to use her legs to swing the brace in a wide arc with all the skill of a lumberjack, to cut down all wood in her path. The brace came off after a few months, which made us all happy except perhaps for Jane who missed her chopper. I think that experience made her the most feisty and independent of our children. She constantly fought tooth and nail with Diana over virtually everything.

Once, as a teenager, she and Diana were in a furious battle in the kitchen. I was working at home and could no longer tolerate the shouting. I charged in.

"Jane, go to your room!"

She threw down the gauntlet. "You can't make me."

"You're not too old to be spanked young lady," I warned.

Hands on hips she faced me. "You wouldn't dare!"

It was a challenge. I could not refuse. Grabbing her arm, I gave her two slaps on her derriere, sending a furious daughter scurrying to her room.

Let's step back in time for a moment. A few miles from our home in Cleveland, there is an Outreach center in the next community south of us, Solon, for teens in trouble. We had always told our kids that if they were in trouble and felt they could not come to us, they should call Outreach for help. Of course, we had in mind problems of drugs and pregnancy.

The next day a Cleveland Police detective showed up at my office.

"We have a complaint from Outreach in Solon that you abused your daughter."

"Listen officer, if you were my son and acted like my daughter did to my wife and me, I would have spanked you too."

"Tell me about it."

I did and he shook my hand left, and I never heard another word about it.

When I got home, I discussed it with Diana and together we came to the conclusion that at the bottom line, we were glad that at least one of our children took our advice and sought help from Outreach, regardless of the reason. So we never threw that up to Jane.

I'll say one thing about Jane. She was the most exuberant and emotional one in our household. You always knew where you stood with her. Unlike my other children, she practiced the art of confrontation, not stealth. Our other children weren't angels but most of their exploits we didn't discover until much later in life and a lot of it, I'm sure, we'll never know.

Jane, center, after having just received her high school diploma, reacting in a typical Jane way

After some rough years during and after college, she made her own way as a counseling psychologist and

later, a massage therapist. She became a loving and
concerned daughter and then, a loving wife to her
professor husband, Max, and a devoted mother to the
delightful and beautiful girl Sophia that she and Max
adopted from China. Now, only occasionally does an
acerbic comment slip out from Jane's lips. But that's
okay because little Sophia has a mind and a mouth of her
own, giving Jane back a little of what she dished out to
us. Sophia, born on Mao Tse-tung's birthday, is the little
dictator in their household; so much so that they've
gotten to calling her "Mini-Mao,"

NOW WHAT?

I Should Have Gotten the Damn Gold Watch

It wasn't all roses for Frank and me. He cost me my straight A average in the first year. We had an Arguments class where, based on court decisions, we paired off and argued against each other taking one side of the case or the other. But we were supposed to stick to the facts in the reported case. This one night I drew Frank as my opponent and flipping a coin I won the winning side of the case with all the good facts supporting my argument. Frank went first. Rather than argue the facts he found in the case, he made up new facts totally reversing our positions.

I jumped up. "I object, professor. He's making up facts not in the record. These shysters will do anything to win an argument."

That was a big mistake. The professor, all five-foot-one of him, stood up and pounded his desk in a fury. "How dare you use that word 'shyster' in *my* class?" That apparently was a very big no-no in law school. I suppose jokes equating lawyers to sharks are in the same category.

Anyway, he threw me out of class for that evening and I could never recover with that professor, no matter what I did or how hard I tried. End result: Five A's and one C (the only C I ever received in law school). Al, another member of our study group was delighted, because he did as well as me and at the end of the first year he edged me out for the first spot, thanks to Frank. I thought, however, I had the last laugh, because when we graduated law school, I was first in the evening class, barely ahead of Al. As it turns out, I did not have the last laugh. I was awarded a two-volume set of *Prince on Evidence*. And Al? He received an inscribed *gold watch.* Life is so unfair! It was even worse than it sounds because several weeks later, I received notice from the publisher that my prize was out of print so they were sending me instead, a two-volume set of *Merrill on Notice*! I ask you: What am I going to do with the two-volume treatise on notice? And who the hell is Merrill?

NOW WHAT?

It Wasn't a Tough Decision

Facing graduation from law school in 1959, I finally received some recognition for my class standing when I received an offer from the Justice Department under its Attorney General's Honor Graduate program. It wasn't a tough decision for me. I jumped at it. They asked me where I wanted to work and I picked the Tax Division (after all, I was a reluctant accountant), the Civil Rights Division (then the darling of the Department), and the Civil Division. The government, being not too terribly dissimilar from the army, assigned me to the Antitrust Division. Antitrust, of course, was one subject about which I know absolutely nothing. So I guess, in the government's way of thinking, it made absolute sense.

The day after I graduated I quit my accounting position and began work in the Antitrust Division in downtown Manhattan on Foley Square. My decision made my accounting boss very unhappy because I had passed the first two parts of the CPA exam and needed only two more months of public accounting experience to be eligible to take the remaining exam and become a CPA. But not a day longer would I spend in accounting. Did I tell you? My boss was also my stepfather. He was in partnership with Bernard, my stepbrother, and he wanted me to come into the partnership. You may think that's too great a deal to turn down. Wrong, I wasn't even tempted. But out of respect for my stepfather, I went through the motions. I agreed to see his other partner, my stepbrother.

CARL L. STEINHOUSE

Stepfather at his accounting/law office

"Tell me, Bernard, do you want me in the business as a partner? I would appreciate brutal honesty." I knew that his wife looked on my family and me as usurpers that would share in the inheritance of my stepfather (and Bernard's father). I could feel the resentment emanating from her over the years and felt reasonably certain that she was pressuring Bernard to keep me at arm's length. Bernard was a great guy and, to his credit, notwithstanding his wife, treated me like one of the family, so I knew on the subject of partnership he was between the frying pan and the fire. His reply was what I expected--and welcomed.

"Frankly, Carl, it would be easier for me if you did not come into the firm. I'm sorry."

"That's okay, Bernard, you don't have to apologize, I understand fully. It makes it easier for me now to turn down Dad's offer of a partnership."

My stepfather warned me I was making a terrible mistake turning down this opportunity. It took twenty years, but after I'd entered private practice, earning more than him, Dad had to admit that I did the right thing after all.

My education behind me, my career as a federal prosecutor was about to begin.

Lad, a Dog, and Beach Trauma

Did you ever read *Lad, a Dog* and other books about this intrepid collie by Albert Pierson Terhune? Like Lassie, Lad seemed to have human-like intelligence, the ability to communicate and warn his masters, and the smarts to outwit the villains while at the same time saving the young girl by carrying her in his teeth back to safety at home and hearth. As a result, for me at least, the collie took on an aura of respect and adoration that lasted well into adulthood--a respect beyond what any canine should have or could have merited or deserved. I know now that dogs are creatures mostly of instinct, of attachment to their food source, and of training, possessing miniscule intelligence. But I had to have it proven to me.

Since our marriage began, I always wanted a collie, not the tri-colors, but one looking like Lad or Lassie. Diana resisted that idea very vigorously and in a small apartment in the Bronx, I didn't blame her, though I'd never admit it. When she broached the subject of moving up to Yonkers to a larger apartment in a condo development, I seized my chance and conditioned such a move upon acquiring a collie. In a weak moment, she agreed. What did I name him? Lad, of course.

Lad was a beautiful dog, just as I imagined the Lad of fiction would have looked. That's where the resemblance ended. Basically, this dog was a crybaby, a coward, and a thief. He came into our household just about the time our second child, Jane, was born.

Lad

133

First of all, collies are prolific hair machines. It appears that no one has ever had to brush the fictional Lad, or at least Terhune conveniently forgot to tell us all about this important matter of upkeep. No matter how many times I brushed him I managed to collect enough hair to make a second dog. If I didn't brush him, well, we'd be eating hair soup, sleeping in hair beds, wearing hair clothes, and sliding on hair floors. As for intelligence, alongside my dog, the fictional Lad was an Einstein.

I can say some good things about my Lad. He was beautiful and affectionate, that is, if you like constant slobbering kisses from him--something Terhune's Lad never seem to do. My Lad did not have a vicious bone in his body but that did not mean he didn't scare some people. He was, after all, a large dog and, when standing on his hind legs, he could reach your shoulders with his paws. As a matter of fact that's just what he did to an elderly lady who smiled at him in passing. Lad, to show his gratitude, jumped up putting his paws on her shoulders, trying to lick her face, promptly knocking over the terrified woman. We had all to do to stop her from calling the police and the dogcatcher. When she had screamed, the dog immediately assumed the head down and tail between the legs position, knowing he did something wrong. He also shit. Oh, he was housebroken all right, but he always shit when he got upset. You remember Nabisco's Mallowmars, the cookie topped with marshmallow and rich dark chocolate? Diana would save empty boxes of Mallowmars just to scoop up and dispose of his droppings. Pity the child looking for a cookie that made a mistake! It was hard to leave him for any significant amount of time because he'd get unhappy and shit all over the house. After several of those occurrences, my poor neighbors didn't want any responsibility for taking care of Lad.

But Lad also had assets; he showed off his
sheepdog herding instincts. When our young children
were playing on the sidewalk in front of our building, as
soon as they headed toward the street, Lad would herd
them back away from the road, putting himself between
the child and the danger, gently bumping the child back
to safety.

But he was also a coward who'd whimper at the
drop of a, well, janitor. It seems that while Diana was out
walking Lad, the new janitor for the building had let
himself in to repair a leaky faucet. Diana didn't
remember he was coming and when she opened the door
with Lad trailing behind, she confronted a rather rough-
looking stranger in dirty jeans and a scruffy shirt. She
became startled and jumped. Brave Lad--all sixty pounds
of him and with all four feet--jumped into Diana's arms.
There Diana stood with the large dog whimpering in her
arms as the new janitor explained himself.

And Lad was a domestic thief. If any food was
left unattended on a counter or table you could bet your
home that he'd find a way to snatch the treat and gobble
it down. That's what happened to Dad's (I'll stop calling
him stepfather because he was a true dad to me) dinner
one evening at his summer cottage in Long Beach where
we spent the summer with him and my mom. He'd never
owned a dog himself, but he was gracious enough not to
withdraw the invitation when we brought along Lad.
Something I am sure he later regretted but never voiced.

Here's what happened. Mom picked up Dad
every weekday at the Long Island Railroad station after
he came in on the commuter train from his office in
midtown Manhattan. Dad expected his meals promptly at
six in the evening, so Mom left the fish on the counter,
intending to broil it as soon as she got home. Dad would
relax with his evening scotch neat and by the time he
finished the drink and the New York Post, dinner would

be ready. Not this time. While mom put it on a counter higher than the dining room table, well back from the edge, Lad, pretty tall himself, managed to swat the fish onto the linoleum kitchen floor and treat himself to the meal for four. Dad grumbled for a while but then graciously took us out to the steak house for dinner-- without Lad, of course.

The summer place presented new problems for Lad. I took him down to the beach early one morning figuring he'd be in for a real treat being able to romp around in the ocean, as I had seen many other dog owners and their pets do--but, no, not my Lad. Leashed, I led him to the Atlantic Ocean at the water's edge, with him trying to dig in his heels, which was pretty tough in the soft sand. As soon as he hit the water, he let out a yowl and bolted, yanking the leash out of my surprised hands. He took off like a scared rabbit down the beach and it took me the better part of a day to find him, many miles away.

Remember me telling you Lad was a coward? Well, that's not entirely true. When it comes to other dogs, regardless of size, he exhibited no fear. My dad discovered this first-hand. He'd walk Lad down the street, passing an empty lot that had this huge, nasty-tempered dog chained to a post in the hot sun. The dog would strain against those chains and growl and bark at passersby. My dad and Lad would ignore this nuisance and keep walking until one day the beast straining against his chains pulled up post clean out of the ground and came charging at his intended victims dragging the chain and post behind him. Terhune says collies are excellent scrappers, and like wolves, are very fast at slashing their enemy's legs. Well, for once, Terhune was correct. Lad wheeled around, wrapping the leash around my father's legs, unceremoniously upending him. Lad, much quicker than his foe, attacked the other dog's feet, sending him scrambling and yowling to the back of his yard where he came from.

NOW WHAT?

His dignity somewhat bruised but otherwise unhurt, Dad untangled himself from the leash, slowly got up and he and Lad resumed their walk as if nothing happened.

The summer cottage had its problems for us humans as well. One pleasant afternoon, Mom and Diana were sitting on the bed in the guest room, Mom crocheting and talking to Diana. I went searching for something in the attic. Now you have to understand that up to this time, I never lived in a house, always an apartment, so exploring attics was a new experience for me. For one, I did not know that all attics weren't floored. I climbed up to the attic and saw what I assumed to be a floor. It wasn't. It was the other side of the plasterboard ceiling of the room below. After walking around on the beams I spotted what I was looking for and stepped down onto what I thought was a floor. I came crashing through, taking part of the ceiling with me into the room below, where my mother and wife were holding their *tete a tete.* I not only crashed down into the room, I landed on the bed right between the two women. Diana screamed and jumped up. Mother, barely wincing, just sat there staring at me. Her first words were not "are you hurt?" or "are you okay?" She shook head. "Why in heaven's name did you do that?" Like I was engaging in the sport of falling through ceilings.

V. MY DAYS WITH THE JUSTICE DEPARTMENT

UNITED STATES DEPARTMENT OF JUSTICE
OFFICE OF THE DEPUTY ATTORNEY GENERAL
WASHINGTON, D. C.

Mr. Carl L. Steinhouse
2 Gateway Road
Yonkers, New York

Dear Mr. Steinhouse:

It is a great pleasure to announce that you have been chosen under the Attorney General's 1959 Recruitment Program for Honor Law Graduates.

I wish to congratulate you on your record of achievement in law school and upon being chosen for participation in the Attorney General's select recruitment program.

Sincerely,

Lawrence E. Walsh
Deputy Attorney General

138

NOW WHAT?

Initiation into the Justice Department--My First Day--the New York Field Office--1959

Eschewing my father's advice to remain in accounting, I arrived at Foley Square in lower Manhattan to show up for work at the Department of Justice's New York Field Office of the Antitrust Division in September 1959. My first day as a lawyer and was I scared. *How could I leave the safety of my father's accounting firm for this dangerous leap into the great unknown? What did I know about antitrust? Am I going to make a fool of myself trying to act like a lawyer, much less a prosecutor?* All these questions raced through my mind. Over the summer, I frantically read about price-fixing, restraints of trade, monopolies, and price discrimination, from what amounted to the Cliff Notes of antitrust, "Understanding the Antitrust Laws." But to be honest, I really didn't have any idea which end was up--and I knew it.

That fateful Monday after Labor Day, I waited in the outer office of the Chief of the New York Office, Richard O'D, trying to keep my terror in check. Sitting there across from me was another new attorney, Don E. Cool as a cucumber he was. I was envious. (Later, he told me he was nervous as hell and admired *my* calm demeanor!)

Don E. and I got to talking. The coincidences were beyond amazing. To start, we were the same age--not so surprising. We were both married; each had a son five years old and a daughter three years old. Now things started to get downright weird. We went to the same university and law school, graduating in the same years, both were drafted in the army in November 1952, both attended the Counter Intelligence Corps school at Fort Holabird at about the same time and yet, we had never seen each other before showing up for work on the same

139

day in the same office, both hired by Justice under the Attorney General's Honor Graduate Program. (Thereafter, our destinies parted, he leaving the Justice Department after only two years for a job with a law firm on the West Coast and me staying on for some fifteen years.)

The chief of the office called me in.

"Welcome, Mr. Steinhouse," he began. Not wasting any time he got right to the point. "How do you feel about working under a woman?"

"It's no problem for me," I assured him.

"Good, because you'll be working with Mary Gardiner Jones on the Swiss Watch Cartel case."

I later found out that none of the male attorneys wanted to work with a woman boss, and one that was pretty aggressive to say the least. They'd agreed among themselves to turn down assignments to work with her. I also found out that Mary came from a family of blue bloods, the Gardiners of Gardiner Island and the Joneses of Jones Beach.

Author in 1959

Unfortunately, agreeing to work with Mary earned me the enmity of some, but certainly not all, of the male attorneys in the office. One particularly nasty individual, a bully, I'll call him Joe Murano, who rode me unmercifully, deriding my lack of antitrust knowledge (which was true enough) and somehow equating my willingness to work with Mary to being a namby-pamby boy. That was not true, as he later found out, much to his regret. But that's a later story.

The Swiss Watch Cartel Case

It turned out I had the last laugh over my male counterparts in the office, because eight months in the Division and I was already getting trial experience in the *Swiss Watch Cartel* case. If Mary was a blue blood, she didn't show it. We got along famously. Since there were only two of us up against a phalanx of the top Wall Street attorneys, she willingly gave me trial responsibilities. Trial experience was a sought-after commodity among the young division attorneys as a means of advancement and a way to build a reputation for use on the private job market. Mary was a tough litigator giving no quarter to the highly paid New York attorneys and fighting with fury for every point.

Author and Mary

I butchered my first examination of a witness, attempting to argue my case, asking leading questions, and generally getting most of my witness's testimony excluded on defense counsel objections. Judge C, feeling sorry for me, called an early halt to the day's proceeding and suggested I try again tomorrow, based I what I had learned today. After a night of studying, with the help of Mary, the next day's examination went smoothly with very few objections sustained. After the day ended, defense counsel Gene Gordon, a respected trial attorney and a fine gentleman, came up to me and congratulated me on getting my act together.

"I thought we had you on the ropes for good but clearly, I was wrong. Good job, Carl."

That comment acted as a tremendous boost to my confidence. Needless to say, I needed it.

During the case, we added another attorney, W. Louise Florencourt, a true lady in the southern tradition, who was on temporary transfer from the Washington Office for reasons known only to herself. She set up quarters in the Barbizon Hotel for women and her fine legal writing contributed significantly to the post-trial phase of the case. It must have been in her blood, being related to the famous writer, Flannery O'Connor. A little while later, we were assigned Jean deLouise Brown, an African-American brought up at an exclusive boarding school, college, and law school in the Northeast. So now I had been in the Division for two years, and had worked with three women attorneys and no men. I had no regrets. The blue blood Mary, southern belle Florencourt, and the northeastern African-American Brown got along famously with each other and with me. What we lacked in experience we made up in enthusiasm. Ultimately, the Judge found in our favor and against the Swiss Watch Cartel.

During the trial I had prepared and enforced subpoenas for documents and testimony against the watch companies in Switzerland who fought me tooth and nail, claiming Swiss secrecy laws precluded production pursuant to those subpoenas. The judge, in a precedent-setting opinion, ruled that since the court had personal jurisdiction over the defendants, they must produce the documents and witnesses pursuant to his order, the Swiss secrecy laws notwithstanding.

After the defendants were forced to comply with the discovery demands, I met the Swiss consul at one of our court hearings; he advised me in a very serious voice that because I broke the sacrosanct Swiss secrecy laws, if I ever set foot in Switzerland, I will be arrested, prosecuted, and jailed. I wasn't about to test their determination so I avoided Switzerland in my subsequent trips to Europe, except forty years later. I considered a river tour that would take me a few days into Switzerland. What the hell, I figured, I'm damn curious if they'd remember me after forty years. Foolhardy you say? Probably. But they did not remember and I got through the Swiss part of the trip without incident. On reflection, I shouldn't have worried: they didn't have computers back in those days. Now, computers never forget.

The Life and Hard Times of the Subway Commuter

By this time, Diana and I had two children, Sam and Jane, living in the larger co-op apartment in Yonkers, New York. Whereas in the Bronx, I could simply hop the Lexington Avenue subway line down to Foley Square, now my commute became much more complicated, requiring me first to drive into the Bronx, and find a space to park my car. Only then could I first take the same Lexington Avenue train downtown, the train that used to be only two blocks from my apartment building. This day, it took me twenty minutes to find a space and then I parked partially in a crosswalk so the chance of getting a parking ticket was even money. I also ended up eight blocks from the station and already late for work, so I wasn't in a particularly good frame of mind when I finally boarded the subway, which could explain why "the incident" occurred.

The seating setup on the Lexington Avenue Line, part of the IRT subway system, is important to understanding just what happened. Seating is simply one long bench that runs parallel to and along each side wall of the subway car. In the rush hour, the standees hang on to straps attached to a long pole, about five and a half feet high, the pole running parallel to and just above the seats. So the lucky riders who were seated generally faced the crotches of the standees that were swaying back and forth as the train lurched along the tracks. Believe me, the subways were far from bullet train technology, and a rider either hung on to something for dear life or got seriously tossed around.

That was the scenario as I entered into subway car at River Avenue and 161st Street in the Bronx, the last stop before the train went underground heading for

145

downtown. As usual, the rush-hour subway was cram-packed full. I managed to reach a hanging strap and just to my left, sat a mean-looking heavy-set woman whom I'll call Madame Sadistic. She had a huge purse in her lap, facing a small man standing in front of her who, I would guess, was barely five-feet tall with large thick glasses. He could double for Mr. Peepers, a milquetoast character on a TV show popular at that time.

The train lurched violently and I leaned against the occupant of the seat in front of me while tightening my grip on the strap to keep from falling into his lap. He looked up and smiled understandingly, happy he was seated and I was standing. Mr. Peepers wasn't as lucky. When he leaned into Madame Sadistic, she screamed "masher," and with one swing of her purse bashed him across the face, his thick glasses went flying.

"My glasses, my glasses," he cried.

The man standing on the other side of Mr. Peepers, five-feet-four at best, grabbed a hold of the five-foot Mr. Peepers. "Is this man bothering you, Lady?"

"Yes, he was trying to molest me."

He cocked his fist, aiming for Mr. Peepers, whose eyes were focused on the floor, frantically looking for his glasses. Now normally, I keep to myself on the train and never involve myself in other people's disputes. But I was in a foul mood and this was simply too much.

I grabbed Five-Foot-Four's arm that sported the fist. "If you punch him," I growled (well, it was more like yell, since the trains were so noisy), "I'll give it back to you in spades."

Madame Sadistic raised her purse to give Mr. Peepers another shot, he being particularly vulnerable as he had sunk to his knees searching for his glasses. I grabbed her purse with my other hand, warning her that while I don't normally hit ladies, I'd make an exception here and punch her out.

That's how things stood as the Lexington Avenue Express left 86th Street and roared downtown until the

next express stop at 59th Street, an eight to ten minute
ride. I held Five-Foot-Four's arm with one hand and
Madame Sadistic's purse with the other, desperately
trying to defy gravity and keep my balance in the
swaying subway car, while Mr. Peepers crawled around
my feet trying to locate his glasses.

The train finally arrived at 59th Street; I let go the
arm and the purse and made a beeline for the doors.
"Hold on there mister," a voice shouted at me. "You're
under arrest for disturbing the peace." He flashed his
detective's badge. He rounded up Madame Sadistic, Mr.
Peepers, and Five-Foot-Four and herded all of us away
from the crowds piling onto the express, to the other side
of the platform. All the perps, naturally, were protesting
their innocence.

"We'll sort this out at the stationhouse. Just stand
here while I find a patrolman," he said gruffly, clearly
unwilling to take any crap from us.

Just then the local came roaring into the station
with me, not more than a foot from the edge of the
platform. I could feel the strong rush of air behind me as
several cars raced passed before coming to a halt. The
doors opened and the people piled out. I was in luck; the
open door was right behind me. I watched that door with
the eyes of a hawk. As soon as I saw it moving to close, I
took one step back onto the local as the doors slammed
shut in my face. I watched Madame Sadistic, Mr.
Peepers, and the Five-Foot-Four quickly recede out of
sight as the train picked up speed. It was just another
rush hour day on the subways of New York.

The Memo from Washington

Having survived another subway commute, I waded through the post-trial briefs in the Swiss Watch Case, a boring downside to federal trial work. While wrestling to frame the reply to defense counsel arguments characterizing our tactics as being falling somewhere between those of Attila the Hun and Charles Manson, the serial killer, I took a break, confident that the judge would ignore most of the hyperbole, which, I decided, was worth very few words in response.

I poured myself some high-test coffee (decaf was unknown in those days) and started absentmindedly going through my In Box, not really paying much attention until a memo from a Washington superior caught my attention. He announced that, now that Hawaii had become a state, the Antitrust Division planned to open a Honolulu office to enforce the antitrust laws there. He sought two attorneys, one senior litigator and one junior attorney with some trial experience, to man the new Honolulu office for an unspecified period of time. I folded the memo and put it in my pocket.

That night, over dinner in our Yonkers condo apartment, I remembered the memo in my jacket pocket. I fetched it and showed it to Diana.

"Who would want to go to Hawaii?" I mused out loud.

Diana looked up from the memo. "You and me, baby."

"Are you serious?"

She nodded her head. "Damn serious. Now what do you have to do to get the assignment?"

Memo to Washington
I Am the Greatest
A Lesson Learned

I prepared a memo for my Washington superior requesting the assignment to Honolulu, stating that I had been in the Division for over two years and had received excellent evaluations.

I walked into Mary Jones' office. "Mary, I'm thinking of applying for the Hawaii position, but I don't want to leave the staff in the lurch and wouldn't do anything without checking with you first."

"Sounds like a great opportunity, Carl, go for it. With Louise and Jean now on my staff, we can handle the post-trial briefing."

I nodded appreciatively and pulled out the memo I had just drafted for Washington and handed it to her. "What do you think?"

It took her only a few seconds to read it. She shook her head and frowned. "Carl, when are you going to start promoting yourself? You want that Hawaii job? This memo will not do it. Shed the damn modesty and tell them what a great trial lawyer you are and trumpet all the experience in court you have under your belt. After all, how many young attorneys in the Division for only two years have such trial experience? Tell them they are going to have two experienced trial lawyers instead of only one if they select you as the second attorney."

I went back to my office and wrote a shameless I-am-the-greatest memo extolling my virtues, youth, and trial experience and, lo and behold, two weeks later, Washington notified me that I was to leave for the Honolulu Office as soon as possible. Mary had taught me a lifelong lesson, even if it was at the loss of my naivety and modesty.

CARL L. STEINHOUSE

Goodbye New York, Hello Hawaii--Confronting King Kamehameha

Hawaii, here I come! I traded in my staid gunmetal gray Valiant station wagon for a spiffy-looking brand-new light blue Rambler convertible with a white ragtop, after the Division agreed to send my family, my car, and me to Hawaii, sailing on the Matson Lines. Pursuant to my father's advice, I purchased a white dinner jacket to wear at all those shipboard and Island parties. (Hawaii was so casual, I never got to use it. So I gave it away when it started turning yellow.)

On the ship, the *Matsonia*, I boned up on Hawaiian history by reading *Hawaii Pono*. Many of the Hawaiian names I read only in my mind's eye. When we arrived in Honolulu, the ship was escorted into the harbor by colorful catamarans before docking at Aloha Tower. The arrival of the Antitrust Division was a big event in Hawaii and when we disembarked from the ship, the governor and the attorney general, as well as my new boss, senior attorney Wilbur F., greeted us, gave us leis, and escorted us in a limousine to our hotel.

On the way, we passed Iolani Palace, the seat of government, prominently featuring a large statue of King Kamehameha. Wanting to show off my knowledge of Hawaiian history, I pointed to the statue and exclaimed, "Isn't that King Kamehameha?"

Gales of laughter came from the governor and the attorney general. I had pronounced it Kamy-Hamy-Ha; not the correct pronunciation, Ka-may-ha-may-ha. Wilbur F. shook his head, probably wondering what kind of assistant he inherited. Red-faced, I shut my mouth on any further expositions of my knowledge of Hawaiian culture.

150

NOW WHAT?

Statue of King Kamehameha

Lanikai

We found a place to rent in Lanikai, a cul-de-sac community with no stores or commercial enterprises save for Buzz's Steakhouse on the border of Lanikai and Kailua. The beach was at our doorstep. Our home, formerly a Japanese bathhouse, had walls that slid open so that we could have one big room from one end of the house to the other. Our living room had a huge picture window looking out on Lanikai Bay, with a beautiful beach and twin islands called the Mokuluas situated about a half-mile out. The Mokuluas marked the end of the coral reef that protected the bay. If you sailed out to the islands, landing was forbidden because the islands were designated bird sanctuaries. Of course, that did not stop people from climbing onto to them. But there was really not much to explore. Each island comprised only a few hundred square feet of rock and guano. To swim on the other side of the islands was not smart. Unprotected by the reef, a swimmer could, and some did, encounter sharks.

The Mokuluas

Living on the beach was great, especially with kids. I could come home from a day's work and take Sam and Jane out for a sail on my Sunfish or take a walk on the beach. After a storm, we'd go scavenging on the beach for Japanese float balls, balls that broke free from fishing nets in Japan and floated across the Pacific, winding up on our beach. Most were dark green in color surrounded by thick netting, and of every size, ranging

NOW WHAT?

from the size of a baseball to that of a basketball.

Fly In the Ointment—Tsunamis and the S.O.S.

Beach living was idyllic, except when there was a tsunami, or tidal wave alert, usually a few days after an earthquake occurred in Japan or Alaska. The alerts were serious stuff. A year before, Hilo on the Big Island was wiped out by a tsunami, being hit by mountainous waves many stories high with a large loss of life.

When an alert sounded, we'd pack our cars-- Diana would be sure to take the kids and my priority was to secure the stereo equipment--and we'd drive up the hills of Lanikai where we could always find welcoming homes, safe from the tidal waves, holding "tsunami parties." We'd drink and party until the threat was ended. It got so that we actually looked forward to the tsunami alerts.

* * *

One peaceful night, looking out our picture window onto Lanikai Bay, we saw a light flashing what seemed to be the Morse code, which I never learned to read. It kept flashing over and over.

"It looks like an S.O.S. from a boat in distress," I opined.

"Let's call the police," Diana offered. "They'll know what to do."

A Hawaiian policeman arrived and watched the flashes for a few minutes, rubbing his chin. "Gee, I don't know Morse code either but it sure looks like someone's in trouble." He radioed headquarters.

"What's happening?" I inquired.

"The marines, they're sending out a helicopter from the Kaneohe Marine Base to investigate."

The base was at the other end of the bay and visible from where we were.

We saw the helicopter rise up and approach the flashing lights. Suddenly, the copter turned on its huge searchlights and came down to a few feet above the water and coupled with the roar of its engines, it was enough to scare the living hell out of anyone underneath all that mayhem.

Finally the copter rose up and returned to its base.

The policeman's radio buzzed. He listened and nodded.

"Was it a boat in distress?" I asked.

He shook his head. "Nah, it was a bunch of Japanese fishermen night fishing. The helicopter scared away all the fish and now they are as mad as hell."

"It doesn't make sense," I insisted. "Why did they flash for help?"

He laughed. "They didn't. They wear flashlights strapped to their heads so they can see underwater. What we saw were their heads bobbing in and out of the water as they dove for fish."

CARL L. STEINHOUSE

The Thing about Shoes and Care Packages

We arrived in Hawaii in January 1962 and the first order of business: find a school for Sam, who was approaching his fifth birthday. We'd heard about Punahou, an outstanding private school in Honolulu. I drove to the school and picked up an application. Right on the first page, in severe and bold language, was the dress code. It went something like this: "Students must come to school appropriately dressed in a clean, white-buttoned shirt and pressed dark pants, however shoes are optional."

Shoes are optional? It must be a joke. It wasn't. Kids here do not wear shoes; occasionally, they'll wear go-aheads. In Hawaii, brief showers can inundate those caught in it, but just as quickly, the sun reappears and dries out everyone and everything--except those with shoes and socks. My children were no exception and within several months of living in Hawaii, I'm not sure they even owned a pair of shoes.

We're over five thousand miles from New York, and if Diana thought she could escape her in-laws by moving to Hawaii, she had another think coming. Distance did not stop my parents from visiting their grandkids at least twice a year, staying for several weeks each time. My children's lack of shoes horrified my mother and reaffirmed her belief that we could not adequately care for our children without her guidance and presence. She gave me a baleful look when I simply shrugged in answer to her question of where the children's shoes were. She immediately took the kids to the Liberty House department store to buy them shoes. Children are perceptive, especially about grandmothers that supply them with all sorts of goodies they couldn't squeeze out of their parents. They had no intention of wearing shoes, but humored grandma as she had them fitted for two pairs each. They suffered the shoes while

156

my mother was present. After she left for New York, the shoes came off, never to see the light of day.

A lei greeting for the Carl's parents' visit to Hawaii

Speaking of my mother, all my friends loved her. If you were my friend you were on her list, which meant when my parents went abroad, such as to Europe, which was about every other year, Mom would bring back Lanvin, Hermes, or Longchamps silk ties for all my friends and comparable silk scarves for their wives. She found out the attorney with whom I worked in the Honolulu Office loved Corenella cigars, but he couldn't find them in Hawaii. Every few months, he'd receive a huge box of Corenellas from Macy's in New York, courtesy of Mom.

Despite the fact that I was an adult and certainly earning an adequate living (that's the best you could say for a government salary at my level) she insisted on sending me care packages--like I lived in poverty in a Third World country. I've received canned food, boxes of candy bars, six-packs of beer, and even socks. She'd found out I liked Macy's Gold Toe brand socks, so every few months I'd get a package of them. (Unlike the kids, my work attire did include shoes and socks.) Once she sent a kosher salami. It came by boat and by the time it arrived, it reeked. The postman delivers through rain, snow, and sleet; well, you can include odors. The poor man held this salami at arm's length and handed it to me.

157

I promised him I'd put my foot down, which is no mean feat with my mother. I begged Mom not to send any more salamis, or they'd stop delivering my mail. She was a great mother and friend, but did have one flaw in her personality--she couldn't stand poor spellers. When I was in elementary school at PS 35 in the Bronx, her idea of helping me practice my spelling was to give me a word to spell, and if I missed it, she'd cuff me. I'll tell you this though; now, I'm a damn good speller.

Mom and me on the roof of our apartment house in the Bronx, when I was 12

Strange Guests

As you would expect, living in Hawaii, meant we would be entertaining guests we would otherwise rarely see--but now we suddenly became a must-stop on their itinerary. I won't bore you with a list of all the guests we had, just the unusual ones.

One of our first guests was my old neighborhood chum, Harry Rothman. By now he was a prominent electrical engineer in Northern California, and he showed up with his wife and three daughters in tow. One of his daughters, about three and a half years old, had a stubborn streak that, if they gave an Oscar for that category, she'd win it, hands down. Meals became a battle of wills between her and her mother. The mother did not stand a chance. When the daughter decided she did not want to eat, invariably her mother would insist and try to feed her. The daughter would take the first mouthful and simply hold it in her mouth. No amount of coaxing, threats, or bribery could cause her to swallow. Her mother would not let her leave the table until it was time for bed. The daughter sat there, arms folded, a sour look on her face, and then went to bed, still with the full mouth.

You would think in the quiet of her bed, the daughter would slowly swallow the food, or at least spit it out. No such luck. She woke up in the morning and lo and behold, had the same morsels still in her mouth. Now that's what I call endurance.

Diana greeting Harry with a lei

Another time a cousin of mine, Roz Rosenthal, came calling all the way from New York. Roz had an unusual career. She never went to college or law school, yet she worked her way up from being an assistant in Columbia Law School administrative offices to *Dean* of Student Affairs. So this was a rather assertive woman.

After the appropriate lei greeting, we escorted Roz to her hotel.

"I'm sorry, M'am," the room clerk advised, "we're overbooked and we have no rooms. But we can put you up at the Royal Hawaiian."

Well, you never heard a fiercer dressing-down than Roz gave this poor room clerk. "I have a reservation, damn it, and I won't move until you give me a room."

"Roz," I whispered in her ear, "don't fuss, and just take him up on his offer."

The Dean shook her head. "I'm not going stand for such treatment. They can't just stick me in a hole-in-the-wall."

I kicked her shoe and when she ignored me, I grabbed her elbow firmly and forced her away from the desk while smiling at the room clerk. "She'll take that room at the Royal Hawaiian" I told the clerk. "Just ignore her, it's been a long trip and she's very tired."

I drove my very angry and reluctant cousin to the Royal Hawaiian, where the doorman, dressed in an outfit that would make a fleet admiral proud, greeted her like royalty. Her jaw dropped. She entered the lobby, her eyes popped open. The most exotic Hawaiian flora filled the area as she approached the reception desk of the hotel that, at that time, was by far the most luxurious in all of Honolulu. For her economy room rate, she was given a suite. She must have asked five times what rate she'd be paying and the answer was always the same--the economy rate of the overbooked hotel. She almost swooned on reaching her room--they had laid out fresh Hawaiian fruit, puupuus (Hawaiian hors d'oeuvres), and a bottle of Champaign.

"Next time, warn me," she complained.

I could only roll my eyes.

We sometimes bid aloha to guests on shipboard, here to my former Swiss Watch case colleague, Louise Florencourt, standing, center

More Guests--the Disagreeable Wife

Into my second year in the Antitrust Division office in Hawaii, I received a call from a judge I had appeared before and to whom, on my leaving for Hawaii, I politely uttered, "Look me up if you ever get to Hawaii." A polite but insincere invitation; I did not expect him to follow up on it. But he did.

Picking up the phone at my Honolulu office, I found myself talking to Judge _. I sat there in stunned silence, never expecting to hear from him again. Recovering my wits quickly from that embarrassing moment of silence, I asked about the Judge's health.

"I'm fine. I called because I just arrived in Hawaii with my wife and we would like to come visit you. We're staying at the Hilton Hawaiian Village."

* * *

While Diana grumbled to me about the short notice to prepare a fancy dinner, she was most gracious to the judge and his wife and prepared a sumptuous meal, thanks to her recent education in Mary Sia's cooking school, which Diana characterizes as the Cordon Bleu of Chinese cooking. Indeed, our guests were most impressed by the meal.

After dinner, the Judge settled comfortably into one of the club chairs in our living room, admiring the view of Lanikai Bay and the twin Mokulua Islands. He lit a large corona cigar and we engaged in small talk. As the ash on his cigar accumulated, his wife would admonish him, "Now, Judge, flick that ash into the ashtray before you get it all over the place."

At the fifth "Now, Judge" reminder, His Honor had finally had it. This Judge, who always displayed a gracious and gentle demeanor on the bench, leaned forward, flicked his ash in the ashtray, and growled,

162

NOW WHAT?

"Listen, woman, if you open your trap to nag me one more time, I'm going to punch you in the nose."

Now, I don't know if he would have really carried out that threat. I sincerely doubt it. But we'll never know because it shut her up for the rest of the evening.

* * *

The judge felt obligated to reciprocate and the night before he was scheduled to return to New York, he invited Diana and me to dinner at the Hilton Hawaiian Village main dining room. This restaurant is a huge room with cylindrical white pillars judiciously placed to hold up the large hanging ceiling. You need to understand this.

The judge and his wife were seated when we arrived at the dining room. The judge got up to greet us. His wife did not--and I saw why. She sat in a wheelchair, her right leg straight out swathing in bandages and a brace.

Did he carry out his threat after all? No, it seems that they went to see Don Ho at the Down Under Bar, and that's just what it is--down under. Taking the stairs down to the bar, the judge's wife lost her footing, fell down a few steps and broke her leg.

Halfway through the meal, the Judge's wife leaned over to Diana. "Be a dearie and wheel me to the powder room, will you?' she said in a low voice.

"Of course, I'll be glad to." So Diana got up, moved behind the wheelchair, backing away it from the table and in the direction of the restrooms.

"We'll see you shortly," the invalid sang out. I wasn't sure if that was a promise or a threat.

Half way to their destination Diana greeted someone she knew and began talking and wheeling--a big mistake because distracted by the conversation, she wheeled the judge's wife, the injured right leg straight out

163

and leading the way, directly into one of those cylindrical white pillars. The result? A blood-curdling scream that silenced the entire large dining room.

Both the judge and I turned to discover the source of that horrible cry. Focusing on Diana and his wife and immediately realizing what had happened, I was about to apologize when the judge leaned over and whispered in my ear, "You know, Carl, I'm getting to like your wife more and more with each passing minute."

NOW WHAT?

Enforcing the Law in Hawaii

You Did What?

Having learned how to pronounce King
Kamehameha, I had another surprise in store for me. I
began working with my boss and senior attorney, Wilbur
F. Everyone called him Bill. I found him to be a fine
gentleman and an expert in the international application
of the antitrust laws, a fine esoteric field, but with little
application to our assignment in Hawaii. Also, he had
zilch experience in trying cases. I, the junior attorney,
with one civil case under my belt, had more trial
experience! And neither of us had criminal trial or grand
jury experience. And here we were, the entire attorney
staff of the Honolulu Office of the federal Antitrust
Division. Vernon C, the head of the Hawaii Antitrust
Division, even younger than me, had more experience
than either of us.

It seems also that neither of us was well versed in
the Division protocol of opening investigations and filing
cases, which required the approval of the Attorney
General of the United States and the Assistant Attorney
General in charge of the Antitrust Division. Going on
our merry way, we began several price fixing
investigations, and a few merger investigations--all
without the requisite authority. That was the first
mistake. We tackled the easiest one first under a little-
used statute barring interlocking directors on the boards
of competing companies. The theory of the law was
simple: the potential for anticompetitive hank-panky was
much greater if the same people sat on the boards of two
or more direct competitors. It sounded logical but the
statute was rarely enforced by the Antitrust Division.

It didn't take long to investigate. The companies in Hawaii were clearly competitors and we found a whole slew of the directors that sat on the boards of two or more of these companies. We put together what I considered to be an airtight civil complaint and a brilliant pleading and sued all the bastards--our second mistake. We sent Washington a copy of the pleadings and the date the case was filed.

As quick as it takes the mail to reach Antitrust Division headquarters, the phone rang. I happened to pick it up. Our direct superior in Washington, Gordon, the Director of Operations, was on the line.

"You did what?" Gordon screamed. He knew what we did so I considered that a rhetorical question that didn't require a response, so I decided to sit there silently, five thousand miles away, knowing from his tone that I was in trouble, but not precisely why.

"Did you ever hear of obtaining authority to conduct investigations?"

I never had really thought about it but it didn't take a genius to know the answer should be affirmative. "I guess so."

"Did you ever hear of obtaining authority to file a case?"

Again, I mumbled, "I guess so."

"Can you withdraw the complaint?" he asked. I detected a lot of anger in Gordon's voice.

"I don't think so."

"Why the hell not?"

"The directors have already resigned and the Honolulu newspapers have been waxing eloquent about, and I quote, 'the quick and effective action of the newly-created office. They are to be congratulated.'"

"What are you reading from?"

"An editorial in the Honolulu Star-Bulletin, the largest daily newspaper in Hawaii. As a matter of fact, we received banner headlines in all the Hawaii newspapers about our great victory. The newspapers are already in the mail to you."

There was silence on the other end of the line. I abhor a vacuum so I asked, "Do you still want me to withdraw the complaint?"

"No, you idiot, it would make us look like horse's asses. Steinhouse, you're one lucky bastard. If that case had blown up in your face, you'd be out of there faster that you could ignore more of our procedures."

"Uh, we have begun about five other investigations and ..."

"Without authority?"

"Fraid so."

"Let me speak to the Bill, the senior attorney."

I handed the phone to Bill. His face turned red. "There's really no need for profanity, Gordon. I understand; you were provoked. Yes, yes, we will seek authority for each of those investigations we've already opened before we do another thing."

Within the year, Bill was transferred back to Washington to a job in his specialty, international commerce, shortly after a new senior attorney, Ray Carlson, arrived. A tough, by the book, no-nonsense trial attorney with several civil and criminal trials under Carlson's belt, things changed for the better--and I learned a lot.

CARL L. STEINHOUSE

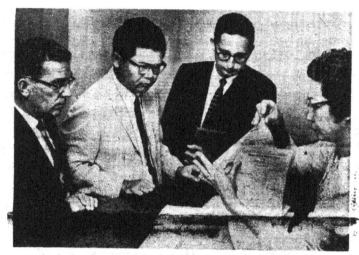

Mrs. Elizabeth Robinson, Federal Court deputy clerk, formally files the anti-trust papers. Attorneys from the left are Raymond M. Carlson, Herman Lum and Carl L. Steinhouse. Lum is the U.S. District Attorney. The other men are with the Department of Justice anti-trust division in Honolulu.—Star-Bulletin Photo.

(Reprinted with permission from the Honolulu Star-Advertiser)

Our cases were front-page news in Honolulu

NOW WHAT?

A Great Interview I Conducted, Too Bad I Wasn't There

A majority of the stock of virtually the only shipping line carrying freight between Hawaii and the mainland was controlled by the dominant companies in Hawaii in retail, wholesale, drugs, and agriculture and we felt it was an anticompetitive mechanism to keep competition out of the Islands--and it seemed to be successful, keeping out all but Sears, which was big enough to afford its own ocean shipping vessels. We launched an investigation and issued civil subpoenas with the idea of divesting such control of the shipping line.

The Hawaii Attorney General, who, at least at that point in time, expressed his excitement and support for our investigation, invited Ray and me to lunch. A pleasant and tropical dining spot in the mountains overlooking Honolulu, the Willows was a popular lunch spot for businessmen and tourists, with its ponds filled with large bright orange carp, underneath the thatched roof of a building with no walls.

We had a round of martinis, mine with a marinated onion, no olive. That was my drink of favor then. I would not dare one touch now.

"Bring another round," the AG ordered without asking us. I ended up drinking three martinis with the attorney general. I think Ray stopped at one and a half martinis.

When we left the restaurant and bid farewell to the AG, we hurried down by the docks for our appointment with the Army Corps of Engineers in connection with our shipping line investigation. I had prepared very hard for this important interview, my questions all carefully thought out and put down on paper.

169

Having introduced ourselves and produced our credentials, I began the interview.

"For the record, would you state your name, rank and position with the Corps of Engineers?"

Ray nudged me. "Let's go," he said sharply.

I looked at him quizzically. "But I haven't even started to ..."

"Never mind that, just get up and leave." Ray was not tall, but he was powerful. He grabbed my arm roughly and would have, I am sure, dragged me out, if I didn't finally stand up and walk out with him.

"What's the idea?" I said with much surprise and a great deal of annoyance after we left the meeting. "This is an important interview and . . ."

"I conducted the interview and obtained all the information we needed."

I blinked and shook my head. "But I don't understand?"

"It's rather simple. You asked the interviewee his name and then fell dead asleep. I did the interview from your notes. He was a little put out by your snooze. 'Am I that boring?' he asked. I assured that was not the case."

I shook my head in disbelief. "No more martini lunches for me."

"You're damn right," Ray affirmed.

And we both meant it.

Let Someone Else Screw Us

Author

When we finally brought the case against the shipping line and the companies controlling it, the AG's ardor for out cause cooled, undoubtedly from the pressure of Island politics in which the defendants were highly influential.

The attorneys for the defendants arranged a meeting with the United States Attorney General to convince him to drop the case and I traveled to Washington to argue against it. The Hawaiian AG, our great initial supporter also attended. After the defense counsel made their argument the US AG turned to the Hawaiian AG and asked his opinion.

"It would be better for the State if the case was dropped," the Hawaiian AG said in a low voice, looking down and away from me while dropping the bomb.

What also dropped was my jaw. Out of the blue, my friend suddenly switched sides.

"With all due respect Mr. Attorney General, you are full of crap. Why just last week . . ."

"What did you say?" my ultimate boss, the US AG, interrupted.

"Well, Sir . . ."

He did not let me continue. All 6' 6" rose out of his chair. "How dare you insult the Attorney General of the sovereign State of Hawaii?" He pointed to the door. "Out, get out of my office--now!"

Well, that was certainly a clear command, not subject to interpretation, so I got up and left, glaring at the State AG on my way out. He simply shrugged.

I knew our case, the most important one we'd ever bring in Hawaii, was in trouble. I called Ray in Honolulu.

"We have strong support from Congressman Tom Gill," Ray said. "Try to get in touch with him now and have him call our AG."

On Capitol Hill, the House was in session considering the Civil Rights Act and Gill was reluctant to leave the chamber. I had the page deliver a message that it was an emergency. He finally came out and I explained the situation to him.

"Get me a phone," Gill ordered of the page. He dialed the AG's number. I could only hear his end of the conversation.

"Mr. Attorney General, I understand that the defendants and the Hawaiian AG are trying to convince you to drop the shipping case." He paused.

"What do I think of it? I have only one thing to say, and then I have to get back into the chamber to vote on the Civil Rights Act. We have been screwed by those defendants for one hundred years now, give us the opportunity to be screwed by someone else for a change. Don't dismiss the case."

He hung up the phone and looked at me. "I'm afraid that's the best I can do right now" and disappeared back into the House chamber.

The case was not dismissed and ultimately the defendants settled by agreeing to have four of the five companies controlling the shipping line divest their interests. The independence of the shipping line was, for the first time, established.

CARL L. STEINHOUSE

Ukulele Court—1963

The senior trial attorney and I were prosecuting several scrap metal dealers in federal District Court in Hawaii. The defendants had conspired to fix the prices of the scrap they bought from the military in Hawaii. A lot was at stake because businessmen don't like to go to jail.

The criminal trial started uneventfully enough, with a little humor to relieve the tension--and if you've ever tried a case, you know there is TENSION, in capital letters.

In any event, on the first day, the court seated twelve jurors and was questioning them to see if there was any bias or other reason why any juror on the panel should be dismissed for cause.

The judge completed his questioning of the jurors and then turned to address each of the attorneys: "Do you know any of the potential jurors seated in the jury box? Now take a good look."

I gave the jurors no more than a passing glance--there was no need--I had been in Hawaii for only a year and there was no way I would recognize any of the faces--all of them were of Asian heritage.

"No, Your Honor," I said. The other attorneys echoed the same answer.

Now the judge turned back to the prospective jurors. "Do you, the jurors, know any of the attorneys standing before you?"

One by one, from right to left, the jurors, in turn, shook their heads no--except when the fourth lady in the second row was reached, a diminutive lady of Japanese extraction. She nodded.

"Is that a yes, Mrs. Fujiyama?" the judge asked.

She smiled--a sweet looking woman. I wondered what her problem was.

"Yes, Your Honor, I know him," pointing an accusing finger directly at me.

174

NOW WHAT?

The judge turned in his chair, and from the high bench, sternly looked down on me. With a scowl, he said two words: "*Mister* Steinhouse . . .?"

The courtroom was hushed; all eyes focused on me, including those of my boss, Carlson, the senior trial attorney. He was probably wondering how I screwed up--and the trial had not yet even started.

I couldn't scream out, "I'm innocent, I swear it!" So all I did was turn a beet red and shrug my shoulders, giving the judge my best "I'll be damned if I know" look.

The Judge turned back to Mrs. Fujiyama and in the most judicial tone he could muster, he said, "Mrs. Fujiyama, just what is the nature of your acquaintance with Mr. Steinhouse." He fairly spit out my name.

Mrs. Fujiyama, still with that now silly smile, said, "I didn't know his name but I sit next to him in his ukulele class."

My baritone ukulele

Howls of laughter reverberated throughout the courtroom. The judge did not help matters. With a wicked grin, he suggested that perhaps over one of the lunch hours, I could serenade the court, my fellow attorneys and, of course, the jurors. This spurred my fellow attorneys to applaud with great gusto. I politely, and still red faced, declined--with "all due respect"--a phrase you always used when you had to say no to, or disagreed with, the court--but most of the time it didn't help.

NOW WHAT?

Another Fantasy--Ukulele Steinhouse of the Justice Department—1963

On reflection, when the judge invited me to play the ukulele over one of the lunch hours and I declined, I really missed a golden opportunity. What if I had been an attorney who goes for the jugular and takes advantage of every opening to defeat my opponent without mercy? I could have played it much cooler. Things might have gone something like this, instead:

The judge with a big grin on his face looked at me. "Perhaps, Mr. Steinhouse, you would care to serenade me, the jurors and the other attorneys before lunch one day during the trial."

Without batting an eye, I stepped up to the bench. "Be glad to Your Honor, you just name the day and I'll have my baritone ukulele in here ready for the concert."

The judge's eyes widened in surprise. "I really wasn't serious Mr. Steinhouse."

"Oh, but I am, Your Honor, very serious," I say. "I accept your invitation."

The judge looked at the rest of the lawyers, shrugging. "Very well, Mr. Steinhouse, Aloha Day would be appropriate." Every Friday was Aloha Day and all the attorneys and the judges were required to shed their suits, white shirts and ties and don aloha shirts, the more colorful the better. It gave us Islanders an advantage over the Mainlanders, who became discombobulated without their three-piece suits and ties. Invariably, it was a day of errors for them.

"That's a date, Your Honor!"

My co-counsel grabbed my arm and whispered frantically in my ear, "Are you crazy, we'll be the laughing stock of the court."

177

Cool Steinhouse turned disdainfully to him. "Just leave it to me; I know what I'm doing."

Actually the judge could hear the whispers and broke out laughing. My co-counsel turned beet-red. If looks could kill... Even the most of the jurors had big smiles. My plan was beginning to work already!

Friday arrived and I showed up with my new baritone ukulele and my old, original, small ukulele. You might ask, why two ukuleles?

That's a fair question, so I'll tell you.

The lunch hour came and I motioned to Mrs. Fujiyama (in my fantasy, she was not kicked off the jury).

She pointed to herself in puzzlement, as if to say, ME?

I nodded and walked over to her, handing her the small ukulele. "Do you remember 'You are My Sunshine'?" It was the only tune we had learned so far in our ukulele class.

A big smile came on her face. "Oh yes, I have been practicing it all week."

"Good, all you have to do is accompany me. I have my own words."

The judge, the attorneys and the jurors still couldn't believe I was actually going to serenade them. I could hear my opponents whispering, "This ought to be good."

They didn't know what was in store for them.

"We'll play it in the key of C." It was the only key in which I could play.

Mrs. Fujiyama winked at me. Who would have believed this shy little lady was such a ham?

"Your Honor, I will sing to the tune of 'You Are My Sunshine.' I'm telling you ahead of time because you may not recognize it from our playing."

The judge looked at defense counsel. "Before we proceed, do you have any objections to the presence of the jury?"

NOW WHAT?

Lead defense stood. "No Your Honor, we welcome the jurors to enjoy the spectacle."

The judge looked at me. "Very well, Mr. Steinhouse, I hope you know what you are doing. You may proceed. But don't take too long. We still have to eat lunch."

"It'll be a quick show, Your Honor, I promise."

I strummed the C chord on my baritone uke. Mrs. Fujiyama matched it on the standard uke.

We strummed the vamp, the lead-in notes to the tune. Just like real professionals.

I sang.

"You think Pearl Harbor was hurt in forty-one,
  That was nothin' compared to what these defendants had done,
  To fix prices for scrap they conspired,
  But alas for them the statute of limitations had not expired,
  They bought the scrap at an artificially low price,
  And cheating our own navy wasn't very nice,
  Leaving less money for our nation's defense,
  Is one damnable and dastardly offense,
  Our Navy and, indeed, our country, will hail
  Putting these bastards directly in jail!"

I bowed and Mrs. Fujiyama gave me a big hug.

The jury applauded wildly. I could hear behind me, defense counsel howling "Objection!" over and over. "Objections were waived and therefore, overruled!" roared the judge. Then he smiled and left the bench.

Carlson just sat there, shaking his head. He knew a flimflam operation when he saw one. He also knew I had the jury in my pocket.

"Now how do we avoid a mistrial?" he mumbled.

The fantasy over, I returned to the real world.

NOW WHAT?

Rubber Hose Enforcement—1963

Of course, there was much more to that trial than the ukulele. As a litigator in criminal white-collar trials, dramatic events come often uninvited and usually, unwanted. The criminal trial we prosecuted for the US Justice Department in Hawaii, however, stands out as more than merely dramatic; it was cataclysmic--almost.

In the criminal price fixing trial, the judge dismissed the ukulele juror since she had the misfortune of sitting next to me in our ukulele class. And that, for me, was the high point in the litigation--it was that kind of trial.

Two companies and several individuals were being tried for price fixing, a felony under the Sherman Act. My star witness, Norman, was an executive in one of the companies on trial--he turned state's evidence to receive immunity from prosecution, thereby implicating his uncle, which owned the large competing company.

Throughout the trial, the witness's parents, Mr. And Mrs. Parent, had front-row seats just behind the bar. Mr. Parent, the owner of the company the witness worked for, sat there expensively dressed, his diamond stick pin anchoring his tie, sparkling from the reflection of the large chandelier hanging in the middle of the courtroom. The mother was resplendent in her mink coat notwithstanding the warm Hawaiian weather.

Previously, the witness had testified before the grand jury that he personally participated in fixing prices with his competitors, the other company, and two individuals on trial. I had the transcript of the grand jury testimony sitting at my elbow as I prepared to examine this witness at trial. It was like shooting fish in a barrel--I thought.

After some preliminary questioning I got down to the meat of the examination--his meeting with the other competitor to fix prices. To my utter surprise he denied everything. Though he was my witness the court nevertheless permitted me to cross-exam him as a "hostile" witness.

"Sir, you have just denied meeting with your competitor to fix prices. I show you your testimony before the grand jury where you stated unequivocally such meetings occurred on a regular basis. Did you lie before the grand jury?"

"No, I told the truth."

He then insisted that his current testimony also was truthful.

I confronted the witness. "How can that be? The statements are contradictory."

"Don't you remember?" The witness continued, "When you were interviewing me prior to the grand jury session, you beat me with a rubber hose and convinced me that your version of events was the truth? I was so fearful, I agreed. My aunt was at the interview and is a witness to your conduct."

Whereupon the witness refused to answer any more questions on the grounds of self-incrimination. His attorney then popped up. He just happened to know of a Supreme Court case from the 1870s holding that a witness physically intimidated could take the Fifth. I knew that I had been set up by the perjury of this witness and the subornation of perjury by his attorney.

The judge called a recess in the trial and held a special hearing as to whether I beat the witness with a rubber hose. I took the stand and explained the events as they actually occurred. The next to testify was the witness' aunt, an 80-year-old woman with flaming red dyed hair whose face definitely had seen better days. I never saw this woman before and believe me, I would have remembered her.

To establish her credibility, she offered that she was an undercover agent for the FBI during World War II, running a bawdy house in San Francisco and reporting on what suspected spies said during their visits to her establishment.

"Presently, I continue to do undercover work," she testified. "I run a gay bar in Honolulu and report on Red agents that frequent my place."

The judge turned to me, saying, "Mr. Steinhouse, it should be easy for you to test her credibility. Why don't you ask your brethren at the local FBI office whether she is lying?"

It seemed like a good idea at the time. Later, I reported back to the court, shaking my head.

"Judge, the Special Agent in charge refuses to comment. He says if the FBI denies those claims that are clearly false and refuses to comment on the others, it will quickly become clear who really are the undercover agents. Your Honor, no amount of pleading and groveling would convince him to change his position. It's FBI policy."

Ultimately, the court held that the witness and his aunt were not credible. The witness was held in contempt.

Throughout this entire drama I feared that someone would discover the one truth--that I do keep a piece of rubber garden hose in my car under the driver's seat for protection.

CARL L. STEINHOUSE

The Alioto Effect—1964

There's an old cliché, "Fact is stranger than fiction." Maybe so, maybe not. This true story may tip the balance slightly in favor of fact. I call it *The Alioto Effect*.

Some attorneys are so good in court that their reputation precedes them, sometimes with devastating effect even before they put a foot into the courtroom. One such attorney was Joe Alioto. You may have heard his name before. For many years, he was the mayor of San Francisco. From my point of view, as you will see, he was far more talented as a courtroom lawyer than as a politician--but I am straying from the story. In any event, this occurred well before Mr. Alioto had become mayor.

Joe Alioto was a commanding presence in court, no doubt about it. At 6'2" and, I would guess, 230 pounds with not an ounce of fat that I could discern, he was an imposing presence. He was immaculately and tasteful dressed--always--and he was an orator of unmatched skill during a trial. As a matter of fact, he was so smooth and charming, he even had my wife rooting for the other side.

Needless to say, opposing Alioto was a daunting task for most thinking lawyers. But what did I know? I was a young lawyer in the Department of Justice, chomping at the bit to make a reputation for myself in the antitrust field as a trial lawyer. Opposing attorneys did not faze me. Not so for my witness, however, and that is the nub of my story.

After the criminal trial, senior trial attorney, Ray Carlson, and I sued the scrap metal dealers, on behalf of the United States, in the same Hawaii Federal District Court. The defendants conspired to fix the prices of the scrap they bought from the military in Hawaii. A ton of money was at stake here because the antitrust laws permitted us to recover triple the damages we could

184

prove. So one of the defendants hired San Francisco attorney, Alioto, one of the best in the business.

Our case was strong on the liability issue--that they did fix prices. It was not as strong on the amount of damages the United States was entitled to recover. The Department of Justice provided us--we couldn't choose for ourselves--with an economist to testify as to the amount of damages. He did not impress me. He was not articulate and he dressed like he just came off the farm. But this is witness I had to use. To tell you the truth, I never trusted economists--when they talk, it's like chalk screeching on a black board, if you know what I mean. There's an old saying I love to quote to economists that doesn't endear me to them: "If you laid all the economists end to end they still would not reach a conclusion."

Every time I talk about economists, I get distracted. I'm sorry. Anyway, getting back on track, the accepted way to get damages into evidence is to use an economist or a statistician as a witness. Now our expert, whom I'll call "Mr. Economist", didn't do the work that was to be the subject of his testimony--I did. Being the junior member of the team, and a former accountant to boot, the tedious task of putting together the numbers fell on my shoulders. I assembled the facts and figures on how much the price of scrap metal should have been absent the conspiracy and gave the package to Mr. Economist who looked it over. He agreed with my analysis and that was no surprise to me. If economists know one thing--it's on which side their bread is buttered.

"Who's the attorney that will question me?" Mr. Economist asked.

"I will," I replied.

"Not Carlson, the senior attorney with more experience?"

I was really getting peeved now. "Not Carlson--me. I will examine you on the stand."

185

"And who will cross-examine me?"

"Joe Alioto."

"*The* Joe Alioto or," he asked hopefully, "his son, Joe, Junior?"

"The big man himself," I said flippantly--big, big mistake.

He turned ash gray with the blood slowly draining from his face. You could actually see it happening--like pulling down a shade.

"Oh dear," he said. He was a devout Mormon with ten children and he never cursed. "I can't go on the stand against Alioto."

I failed to appreciate the depth of his fear and said crossly, "You can and you will. Do you think we paid your way out to Hawaii to provide you with a sun tan?"

Sitting in front of me dumbstruck, he didn't answer. *Great,* I thought. Trying to mollify him, I said, "Don't worry, you'll be well prepared for him--I guarantee it."

Mr. Economist was a frugal man. I suppose being a government employee with ten kids, he had no choice. He booked himself into a room on the fourth floor of the YMCA on Nuuanu Street (don't spend time trying to pronounce it, but if you must, simply pronounce EVERY vowel). And with no elevator--remember that. With those accommodations he could save some of his government per diem which, in those days, was only $16 a day. Believe me; anyone who could save at that per diem rate had to be as thrifty as they come.

He left my office at about seven in the evening, a quivering mass. I had bad vibes about it--but what did I know? This was only my third trial, so I continued to work into the night, preparing for the next day's court battle. That's the life of an attorney in trial--in court all day and preparing all night for the next day. At about ten at night, I received a call from the night manager of the YMCA facility. I knew him because I worked out there three times a week--when I wasn't on trial, of course.

NOW WHAT?

"Carl, you'd better get over here right away, your friend seems to be very ill." The words were like sledgehammer blows to my gut.

Unlike Mr. Economist, my first utterance was not "Oh dear". Uttering every obscenity I ever learned, I raced over to Nuuanu Street. I dashed into the lobby of the "Y".

"Room 405, Carl," the night manager yelled. I could hear Mr. Economist screaming upstairs. I took the stairs, two at a time, up to the top floor to his room. The ambulance crew arrived at about the same time.

Room 405 was quite a sight. Mr. Economist was spread-eagled on the bed, his arms straight out, his legs wide apart, like he was being crucified. He screamed, "The Pain, the pain, I can't stand the pain."

He was stiff as a board, and I don't mean figuratively. His toes pointed straight ahead and if you stood him up he would be standing on his tip toes. His fingers were splayed out and absolutely rigid. If you were strong enough to lift him by one toe, it would be like lifting a large piece of plywood from one of its corners.

The ambulance attendants had to take him down the narrow staircase like a piece of furniture. They maneuvered the spread-eagled economist around a bend in the stairs on the second floor. They would angle him, turn him upright, then horizontal, all the while he screamed about the pain. The same routine got Mr. Economist down to the first floor. It was a nightmare for everyone. So this was the situation: Mr. Economist had his pain, I had no witness for the next morning, and the ambulance attendants had to carry him like a frozen side of beef down four flights of stairs. The entire "Y" turned out for the spectacle. I left him at the hospital at midnight and went back to work. The doctors had advised me that Mr. Economist would not be available

187

tomorrow; that he had and was still having a catatonic fit. Even my inexperienced eye could see that, but I preferred my diagnosis, *The Alioto Effect*.

My boss, Carlson, decided that since I did all the work anyway, I would be the witness. The thought briefly entered my mind, *Hell, now Alioto will cross-examine me.* I quickly dismissed it. In view of Mr. Economist's "illness", the court permitted us to substitute me for him on the stand. Ray Carlson did the examination with my notes.

After the day's session was concluded, we visited Mr. Economist in the hospital. He was bright, cheery and no longer catatonic. He had no memory of the event, or of the pain, or of the trip to the hospital. I know what you're thinking: he was faking. I don't think so; no one could hold himself that stiff for such a sustained period. Believe me, Mr. Economist was not in great physical shape and he certainly was no Olympic gymnast. No, it had to be *The Alioto Effect*.

"They'll release me tomorrow," he said happily, adding, "By the way, how was Mr. Alioto's cross-examination?"

I looked him squarely in the eyes and said through clenched teeth with as much sarcasm as I could muster, "On conclusion of my direct examination, Alioto stood up in court and said, and I quote: 'I have no questions at all, Your Honor'."

Those Hawaiians!

It's always a mistake to try to generalize about people on the basis of ethnicity, nationality, or race, as for example, certain peoples being lazy, nasty, violent, or having other common characteristics. But I can wholeheartedly do that for those with Hawaiian blood with whom I came into contact. At least it was true in the early sixties when Hawaii first became a state. For the most part, they were a caring, naive and helpful people with the true aloha spirit ("aloha" is a fond greeting of hello, a heart-felt goodbye, and a sincerely-caring how-are-you).

Let me give you an example. I spent a lot of time in the Federal Courthouse in Honolulu in the course of enforcing the antitrust laws, conducting grand juries and trying civil and criminal antitrust cases. Being in law enforcement did grant me some privileges. I was permitted to park free at the metered spaces in front of that building. The meter maids respected the small sign on my windshield identifying me as being with the Department of Justice. One day, I came out of the courthouse and headed for my car parked in such a metered space. I stopped. There she was, a heavy-set Hawaiian lady in a long muumuu, sporting several leis, feeding coins into the meter where I parked my car. As I approached, she greeted me with a dazzling smile.

"Aloha. I didn't want you to get a parking ticket so I put coins into the meter."

I didn't have the heart to tell her I could park free. "Thank you so much," I gushed, "you saved me from a visit to traffic court and a fine."

I handed her a dollar for reimbursement. She refused it. "Keep your money. You would do the same for me, I'm sure." Obviously, she did not know me.

She moved away, finding another meter that needed feeding.

The Hawaiians are also wonderfully naïve. When I worked in New York City, I escaped several tickets for moving violations by not hesitating to flash my Department of Justice credentials. As a matter of fact I kept my driver's license in my credentials just for that reason. I never had to say anything. I'd get a warning to drive carefully and be sent on my way. Well, a Hawaiian motorcycle cop stopped me for making a right turn without being fully in the right turn lane. He explained that my left front tire slightly overlapped the line into the straight-ahead lane. An outrageous technicality if there ever was one. He asked for my license, so I took out my credentials and confidently flashed them in his face while fishing out my license. He couldn't miss the large gold lettering, "Department of Justice."

"That where you work, Mr. Steinhouse?"

"Yes, I'm a fellow law enforcement officer, working in the *Department of Justice*," waiting for him to be impressed, return my license, and send me on my merry way.

Instead, he took out his pen and a blank ticket form. "How you spell 'Department of Justice?'" I got the ticket, but the moment was priceless.

Kimchee and Poi

Our two-man office had space in the Justice Department's Immigration Station on Ala Moana Boulevard, the main drag running along the waterfront downtown. We had three rooms, an office for each attorney and one for our secretary of Japanese ancestry, Doris Yokoyama. It turned out to be a great place to be situated because at least half of the Immigration work force was of Hawaiian, Samoan, Japanese, Chinese, Filipino, Korean or Portuguese ancestry, among others. We celebrated all their holidays, and all their New Years. More to the point was the cornucopia of food that showed up at the lunchroom that was for the taking. Every few weeks Sara Kim would honor us with a batch of Korean salad, kimchee, that was spicy hot, but spectacular tasting. Other women brought in sashimi, Mandarin duck, taro root, rice dishes, and the like, and all shared and shared alike. Every few months they'd throw a huge luau on the large center lawn of the station (the station was a two-story rectangular-shaped building with the lawn in the middle and a large covered, but open air, area for dining). Those were real luaus with the roast pig baked in the ground, copious amounts of poi, which some haoles (*i.e.*, those coming from the Mainland and not Hawaiian born) equated with school paste. But not me, I couldn't get enough of it. We washed it all down with Primo Hawaiian Beer.

Luau at the Immigration Station

We became part of the Immigration Service family and frequented the homes and parties of its officers and administrative judges. Those were my martini-drinking days and on more than one occasion I suffered the sin of overdrinking—in other words I had gotten sloshed. Once, I became boisterous and obnoxious and refused to leave the party. Several of the Immigration officers tried and failed to get me in the front passenger seat of my Rambler convertible, so they did the next best thing, they threw me in the trunk and closed the lid so Diana could drive me home. She wasn't too friendly to me after such incidents and I don't blame her. It seems alcohol brings out the nastiness in me.

The Gasoline Scam

While we worked hard enforcing the antitrust laws, we were not above having a good time too. One of the Immigration officers, John C., purchased a new 1963 Volkswagen Beetle and kept bragging its wonderful gas mileage. It was tiresome because most of us had small cars with good mileage especially with gas being priced some 75 cents above that on mainland (in Hawaii you always referred to the 48 contiguous states as the "mainland," never as the insulting "United States," since Hawaii strongly felt it was part of the United States, as indeed it was). A bunch of us got together and we chipped in to buy gas and surreptitiously poured it into the gas tank of his Beetle. He couldn't believe it; he boasted getting between 60 and 70 miles a gallon. We gave him a hard time, saying he was full of it and this frustrated him mightily. He wanted to bet us; but there were no takers. "Damn it," he'd yell, "I am really getting that mileage, no kidding."

"Yeah, sure," was the response.

Then we switched tactics. Again surreptitiously, we began siphoning gas out of his gas tank. Now, he was getting 9 to 11 miles per gallon.

"I don't understand it. How could it drop so precipitously," he'd moan. His auto repairman couldn't find anything wrong. It was a new car in tip-top condition, he told John C. One of John's buddies finally took pity on him and told him. You know what we found out? John C. definitely did not have a sense of humor. But also, we never heard again about his great gas mileage.

CARL L. STEINHOUSE

Say That Again?

The first time I visited the bar across the street
from the Immigration Station, I discovered two important
things. One, the bar had great fried mahi-mahi
sandwiches, and two, I had a Bronx accent. Having
heretofore lived in New York City all my life, that fact
had never occurred to me. Everyone in the City had
some form of New York accent, be it from the Bronx,
Brooklyn, or another borough. But to us New Yorkers,
we had no accent, but everyone else did.

The discovery came about when I ordered my first
bottle of beer at the bar. "A bottul a bee-a, please."

"Say that again?" the bar tender responded.

"A bottul a bee-a."

The bartender broke out laughing (I don't know
why, you should hear the Hawaiian accent and Pidgin
English they speak) and called over other patrons. I
finally got my beer after entertaining the patrons over that
lunch hour and subsequent lunch hours until I finally
mastered the pronunciation that did not excite the locals.

That Devil Attacked Me but I Had the Last Laugh and Not So Sweet Revenge

My investigations and trial preparation often took me to the other islands in search of evidence and to speak to potential witnesses. One trip took me to the Big Island (Island of Hawaii). I drove to a ranch about an hour out of Hilo to prepare its owner, Jack R., an important witness in one of our trials.

"Jeez, Carl, I'm sorry," Jack said, with a hang-dog look, "I know we had an appointment today but I forgot I've got to round up my cattle first. All the small ranchers in this area join together to round up each of our herds and it today they're going to round up my cattle. Can you stay over until tomorrow?"

"No problem, Jack."

"You ride a horse, Carl?"

"Haven't for many years, but I used to help teach horseback riding at summer camp." (Actually, I cleaned out the stables, but why tell him that. I did, after all, know how to ride.)

Jack smiled. "Great, I'll have you outfitted in riding gear, boots and a horse and you can join the roundup."

Not knowing what I was letting myself in for I gushed, "Now that sounds like something I would really enjoy."

Properly outfitted, they led me to my horse. Now you have to understand something that I did not at that time, that is, there is a huge difference riding English style with the double reins, for which I was trained, and riding western style with the single rein, a style I didn't even know existed. English-style riders ride with two hands on the reins, each hand controlling different commands to the horse, whereas western riders ride with one hand, which controlled all rein commands, because they need the other hand free for various tasks associated with the roundup such lassoing stray cattle, or to waving them into the corral with their hats coupled with a lots of loud yeehaws.

I mounted the horse and to steady him, I pulled on the reins, the stop command, I thought. The horse backed up and the more I pulled on the reins, the more he backed up. My host grabbed the reins to halt the beast. "I thought you knew how to ride?"

"I do but this horse won't obey." Thereupon I received a crash course in western riding: "Whoa" stops the horse, pulling on the reins backs him up, laying the rein on the left side of his neck commands him to go right and on the right side, to go left.

Actually, the western style turned out to be a lot easier and the horse, more responsive than eastern-style riding. Now we were ready to round up the cattle in the brush. The object was through noise and the use of our horses, to steer the cattle into the corral. As I was about to take off for the brush, Jack pulled alongside me. He patted me on the shoulder. "If you get into trouble, drop the reins, the horse knows what to do."

It seemed to me like a strange comment. What kind of trouble could I possibly get into? I soon found out.

I spotted a young bull wandering on the hillside in the bushes. I rode up to him waving my hat and yelling "yeehaw." The bull was unimpressed. I kept at it until the bull became irritated. Suddenly, he lowered his head, pawed the ground a few times and charged. It was then that I remembered Jack's advice and dropped the reins. The horse wheeled about and took off down the road like a jackrabbit, the raging bull just behind. I hung on for dear life. This was no time to fall off. I worried: who had more stamina, my horse or the bull? I needn't have been concerned, because as we passed the entrance to the corral, the bull suddenly wheeled into the corral and joined the other steers.

Jack congratulated me on a job well done.

"Oh, it was nothing," I said, patting the neck of my mount with some affection. "It seemed, though, that young bull had it in for me."

Jack winked at me. "Never fear, you'll get your revenge!"

I wondered what he meant.

All steers accounted for, the next phase of the roundup began: branding the younger bulls. One of the cowboys would grab the steer by the horns and wrestle it down while another cowboy branded it. Jack invited to me take a hand at downing a steer. I didn't think so.

"There's real young 'un, maybe just a week old. Think you could handle 'er?"

I nodded and approached the calf. I grabbed it by the horns and it became a whirling dervish, biting me, kicking, and spitting, totally frustrating my attempts to down it. Indeed, I came out of the wrestling match more the worse for wear. The cowboys were slapping their thighs, laughing uproariously.

Jack put his arm around me. "Don't feel bad. That's how all the very young 'uns act--hysterically. We don't even bother with them until they get a little older."

"Thanks a lot!"

He shrugged. "Don't feel bad, that was just your initiation into the world of roundup."

Next, they castrated the young bulls that were not going to be used for stud service, roping them, bringing them down, and swiftly cutting open the sac, popping out the testicles, and applying some astringent.

That night Jack hosted a feast for the roundup crew, featuring, of course, prime beef, and plenty of it. Jack handed me a plate piled high with vittles. I didn't recognize one item. "What's that, Jack?"

197

"Rocky Mountain oysters."

I gave him a quizzical look.

He laughed. "Them's the balls of the bull that had the temerity to charge you."

So that was my revenge. They tasted like something between chopped liver and sweetbreads.

NOW WHAT?

Lani and Our Exit from Hawaii

It was 1965, the year of the infamous Northeast blackout, the enactment of the Voting Rights Act, the arrival of the first U.S. troops in Vietnam, and the premier of "The Sound of Music" in the movie theaters. Winston Churchill, Adlai Stevenson, and Nat King Cole died that year.

I don't know what got into us. We had two children, eight and six, now both in school, freeing up Diana for more outside activities. We led an idyllic life in Hawaii. I was busy with trials, tennis, and sailing; Diana occupied her time with Hawaiian quilting, flower arranging, Chinese cuisine preparation, and motherhood. Life was too good, so we decided to have another child to bring us back to reality.

Diana remembered all too vividly the painful deliveries she had endured with both Sam and Jane. In Honolulu, she found an obstetrician who was also a hypnotist.

"I can have my baby by hypnosis?" she asked.

"Absolutely. You'll feel the pangs of birth but you won't mind it a bit and in recovery, you'll feel wonderful."

"No spinal block?"

"Nope, none will be needed."

Diana smiled. "Sounds like a plan to me."

Every few weeks, Diana would see the doctor who, after the usual examination, spent time acclimating her to hypnosis until one chosen word, let's say "sleep," would instantly put her in the hypnotic state.

On the big day, I drove Diana to the hospital, and met her doctor. Before wheeling her into the delivery room, the doctor said the magic word and put her under his spell. But I was worried, because she was still wide-awake and fully involved.

"Why isn't she asleep," I whined.

The doctor laughed. "Oh, she's hypnotized, all right, but only insofar as she won't mind pain."

"Why not put her out completely?" I persisted.

He sighed. "This way, she can tell us precisely what she is feeling, which will be a great help to us in the course of the delivery. I've also given her a post-hypnotic suggestion that she will feel fine after the birth."

There were no complications and on February 16, 1965, a fully awake Diana gave birth to an eight-pound girl. I wasn't there for the actual birth because it wasn't permitted in those days to have the father in the delivery room--not that I'm sure I would want to be there.

I saw Diana in recovery and whereas the other new mothers were moaning, groaning, or sleeping, Diana was wide awake and chipper, a real chatty Cathy.

"Since the hypnosis went so well," I postulated, "perhaps in a few years we should have another."

The post-hypnotic suggestion didn't soften her that much. "Not on your life, buster, except if you can figure out a way for you to carry and deliver the next one."

"The hills are alive with the sound of music." These lyrics introduced the new movie, *Sound of Music, and also* heralded into the world our youngest, Laura Aolani, AKA Lani. After her birth, I celebrated with Sam and Jane, taking them to see that motion picture, which was premiering in Honolulu.

NOW WHAT?

Laura Aolani: The Laura was for a dear friend of the family and as I explained earlier, the Aolani, meaning "heavenly cloud" in Hawaiian was suggested by the tutus (Hawaiian grandmothers) with whom Diana quilted. And indeed she was. The Laura part was dropped by our daughter in grade school when another classmate named Laura made it one Laura too many. So our daughter opted to be called Lani, short for Aolani. The name has stuck ever since.

An interesting sidelight on the name Laura: Much later, when Lani was out on her own working at a high-end leather jacket manufacturer and seller in New York, she began dating one of the salesmen at the company.

"My father recognized your name," he told her. "He thinks he knows your parents from childhood days."

Lani asked me, "Do you know Stanley?"

"Of course," I said, "he's the son of Laura a dear friend of our family. Why do you ask?"

"Because I dated Stanley's son."

"Well, Lani, then it may interest you to know that you are dating the grandson of the Laura for whom you were named."

It didn't help the relationship. They broke it off a few weeks later.

* * *

Lani was a beautiful baby from the get-go and fawned over by her siblings and my parents who, of course, dropped everything to fly from New York to Hawaii to see their new granddaughter. We also appreciated her since she slept through the night, rarely cried, and generally, had a sunny disposition--a far cry from Sam and Jane--at least regarding the sleeping and crying parts.

By now, we had made our third move, and instead of being on the beach and evacuating at every tsunami

201

alert, we rented a house on Lanipo Drive in the hills overlooking Lanikai Bay and the Mokulua islands.

The House on Lanipo

So now we were the ones who threw the tsunami parties while the beach dwellers fled to us on the higher ground. We left the first home on the beach because we couldn't afford the rent. We found another house on the beach. We couldn't believe our luck until we found out why the rent was so low--the house was termite-infested and on the second floor, where our bedrooms were located, we had to feel our way very carefully in the halls so as not to put a foot through the floor. Also, the landlord was a cranky old bastard who checked his property every day and threatened to evict us if I didn't keep the grass short enough for his taste--and all he supplied was an old non-powered push mower. Yeah, right. I wasn't about to become his personal gardener. When we went back to New York on "home leave" we vacated and left the termites. (Can you imagine having so tough a duty in Hawaii that the government gave us home leave? Thank heavens for the bureaucracy.) On our return we rented the house in the hills of Lanikai on Lanipo Drive.

Diana and Lani on the deck of our home in the Lanikai hills. Note the reflection of Lanikai Bay and the one of the Mokulua islands. That other reflection is the author taking the snapshot

Author's mother and stepfather standing on the deck of the Lanipo house, while visiting their new granddaughter, The Mokuluas are in the background

Diana in muumuu and lei at front door of Lanipo House

The owners of the house were on the Mainland for two years and were anxious to have a renter that would not abuse the property that they planned to call home. We apparently filled the bill and they pegged the rent within our budget. The owners had a beautiful stepped garden and orchard on the hill behind the house that was cared for by a Japanese gardener paid by them. We, however, were free to partake of the growth—the bananas, papayas, mangos, and other exotic fruits.

Diana led an active life, doing Japanese flower arranging through Ikebana, playing tennis and beginning her third Hawaiian quilt, working with the tutus.

One of Diana's Japanese flower arrangement

About the Hawaiian quilts: These are long-term undertakings, not to be embarked upon lightly. The quilts are built in stages: preparing the underlying fabric and filling, designing, and cutting out a pattern to be pinned and then basted to the quilt, sewing it all together and then the hard part--the actual quilting, which in Hawaiian quilts requires tens of thousands of close-knit stitches following the pattern of the quilt in ripple-like fashion. So when I say Diana began her third quilt, I did not mean to imply that the first two were finished--far from it. It took some thirty years to complete them, one for each child. A blue silver sword (rare Hawaiian plant found only in the volcanic crater of Haleakala where Sam and I had hiked) pattern for Sam, a pink angel's trumpet pattern for Jane, and for Lani—what else? A heavenly cloud pattern in light blue. Many years later, Jane's quilt won first prize in the Naples Guild Quilt show.

Diana at work in Hawaii on Sam's silver sword quilt

Jane and husband Max standing by her quilt for which Diana won first prize in the quilt show in Naples, Florida

What I am trying to say is that Diana was having a glorious time in Hawaii with her activities and in her muumuus. And so was I. My boss Ray was scheduled to leave Hawaii for reassignment in Washington and I figured I was now experienced enough to run the Honolulu Office. It would be nice to have help, but I could, if necessary, run the operation myself. I even put down $100 with my application to take the Hawaii bar exam.

So it was with great surprise, after Ray left and several months had passed, to get a telephone call from my boss in Washington in response to my request for authority to open an investigation (see, I learned).

"Carl, what are you still doing in Hawaii?"

"Gordon, what do you mean what am I doing in Hawaii?"

"You were supposed to close the office and come to Washington."

"It's news to me. I was never informed. I thought I was going to stay and run the office."

"The head of the Antitrust Division decided to close it for economic reasons."

I recalled the head of the Antitrust Division coming out to Hawaii and looking over the office on the way to a boondoggle to Japan. We wined and dined the boss, but had a bad feeling about him. He certainly wasn't among the brightest brains to hold that office. I told of my plans for the office and he just listened and complimented me on my work in the office. I found out later that the S.O.B. had planned to close it all along. Economic reasons, huh? I wonder how much that boondoggle to Japan cost?

"Gordon, you close the Honolulu Office and I will quit. That's how pissed off I am about it."

Then he cast out the bait and I bit.

"How would it be if I made you assistant chief of the Great Lakes Field Office?"

"Where's that?"

"Cleveland."

"You are kidding, aren't you? That's supposed to be an inducement?"

"Yes. I expect in a very short time you may be chief, with a two grade boost in pay."

"Do you know something I don't?"

"Yes."

"And you're not going to tell me?"

"That's right."

I sighed. "I really don't want to leave Hawaii and Diana will have a fit."

"I know. I visited you guys two years ago and I can totally understand your feelings, but the matter is out of my hands. That's why I offered the inducement."

"Can I take the Matson Lines back with my car?"

"Yes."

"You make it difficult to refuse."

"That was my intention."

Another government snafu. But I did close the office and in September 1965, we began our return to the Mainland on the Luraline, a ship of the Matson Line, the company that I had recently freed from Big Five control.

Diana modeling a muumuu on the Luraline after leaving Hawaii

We docked in San Francisco, off-loaded my automobile, a Rambler station wagon and took the northern route to Cleveland. Sam and Jane were in the rear seats and Lani was in a playpen-like enclosure in the back of the station wagon. We had purchased food supplies to picnic along this route with the glorious scenery. We stored them also in the back of the station wagon. It was a fairly warm day and back then my cars did not have air conditioning.

While driving on the highway we seemed to attract an undue amount of attention from the occupants of other cars--they waved, pointed, and laughed.

"Something's going on," I said. "Did we lose a fender or something? Everyone seems to be focused on us."

Diana turned around to check the children and emitted a short scream.

"Oh my God, look at Lani."

I learned never to turn around when driving seventy on the highway so I pulled off the road and stopped the car. Turning around, I saw Lani with a big smile covered head to foot in what looked like white paint.

I frowned. "What the hell is that stuff?"

Diana opened the back of the station wagon and put some of this white mass on her finger. She smelled it, and then tasted it.

"It's the powdered milk!"

Somehow, she had gotten into the grocery supplies and emptied the entire contents of a box of powdered milk over her sweaty self, making an unbelievable gloppy mess. She looked like a mime ready to perform on stage.

We figured she couldn't do much more damage, so we just kept driving for a few more hours until we stopped at a motel for the night and a badly needed bath, first for Lani and then for all of us, by the time we got finished cleaning up after her.

* * *

NOW WHAT?

We reached Missoula, Montana on a rainy afternoon following a large tractor-trailer on a winding slick road. Suddenly the truck fishtailed and then jackknifed, running off the road and down into a gully, about fifteen feet below.

I pulled over to the side of the road and scrambled down the embankment to the trailer-tractor that was lying on its side. The driver was semi-conscious having severely cracked his head on the dashboard.

He opened his eyes as I climbed up onto the driver's door. "Get out of here; I have a load of nitroglycerin. I smell smoke and it could explode at any time. I told the bastards that I couldn't manage such a light load on these roads, but they didn't believe me."

"Where's your fire extinguisher?"

"Hooked up behind my right shoulder."

I reached in the window and found it, traced the source of the smoke, and extinguished the small blaze with a blast of foam.

I then managed to get the driver's door open. By this time several other motorists had joined me and helped pull him out. We laid him out on the grass in the rain.

"You'd better get back up the embankment," I said, "This truck's load is nitroglycerine."

I scrambled up the embankment to get a blanket and an umbrella from my car.

A state trooper arrived and asked me what the situation was.

"There's a truck with nitroglycerin in it and I'm going back down to the driver with a blanket and umbrella."

The state trooper nodded. "Okay, I'll call for an ambulance. I'd better stay up here to direct traffic."

I looked at him but said nothing, then scrambled down into the gully to the injured driver. The truck didn't blow up, the cop stayed safely up top until the ambulance came.

The driver wanted my name. Perhaps his company would reward me, he suggested.

"No thanks. I'm sure if I were in the same situation a trucker would come to my rescue."

With no more untoward incidents we arrived in Cleveland a week later, ready to take on my new position as Assistant Chief of the Great lakes Office, whose territory included Ohio, Kentucky, West Virginia and parts of Michigan.

Cleveland, Here I Come

Whenever my then beloved Yankees played baseball there (the New York sports writers called Cleveland "the wild west" notwithstanding it being in the Eastern time zone) the Cleveland Indians gave the mighty Bronx Bombers fits. That's the only thing I knew about Cleveland.

I wasn't impressed on arrival when I read the newspapers. One reported that the mayor's wife had declined a White House dinner invitation because it was her bowling night. Gimme a break! Another reported that the mayor's hair went up in flames when he cut the ceremonial metal ribbon with a blow torch to celebrate the cleanup of the city's Cuyahoga River, a navigable waterway so polluted that it too had caught on fire. A metal ribbon? I knew Cleveland was a big steel town, but wouldn't a regular ribbon and a good old scissors do?

Finally, reading the headline in the Cleveland Plain Dealer sports page, I learned that Indians' third baseman Max Alvis was out with "a rectal problem." Yech, that was certainly much more information and detail than I ever wanted to know from a sports column. Couldn't the Indians' publicity department make up something like a strained gluttonous maximus, instead of embarrassing the poor man suffering from hemorrhoids?

I did find out something I'd bet you didn't know: that a famous federal crime fighter of the Untouchables ran for mayor of Cleveland in 1947.

CARL L. STEINHOUSE

Wikipedia, the free encyclopedia. Image in the public domain

First impressions can be way off. Cleveland turned out great for me professionally; for Diana, it provided a finding of purpose; and for the children, it resulted in a quality public school education.

It didn't start out that way though. On our way into Cleveland, I was so anxious to get started on the job I insisted that we not spend days looking for a place to live. Not letting any grass to grow under *my* feet, while driving into Cleveland on the last leg of our trip, we passed through the southeastern suburbs of the city and, seeing for-rent signs, signed a lease on the first acceptable place we found, a one-story walk-up with three bedrooms. It turned out to be a dreary place, situated in a town with an unimpressive school system.

Besides Max Alvis' rectal woes, Cleveland had other problems. The Chamber of Commerce claimed there are 160 days of sunshine per year in Cleveland. Obviously, its members don't live there. I figure 100 days is generous. That's versus well over three hundred days we enjoyed in Hawaii, our previous home. The "lake effect" keeps Cleveland either overcast or covered with snow in the winter. Depressed at being tied down in the apartment with young Lani during the winters in Cleveland, especially after the sun and beach-filled life they'd had in Hawaii, Diana determined to change things.

First of all, we purchased a house in an upscale community with a great public school system (the purchase of the house is a story unto itself). Second, she found a job at a hospital close to home in her field of medical research as a lab technician. Better yet, the hospital ran a nursery school for the children of the employees. The job opportunity solved two problems: getting Diana out of the house and Lani into nearby childcare. A few years later, after agonizing over whether she had the brainpower to return to college to complete her education for a bachelor's degree, at my urging, she actually risked doing it. She needn't have worried about her brainpower or lack thereof. This nice Jewish girl sailed through the Catholic College run by the Order of the Ursuline nuns, and she did it with a straight "A" average. But she never convinced herself she could do it: every assignment, every class, and every exam provoked a panicky bout of studying and cramming, certain this time, she would fail.

Diana, Ursuline class of 1975

Graduating with honors and awarded a degree in psychology, Diana rolled the dice again, this time going for a post-graduate Masters degree in psychology at Case Western University and then advanced training at the

213

Gestalt Institute of Cleveland. Eventually, she started her own practice as a counseling psychologist and a hypnotist--and no, I did not let her practice on me--no post-hypnotic suggestions for me, thank you very much, to pick up after myself or put down the toilet seat!

I assumed my duties as assistant chief of the ten-man Great Lakes Field Office. Just as my boss Gordon in Washington predicted, in a little over a year, the chief of the office was reassigned to head the field office in New York and I was appointed chief of the office in Cleveland. Fickle, I abandoned my lifelong love affair with the NY Yankees and became an ardent Cleveland Indians fan. Go Tribe! Things were indeed looking up for the Steinhouses.

Author, far right, Norman Seidler then chief of the Great Lakes Field Office, far left. Seidler left to become chief of the New York Field Office.

The Yankee Mystique

Rooting for the Cleveland Indians simply did not instill the excitement that I experienced as a Yankee fan. As a Yankee fan, I considered the season a failure if the Yankees did not win the World Series and they seemed to win it about every other year, sometimes stringing together several years of world championships in a row. While rooting for the Indians, a happy season was one where the Indians won more games than they lost.

One of the greatest examples of Indian stumbles and Yankee luck occurred while I was still a Yankee fan. The Indians had Roger Maris in its outfield in 1957 and traded him away. Roger ended up with the New York Yankees in 1960 and went on to a glorious career for them, even if Mickey Mantle overshadowed him. But that was the New York Yankees--perennially overstocked with all-star baseball players.

Anyway, the year was 1961 and Mantle and Maris were battling to see who would break Babe Ruth's home run record of 60 home runs in a season. Both were reaching the 50-homer mark in August. In the middle of August a leg infection sidelined Mantle, so it was up to Roger Maris. On September 26, 1961, Maris was at 59 home runs and I had Yankee Stadium tickets to the Yankee-Baltimore Orioles game that day. Each time Maris stepped to the plate it seemed the entire crowd became uncharacteristically silent. Batting third in the lineup, he singled in the first inning. A hit normally would bring a cheer from the crowd; the masses and yours truly only groaned. Mantle, back in the lineup, walked, but Yogi Berra flied out and no runs were scored. In the top of the second inning, hits by Brooks Robinson and others produced a two-run lead for the Orioles.

Mel Allen in the broadcast booth: *It's the bottom of the third inning and there are two outs. The Yankee fans seem to be holding their collective breath as Maris steps to the plate. Jack Fisher of Baltimore goes into his windup; here's the pitch. Maris swings . . . the ball goes deep, very deep; Earl Robinson backs to the warning track but that ball is going, going, GONE! How about that, sports fans! Roger Maris has just hit his sixtieth home run tying the Babe's record! There was no doubt about that one; it landed well back in the third deck of Yankee Stadium and the bounced back onto the field. Robinson, the Oriole right fielder, picks up the ball and tosses back to the infield where the Yankee first base coach intercepts it and tosses into the Yankee dugout, the ball arriving simultaneously with Maris.*

At first there was a stunned silence; then all hell broke loose. Maris had tied Babe Ruth's record set in 1927! I almost peed in my pants. Fans screamed for Maris and he finally emerged from the dugout holding the ball and tipping his cap.

On October 1, the last day of the season, Roger hit number 61, breaking Ruth's 34-year record. Some sportswriters wanted to place an asterisk by Maris's record because he played in a 162-game season while Ruth had only a 154-game season. Screw them; they must be Boston sportswriters.

Compare, if you will, that excitement with my attendance at the Cleveland Indians games where you could feel very lonely in the vast Municipal Stadium with only 5,000 fans in attendance. Until the Indians moved to Jacobs Field and became an exciting team (at least for a while), the most exciting thing that happened was Max Alvis's rectal problem reported earlier by the Cleveland Plain Dealer.

NOW WHAT?

Scorecard maintained by Author on September 26, 1961 at the game where Maris hit his 60th in the third inning (circled).

217

CARL L. STEINHOUSE

The North Strawberry Lane Homeowners Association Does Not Want You

Two years was enough in an apartment in Warrensville Heights, so we decided it was time to own our own home--a first for us. We saw a house we liked for sale in Moreland Hills, an upscale suburb east of Cleveland. It sat on a street with a fetching name, North Strawberry Lane. Who could resist an address like that? So I contacted our realtor, who got in touch with the listing real estate agent and made an offer.

Our realtor, a real sweet lady, came back to us. "I am really embarrassed. The listing agent won't consider our offer because you're Jewish and according to the agent, the owner and the North Strawberry Lane Homeowners Association won't allow it."

I made a beeline for that house on North Strawberry Lane and rang the bell. The owner answered.

"I'm a buyer for your house," I began, "and I understand you won't sell to me because I'm Jewish."

The owner frowned. "What? I put no such restriction on the sale of this house. Of course I'll sell to you if your offer is high enough."

"That's all I want to know. By the way, I withdrew my offer and you can blame your realtor."

"What was your offer?"

I told him.

"That's very close to what I'd accept. If you still want the house we can make a deal."

"No thanks," I said, "I don't want to live in a community that doesn't want me."

Having found out that the owner placed no such restriction on the sale of the house, I immediately contracted the Ohio Civil Rights Commission and lodged a complaint against the realtor.

"Can you do anything?"

"We certainly can," the Commission employee assured. "We'll get right on it. You're the first non-black complainant we've had. The Commission should indeed be very interested."

The Commission investigated and after a hearing imposed a large fine on the realtor, required her to write me a letter of apology, and enjoined such conduct in the future.

I don't think she was sincere about the apology: I attended a Christmas party in Shaker Heights, thrown by one of our friends. The offending realtor's son happened to be a guest at the party and was complaining loudly about the stupidity of the Ohio Civil Rights Commission. I joined the crowd listening to him.

"Who complained?" I asked innocently.

"Some son-of-a-bitch Jew named Steinhouse who wanted a house in my mother's neighborhood."

Many of the listeners who knew us looked at each other, and then at me.

I smiled at the realtor's son. I put out my hand. "Hi, I don't think we've been introduced. I'm that son-of-a-bitch Jew named Steinhouse."

The crowd around him started to laugh. He turned beet red and didn't know where to hide. He left the party shortly thereafter.

Not that I would stand for discrimination in my own community. Many years later, living in Pepper Pike, another upscale community in the eastern suburbs of Cleveland, there was another prominent government attorney living in the same community, Carole Emmerling, the then head of the Federal Trade Commission Office in Cleveland. One day I received a flyer stuffed in my mailbox announcing a meeting of a committee of residents of Pepper Pike to block the sale of a home to a black family in our community. I called

Carole. She'd gotten the flyer also and expressed her outrage.

"Let's you and I go to the meeting," I suggested. "I'll pick you up this evening and tell you my plan on the way to the meeting."

We arrived at this plush home with about thirty other residents from Pepper Pike. A spirited discussion ensued as to the best means to block the purchase by blacks. The most sure-fire method, most agreed, was to have the committee of Pepper Pike homeowners buy the targeted house and then resell it to a person of their choosing. If enough people chipped in, the committee felt, the purchase and sale could be accomplished at minimum expense.

The chairman of the meeting went around the room soliciting each person's views. When the chair came to me, I flashed my Department of Justice credentials, pulled out a pad, and announced, "I want the names of everyone at this meeting here tonight to be turned over to the US Attorney. You are in violation of the federal civil rights laws."

Carole immediately flashed her credentials. "The Federal Trade Commission also will be very interested in the restraints of trade you are conspiring to commit tonight."

I'm not sure there was any federal violation of the law or restraint of trade but by the mere threat, I never saw a meeting empty out faster and tires squeal louder making quit exits from the area.

The committee was never heard from again and the black family bought the house. They were great neighbors and housing prices in the community did not tumble one whit as a result.

As far as the North Strawberry Lane Association is concerned? My son now lives in the area without experiencing any discrimination whatsoever.

But Nobody Buys Open Houses!

I think I got ahead of myself talking about Pepper Pike, so let's back up a little bit. While we were looking for a house, we found a place we liked in the community of Lyndhurst. It was a new development, and a brand-new home in move-in shape--a two-story colonial with a center hallway on a small lot (very little mowing)--just what we were looking for. We saw it on a Thursday afternoon and by Friday, we decided we'd buy it. I called the developer and tried to arrange a meeting that day. He was apologetic; explaining he was taking his kid to summer camp. "Could we do it Monday? I assured him it was no problem, and it wasn't--at least for me.

For the hell of it, we visited several "open houses" on that weekend and discovered this twenty-year old ranch house in Pepper Pike, nothing like the house of our dreams--one-story on almost two acres of land. We fell in love with it and made an offer. $42,500 and the house was ours. A great bargain, I thought.

Monday morning the developer with the Lyndhurst house called me.

"I'm sorry," I said sheepishly, "but we saw this open house we loved on the weekend and made an offer that was accepted."

A pause at the other end of the line: "You're pulling my leg aren't you? Nobody ever buys at those open houses!"

"Well, we did." It took me quite a while to convince him I was serious.

"Son-of-a-bitch," he growled, "do you know how much that damn kid and his lousy camp cost me?" He slammed down the phone.

A footnote: Remember that great bargain of a house I got? Well, while on a lunch hour break in downtown Cleveland, I happened to stroll through the Euclid Arcade and found this interesting aerial photograph, about fifty feet long, showing the path of the proposed Clark Freeway as it wended its way out of downtown through the Shaker Lakes and onto to the Shaker Transit right-of-way. It was fascinating because I could recognize various landmarks in the sharp photography--including my house. Fascinating, that is, until I followed the Freeway to its inevitable end, a large cloverleaf loop that deposited traffic onto the local Pepper Pike street. Where? Right onto my house, right smack in the middle of that cloverleaf. No wonder the former owner gave me a bargain.

Another footnote: After the transfer of ownership of the house closed I saw in the paper that the previous owner was throwing a huge bash in his new home in Gates Mills for a reported $43,000. He blew on that one party, the entire hard-earned wad I paid for the house plus more! He really knew how to hurt a guy. But I had the last laugh--the Clark Freeway was never built, thanks to the influential politicians of Shaker Heights who didn't give a damn about my house in Pepper Pike but wanted to preserve the pristine qualities of their Shaker Lakes.

NOW WHAT?

Big Brother

We were fortunate to pick Pepper Pike to buy our home. It had the Orange School system, which was a great public school learning facility, equal to the fancy private schools in the area. My job as a prosecutor and later as a private practice trial attorney did not give me much leisure time and I spent a great deal of my week on the road. As a result, I wasn't involved as a member of the school board or the PTA board. (Many years later, my son Sam became president of the Orange School Board!) Oh, I went to meetings when I could and tried to attend most of my children's parent-teacher conferences, but that was about it.

So how did I get so involved in school board politics so suddenly one spring? It began with a strike of the blue-collar workers at the school, the janitors, bus drivers, cafeteria workers, and the like. Now, as I said before, the communities that the Orange Schools serve are very affluent and, as a rule, its blue-collar workers don't live in these communities--they couldn't afford to, basically trying to get by on the low wages doled out by the school. In my opinion, they were underpaid and due a well-deserved increase.

It was not an equal battle. The school board, many of them scions of industry and finance, hired a large, prestigious Cleveland law firm to represent them. The blue-collar workers, on the other hand, were unorganized and without legal representation.

I attended a community meeting called by the school board to map a strategy to defeat the strike. I was pretty vocal at the meeting in support of the workers and how the school board had taken advantage these relatively unsophisticated people. That brought out the worse in some of the esteemed members of the community, telling me to shut up and sit down, and from some of the not-so-esteemed members, such as a known racketeer who got up and told the board to "just say the word and I'll have this commie taken care of." The school board, to its credit, turned down his generous offer. Later, I'm sure they were sorry they did.

That was it for me. I left and met with the workers, some of whom had attended the meeting. "One of your problems," I explained to them, "is that you're not organized and you have no legal representation. You must have a spokesman that the board will have to deal with."

I was told they had no money to hire a lawyer.

"That's no problem. I'll represent you."

"You'll be disliked in the community," one worker warned.

"That's okay; they are already dumping on me. I may as well give them a good reason to do so."

I arranged a meeting of all the workers at a motel in the area. We agreed on a strategy.

I set up a meeting with the school board and the officers the workers elected to represent them before the school board. I sat in at the meeting and was challenged by the president of the school board.

"You are not authorized to be here. You're not a member of the school board."

"That's true" I agreed, "but I am not here on behalf of the school board, I am attorney for the workers group."

"What group?"

"The group they just formed to further their demands and deal with your intransigence."

"They don't need a lawyer; we have always looked out for their interests."

"Is that so? Then why are you always represented at these meetings by that fancy lawyer from such a prestigious law firm," pointing to their attorney. "As far as looking out for the workers' interests, it sounds like Big Brother right out of Orwell's *1984*. Frankly, we don't believe it. Just look at the sub-normal wages the workers in this school system have been receiving, compared to other area schools."

The school board conferred off to one side in whispers with their attorney.

I pulled the workers out of the room to confer.

"Where are you going?" the school board president asked.

"To confer with my clients."

"Do it in here so we can all have the benefit of your advice. They've never conferred behind our backs before."

"You've got to be kidding. Here you confer in private before our very faces and then want to deny us the right to do likewise, calling it going 'behind your backs.' No wonder they're so low paid, having to put up with this patronizing abuse all these years."

The workers won their raise and joined the school workers union, never needing my assistance again.

I heard from quite a few members of the community who said they supported my position. Too bad they didn't have the courage to speak up at the community meeting.

CARL L. STEINHOUSE

The Encounter Fad

*"Do not join encounter groups. If you enjoy being made
to feel inadequate, call your mother."* Liz Smith

The seventies were the heydays of encounter
groups, where strangers and acquaintances got together
under the leadership of one purporting to be a
psychologist or counselor, to whom the participants bared
their souls, or at least acted like they were.

Some of the participants were encounter junkies,
dealing with the same issues week after week. They were
like voyeurs, reveling in others' struggles in life and
themselves freely dispensing their inexpert, if seemingly
earnest, advice.

Some participants approached their own issues in
novel physical ways. One fellow got hung up--literally--
he hung from the doorframe, or rafter, or whatever else
was convenient, when his turn to talk and emote came.
Another faced down his problems, well, face down. He'd
belly flop onto the carpet (that is, if he was lucky and the
floor was not tiled instead) and talked to the floor.

Some of the group leaders were themselves not
too swift. One husband-wife team, leading couples'
encounter groups, dispensed advice on successful
marriage relationships and trust. They seemed to know
what they were doing until they broke up after she caught
him having sex with a former participant in one of their
groups.

That's not to say there weren't good group leaders,
there were. One, a real psychologist named Sylvia, was
amazing at gently bringing to the surface the underlying
and unsaid, but real, issues and then dealing with them--
and yet never seeming to give advice. On a personal
level, she helped Diana and me deal with the fear of
change--me, to risk change by moving from the

226

NOW WHAT?

government into private practice and Diana, to risk going back to college to obtain a degree.

I recall in one of Sylvia's sessions, a prominent national weekly news magazine had sent a reporter to cover our session in order to do a story on the encounter movement.

"I'm just here to listen, not participate," the reporter assured.

Sylvia smiled. "Do you have any issues you'd like to deal with?"

"Nah, I'm well adjusted, no problemos, dear."

It took Sylvia only half an hour into the session to open him like peeling the rind off an orange. That happened when she caught him wringing his hands. "Want to tell me about it?"

He separated his hands.

But she persisted. "Why is one hand wringing the other?"

He shrugged. "Means nothing, forget about it."

Sylvia smiled as if she understood. Then, as quick as a cobra, she struck. "Why don't you have one hand talk to the other?"

From then on, it was just a matter of time before we found out he was divorced and had weekly weekend visitation rights with his two children. This resulted in terrible guilt feelings because he did not want, in his own words, "to be tied down with his children every damn weekend."

Of course, it wasn't totally resolved during his few minutes on the hot seat, but now, at least, he could own up to the fact he had a problem--a first step toward resolving it.

Later, a laudatory story appeared in the magazine about that session.

Encounter grouping had a certain gestalt flavor to it. For example, one leader suggested that an interesting

227

home exercise would be an "encounter dinner". The object was to be one with the food, forsaking all accoutrements like silverware, plates, napkins, and the like--touch, feel the texture of the food; smell and taste it, thereby engaging not one, but all your sensory preceptors.

One evening Diana and I announced, "Kids, we're going to have an encounter dinner tonight."

They rolled their eyes. They'd been dragged to family encounter groups and were singularly unimpressed until we explained what we were going to do.

For dinner, we gathered around the brown Formica kitchen counter situated over a tile floor--a perfect venue for such a dinner, as you will see.

Again, in case you missed it, no eating with any implements, no plates, nothing except food; a simple dinner of steak, corn on the cob, and salad, all dumped together on the Formica table.

We each grabbed handfuls of salad off the table, letting the wide leaf of the romaine lettuce, the smooth, red, and plump surface of the grape tomatoes, and the ridged roughness of the celery stalk course though the palms of our hands and the tips of our fingers--a new and different sensory experience of the food beyond merely taste. Grab an ear of corn sitting amid the salad. Feel the contours of the individual kernels, but be careful, the ear's hot. What some butter? Smear it on with your fingers. How does that feel? Finally, clutch the steak with both hands and rip off a chunk. Feel the resistance? Experience the texture of the meat?

What about the used corncob? Just toss it over your shoulder onto the tile floor. That made the kids happy.

Now the place was a mess. Food scattered all over and our kids (and us) covered with what we ate.

A knock on the front door. Whoops, we forgot. We had a date with a very conservative couple down the street. You know the type. He's the crew cut, straight arrow man, his kids toe the line, all are expected to be eagle scouts and varsity athletes, and the wife a stay-at-home mother because no wife of his would ever work, etc.

Anyway, I opened the door, he took one look at the chaos, muttered something about coming at a bad time, and left. His wife, dutifully trailing behind him, never made it into the house. He turned around and steered her into the car. I could catch only a few words of what he whispered to her and it sounded awfully like "socialist weirdoes."

He never got over the trauma of what he called the "Steinhouse food fight." We had little further social relationship with them as a couple. I tolerated his uptight views of life and family because Diana was friendly with his sweet if somewhat submissive wife, so I didn't lose much sleep over the loss. Besides, it took most of that evening to clean up. After all, the encounter dinner didn't release all Diana's inhibitions, especially being a neatnik. Looking at the children's rooms, it was readily apparent they'd not inherited that gene from their mother!

* * *

We actually went so far as to participate in a mountain climbing encounter group in the Colorado Rockies. The encounter may have improved our mental health but did diddlysquat for us physically. This was no simple mountain climb. The peak we aimed for was over 13,000 feet and we camped at over 10,000 feet. Climbing to the peak and back down again was no mean feat. By the time we got down, my right knee that I had injured skiing twenty years before but which hadn't bothered me since, blew up like a balloon and I could hardly walk.

Also, this is where I learned about an illness I never heard of before; it's called altitude or mountain sickness. One afternoon at our 10,000-foot camp, Diana began to have a severe headache and feel nauseous, weak, dizzy and disoriented. We were far from civilization and she became progressively worse. An osteopath doctor on our trip had the same problem with his wife, who also experienced altitude sickness.

The doctor approached Diana. "I know what is the matter with you. It's altitude sickness. I can cure you if you're willing."

"What about your wife?" Diana asked. "Did you cure her?"

He shook his head. "She won't let me touch her. She's a nurse and doesn't believe in osteopathy, only conventional medicine. But don't you worry; I know what I'm doing."

Diana shrugged. "Well, I'll try anything to get rid of this terrible feeling. Go ahead and treat me."

"The treatment is simple and quick. Just stand up."

Diana did.

The doctor stepped behind her and grabbed her under the arms and around her midsection. He suddenly and violently (at least it appeared that way to me) jerked her up in the air; her feet lifted about three feet off the ground.

I winced as I seemed to hear every bone in her body crack or at least protest. Diana let out a scream. He let her down and she collapsed in a bundle.

Concerned, I leaned over her, trying to figure out if I could sue this guy. Before I got very far on this train of thought, she slowly got to a sitting position and then stood up.

"How are you feeling?" I asked.

"All my symptoms are gone. I'm a little shaky but I guess I feel fine."

So, instead of suing him, I shook the doctor's hand.

* * *

230

NOW WHAT?

The encounter craze lasted until we discovered the Maharishi.

CARL L. STEINHOUSE

Maharishi Who?

Exit encounter group; enter transcendental meditation ("TM"). Transcendental what? I don't recall who put us on to it, but we were subject to a hard sell by the TM disciples. These people, the protégés of Maharishi Mahesh Yogi, the guru of this branch of meditation, could hold their own with insurance salesmen.

The Maharishi sat in India, I imagined, on a mountaintop, looking and acting like Gandhi, austere and undernourished, dispensing pearls of wisdom to the faithful who had the perseverance to climb the mountain. Reality, of course, was much different. Maharishi had built a billion dollar business in TM and traveled the world like a jet setter, promoting his brand of meditation. I doubt that he ever graced any mountaintop.

This is not necessarily meant as criticism. If his method works and brings benefits to its practitioners, then more power to him.

The claimed benefits were expansive. In their words it would help us make full use of our mind, body and consciousness--so that we can live a problem-free life in enlightenment. To quote their website, "The Transcendental Meditation® program of Maharishi Mahesh Yogi is the single most effective meditation technique available to gain deep relaxation, eliminate stress, promote good health, increase creativity and intelligence, and attain inner happiness and fulfillment."

But we did this before the advent of websites; back then, Maharishi's advance men claimed meditation would reduce stress and anxiety, reduce blood pressure, and even result in promotions or a new, higher paying job for its practitioners.

Being in a high stress profession, particularly as a trial attorney, I figured what the hell, I'd give it a try and signed up for the family plan, which included Diana, Sam (14), Jane (12), and little Lani (6).

The course of study ran several sessions, teaching relaxation though meditative techniques, such as sitting up straight in your chair, closing your eyes, and becoming aware of your breathing as you recite your mantra. The mantra, they say, is the key to achieving "restful alertness". At the beginning of our training, a Maharishi disciple, touted as a specially trained expert in mantras, talked with each of us privately to "custom fit" a mantra for each individual. The mantra is usually a nonsensical word or sound, for example, "oom." We were told to keep our personal mantra secret. Revealed, it would lose its special power, they warned in all solemnity. Did I believe this? Hell no! Have I ever revealed my mantra to anyone? Hell no! Though I may leave the answer to that secret in a note attached to my will, if anyone is interested.

Let me say this. I did achieve relaxation through TM and some good ideas bubbled up during meditation, both when I worked as a lawyer and now, as a writer. I suspect, however, that any repetitive word would have served just as well as a mantra. Occasionally, I reach such a relaxed state that I seemed to float or have had an out-of-the-body experience. I say "seemed" because I have my doubts. My endorsement of TM is not whole-hearted because it never lowered my blood pressure or reduced stress *during trials*. But one of their representations did pan out--after taking the Maharishi's course, I did leave the government and obtained a higher paying job in private practice. I like to think it was because of my skill and reputation as a prosecutor. But who knows?

CARL L. STEINHOUSE

I'll Make You an Offer You Can't Refuse

After her junior year in high school, Lani was required to intern for a few weeks over the summer at a business. My friend Fred of Fred The Furrier fame offered Lani a job in his fur business in Manhattan and a place to stay at his home in Kings Point on Long Island. But Lani had the idea of staying in Cleveland, working perhaps at Baskin Robbins to earn money to buy clothes, and hanging out for the summer with her pals. I guess we live vicariously through our kids, so if Lani wasn't excited, her mother sure was at this opportunity to work in New York City. But you know teenagers; if Mom wanted it, it was the kiss of death. So Diana hit on a bright idea, attacking Lani's weakness--love of shopping.

"I'll make you an offer you can't refuse," Diana told Lani.

Lani looked skeptical.

"I'll give you my Bloomingdale's credit card to use while you are in New York."

"Your Bloomie card? Really?"

Diana nodded.

That did it. Off to New York Lani went and never looked back. After college, Lani made a beeline for the New York scene and began her fabulous career as a stylist and a wardrobe specialist and embarked upon her family life in the Big Apple.

Now she has her own Bloomingdale card--a Bloomie gal forevermore.

How Do You Test This Hose, Anyway?

One of the first criminal cases I supervised as chief of the Great Lakes Field Office took place in Detroit and involved price fixing of hydraulic hose used in construction equipment, trucks, tools, and the like. An issue arose at the trial on the substitutability of regular hose for the hydraulic variety, the government alleging the stringent testing requirements made hydraulic hose a separate market.

We flew in an expert to testify. The first night in town and on an expense account, he headed for this fancy and expensive steakhouse downtown. It also happened to be the regular hangout of a group of the defense counsel. And why not? They too were on seemingly unlimited expense accounts. As a government attorney, I had to make do on $25 a day for food and expenses. That effectively eliminated the $30 and $40 meals--and the steakhouse as a source of meal choice. Rather, we contented ourselves with the local cafeteria near the hotel. We could eat, if not as well, certainly as much, for a fraction of the cost.

One of the defense counsel, a former government antitrust chief and prosecutor gone over to the other side, had a reputation for being a damn good courtroom lawyer, and also a down and dirty street fighter. Let's call him "Mr. Down and Dirty." Anyway, Mr. Down and Dirty spotted our well-known industry expert as he entered the restaurant and waved him over to his table for a drink with his defense counsel cronies.

The next day, our expert showed up in court, ready to testify. Mr. Down and Dirty came in and, with great flourish, placed a large and conspicuous tape recorder on counsel table. Our expert turned ashen.

That disquieted me. "What's the matter? You look like you're best friend just died."

"It's worse than that," he croaked. "I can't testify."

"What the hell did you mean, you can't testify? You think we're paying you to vacation here?"

"No, but he'll make a fool of me on the stand," pointing to Mr. Down and Dirty. "Look, he's got a tape recorder."

I was confused. "So?"

Then the story came out.

"Mr. Down and Dirty invited me over for a drink and I'm afraid that led to a few more and I had one too many."

Now I was concerned. "What happened?"

Our expert looked sheepish. It was not a good sign.

"We began discussing testing hydraulic hose. Joking, I said, 'Just like regular hose, I piss in it. If it comes out the other end, it passes.'"

"Is that what you actually do?"

He looked at me like I was a simpleton. "Of course not. It requires highly sophisticated testing. We were just joking around."

"Then what's the problem?"

"That tape recorder on the table in front of Mr. Down and Dirty is the problem; he must have recorded my remarks and he'll use them to embarrass me when he cross-examines. That's why I can't go on the witness stand."

"You can and you will. He's just trying to psych you out. He can't have known you'd show up at that restaurant, much less have a tape recorder all primed to take down your every word. He's good, very good, but believe me, he's no psychic. That tape recorder's there just to screw with your mind."

NOW WHAT?

Our expert did testify and at one point in the cross exam, Mr. Down and Dirty retreated back to counsel table and leaned dramatically on the tape recorder.

The expert shot me a furtive glance. I shook my head almost imperceptivity.

"Do you recall speaking with me at the restaurant last evening?"

"Yes."

"And do you recall discussing hydraulic hose?"

"Vaguely."

"Tell the court what you said about testing such hose." Mr. Down and Dirty bent over and fiddled with the tape machine.

What a show!

"Um, I'm not sure."

Mr. Down and Dirty slid the machine to the end of the table. "What do you mean you're 'not sure'?"

Don't be intimidated, I willed.

The witness paused and gathered his thoughts. Good, I thought, he's following instructions of never answering any questions quickly.

"Well, I certainly know about testing hydraulic hose, it's a very sophisticated procedure compared to other types of hose, but I can't recall what I said last night because you bought me too many drinks."

Mr. Down and Dirty shook his head and sat down.

A lot of strange things happened at that trial, and not all of the in the courtroom. Prior to the trial, one of the senior attorneys and I flew up to Detroit to attend a pretrial hearing. My senior attorney checked into his hotel room and the only items of clothing he brought was a tie for the next morning's hearing and a pair of socks. He hung the tie in the closet, put the socks in a drawer, and we went out for dinner (in the cafeteria, of course). Upon returning to the hotel, we found it filled with firemen and police. It seems the closet in the senior attorney's room blew up--literally. Whether it was a bomb or a gas leak, we never found out. The only casualty was the tie, which got blown to smithereens. The police questioned my senior attorney briefly.

I half expected the cops to ask that question, "Do you know anyone with a motive to do in your tie?" but they didn't.

Again, during the pretrial phase of that case, we had an important pleading that had to be filed by the close of court that day. The attorney designated to hand deliver it up to that city came down ill, and I called in a young intern, still in law school, that we'd hired for the summer.

I handed the intern the pleading. "Fly up and file this with the clerk of courts and be sure to get a stamped receipted copy. Here's the ticket."

He took it and looked it over. "But it's not in my name."

"It doesn't matter; no one will ever ask you. Just hand it to the gate attendant. We simply don't have time to issue a new ticket." This was at a time well before the airport security procedures we know today.

He nodded and took off for the airport.

Six thirty that evening I was having a quiet dinner at home when the phone rang. I picked it up.

"This is the FBI in Detroit calling. We just picked up someone impersonating a Department of Justice lawyer. We're questioning him right now and he insists he works for you."

I knew the answer before I even asked the question. "What's his name?"

The agent told me. It is my summer intern.

"Let me speak to him," I requested.

The agent put him on the line.

"What the hell happened?"

"When I went up to the ticket counter on the return leg, I explained I wasn't the ticket holder and whether that was okay. The airline employee disappeared for a few minutes and the next thing I knew I was taken into custody by an FBI agent."

"What didn't you just keep your mouth shut like I told you?"

He grunted an inaudible reply.

"That's great. Congratulations, that's a first; a federal officer arrested for impersonating a federal officer."

Two Ships Passing In the Night

A well-known businessman owned a fleet of ships which plied certain waterway routes. He announced his intention to merge his fleet with another, which, in those routes would give him a virtual monopoly. My office conducted a quick investigation and advised the businessman that we would file a case and move for injunction to block the merger as a violation of the federal antitrust laws. After conferring with me and my associate, the businessman withdrew the offer and assured me that if he ever intended to renew the offer he would give us at least two weeks' notice. The businessman seemed to be a nice enough guy, but it turned out he was a sneaky one.

Several weeks had elapsed since our conversation and one Friday afternoon, just prior to the weekend, an announcement came over the news wires that the businessman's company had *completed* the merger of its competitor. No prior notice, as we had agreed, was given. He accomplished the acquisition by stealth.

Fait accompli? Not quite. One of my lawyers on the Antitrust Division staff, Bob McNew, was a former Coast Guard officer.

"Is there anything we can do?" I asked McNew.

"There's one thing left. We know that the only reason for the merger was to acquire the competing ships. Well, even though they acquired the company, title to the ships cannot be transferred until the Coast Guard processes the ships logs, which cannot be done until the ships reach port."

"What can we do to prevent the transfer of the logs?" I asked.

"Contact the Coast guard commandant's office, and tell them that we have an injunction hearing pending and they cannot transfer the logs."

NOW WHAT?

With one hour left to the work week, we filed the case and injunction papers we had prepared earlier and McNew called the Coast Guard, who agreed to hold up any transfers until the court rules. Then we sat back.

Monday morning, I received a call from an outraged attorney, representing the sneaky businessman, who found out that the Coast Guard would not transfer title to the ships. It seems our sneaky businessman was accusing me of being underhanded and violating his rights.

"My actions underhanded?" I replied incredulously. "Your man sneaked through the merger in secret after promising me he would give us two weeks' notice. I'd like to see you convince a court that we violated your client's rights."

A hearing ensued on whether a preliminary injunction should issue pending a trial on the merits. By the luck of the draw we obtained a judge who historically was anti-government and despite our very strong case that a monopoly would occur if the merger were permitted, the judge ruled against us.

We immediately filed an appeal, which occasioned a call directly from the businessman, who was all honey and sugar. "Carl, we're all reasonable people. Let's meet and reach an accommodation satisfactory to all parties."

I paused and he waited for an answer. "What makes you think I can trust you and your promises after what you tried to pull?"

"Carl, it was nothing personal. It was business, pure and simple."

His rationalization amazed me, but my curiosity got the better of me and I agreed to meet with him and his attorneys.

My senior litigator on the case and I met with the businessman and his lawyers (four of them) in his offices.

The businessman kicked off the meeting by noting that the government had lost the preliminary injunction and could not stop the merger. "We beat you fair and square. Why can't you accept defeat gracefully and not prolong your agony."

Condescension was not a tactic that made me more agreeable. I stood up. "I think we understand your position clear enough. If you think you won this law suit because you prevailed on the preliminary injunction, you've got a big surprise in store for you."

The businessman put up his hands. "Wait a minute. I can make an offer that would interest you."

I sat down. "I'm all ears."

"We will agree not to acquire two ships of *your choosing* from our competitor if you agree not to contest the merger."

I shook my head. "Forget it. No one can compete with you with only two ships. Here's my offer. Abandon the merger and we will withdraw our legal action."

His lead lawyer, a respected attorney interjected, "You are not offering us anything of value."

I smiled. "Well, neither is your client."

The businessman, clearly frustrated, leaned forward, pointing his finger at me. "Why are you so intransigent when you are in such a weak position? It doesn't make sense."

"It makes good sense to me because I understand the law. We will prevail on appeal. I suggest you have your attorneys explain to you the anti-merger section of the antitrust laws and how the Supreme Court has consistently interpreted the statute in situations just like this one in our favor. I lost the preliminary injunction hearing. You were lucky at the judge you drew. But so what? I promise you the Supreme Court will rip those newly acquired assets right out of your gut and force you to set up an effective competitor. Believe me; you're far better off abandoning the merger now. If your attorneys are advising that you will win on appeal, they are bullshitting you."

The businessman looked at his lead lawyer. "Is that true?"

With a little harrumphing and clearing of the throat, the lawyer said, "Well, there is always a chance the government could prevail."

The businessman knew waffling when he heard it. "What kind of chance does the government have?"

The lawyer shrugged. "I suppose better than even chance."

The businessman stared down his attorney. "And could the government prevail in ripping those assets out of our gut, as Mr. Steinhouse so quaintly put it?"

The attorney sighed. "It's certainly possible."

The businessman looked at me. "Look, we've managed already to transfer the title of the two ships that had already been in port to our control. If we can keep just those two ships, we will cancel the merger. Is that agreeable?"

"Yes, provided, your competitor gets a reasonable price for those vessels."

The businessman nodded. "Agreed."

Chalk another up for the good guys.

CARL L. STEINHOUSE

The Jargon Generator

Even in as serious a profession as federal law enforcement a little humor never hurts, and occasionally the imp (some would call it the devil) in me rises to the top. But if you use humor at the expense of your boss, I found out, it's a mistake to own up to it.

Bureaucrats love to search out things that parody the red tape, the bureaucratic language and innumerable rules that infest every government agency. The Justice Department is no exception. Thus, came across my desk, when I was chief of the Great Lakes Field Office of the Antitrust Division, a news story in a leading daily about a table of words called the Jargon Generator created by a bureaucrat in a state government. The first two columns are multisyllabic adjectives followed by the third column containing ambiguous nouns that defy strict definition.

THE JARGON GENERATOR

1. integrated	1. management	1. outputs
2. total	2. organizational	2. flexibility
3. systematized	3. monitored	3. analysis
4. parallel	4. reciprocal	4. mobility
5. functional	5. logistical	5. factors
6. responsive	6. transitional	6. concept
7. synchronized	7. modular	7. capability
8. compatible	8. creative	8. guidelines
9. balanced	9. operational	9 contingencies

The object is to randomly pick any combination of the 1, 2, and 3 columns to create an impressive phrase. Thus, for example, 1-5-9 produces "integrated logistical contingencies," guaranteed to establish your expertise and eruditeness on any subject or issue.

This was simply too good to pass up. I began salting my memos to Washington, including recommendations to indict criminally or sue civilly, with phrases like "compatible transitional concepts," "total creative guidelines," and the like. The phrases were high sounding but basically, gibberish. I'd put one somewhere in a ten-page memo and waited. Nothing. Apparently, if a memo is otherwise understandable, the reviewers will slide over an erudite phrase like any one generated above, without admitting, even to themselves, that they don't know what it means.

On a visit to Washington, instead of resting on my laurels, I asked my boss, "What did you think of my "total creative guidelines," pointing to the phrase in one of my memos sitting on his desk.

He looked at me, thinking hard, and then shrugged. "I have no idea," he said sheepishly.

I smiled. "It's part of my Jargon Generator."

"You're what?"

I could see his color rising as he already suspected I pulled one over on him, but there was no way out now. "I was just testing the theory that if you make phrases sound important enough you can write bullshit without anyone noticing." As soon as the word bullshit slipped out of my mouth, I knew I'd made a big, big mistake.

My boss stood up, leaning his fists on his desk. "You put BULLSHIT in your memos, some of which are forwarded to the Assistant Attorney General and then the Attorney General OF THESE UNITED STATES? Is THAT what you're telling me?" He dramatized the attorney general's title for effect.

"Jeezy peezy, Boss, I didn't USE the word bullshit."

He walked around his desk, grabbing my memo in one hand and my arm none too gently in the other. "Come with me," he growled.

We walked over to the office of the Assistant Attorney General, the big boss of the Antitrust Division.

Well, if my boss did not have a sense of humor, the big boss certainly did, laughing heartily at my indiscretions. Once alone in his office, the assistant attorney general gently suggested that I refrain from future bullshit phrases if I did not want my boss to make my job a living hell. It was certainly good advice, but then he insisted I give *him* a copy of my Jargon Generator. Attorney General of THESE UNITED STATES, watch out!

NOW WHAT?

Vignettes of a Prosecutor

Bobby

During my early years in the Justice Department in the New York Office, Bobby Kennedy, the attorney general had occasion to visit and figured it would be a good idea to meet all the government antitrust attorneys in the office. He felt it was important to give us individual attention so he met us two at a time.

Kennedy sat in the chief's office behind a large mahogany desk. I was paired up with this old attorney who'd been around thirty years and was ready for retirement. (Old, I discovered later, is a relative term. From my perspective now, he hardly seemed so old.)

As we walked into the office, Kennedy gave us a broad smile, as only the Kennedys can give, stood up, leaped over the desk, and stuck out his hand. The poor old attorney almost dumped in his pants, backing out of the office in a minor panic. I stood my ground.

"Good to meet you," he said enthusiastically pumping my hand with a firm grip and a vigorous shaking motion. "What have you been working on?"

I mumbled something about the Swiss Watch Cartel case while Kennedy looked over my shoulder at the scuffle going on behind me as our chief pushed the reluctant old attorney back into the room. You'd think he was being fed to the lions in the Roman Coliseum.

CARL L. STEINHOUSE

Business as Usual

Conducting a grand jury investigation into price fixing by building contractors in a state in the southern part of our jurisdiction, we came across the strange situation of a lesson never learned. It started with an indictment handed down by the grand jury and ultimately resulted convictions for price fixing of five individual owners of contracting businesses. Then things got weird.

The defendants received jail time and were incarcerated together in a local prison. That gave them a lot of time to spend with each other. I should have known better.

A month after their incarceration, I received a frantic call from one of the convicted contractors. "I have to whisper, so they don't hear me," he said breathlessly into the phone.

"What's the problem?"

"I don't want to go to jail again!"

"Now why should that happen?"

"Because those dumb bastards are running their businesses from the jail and are fixing prices again, bold as you please. They're really leaning on me to go along."

That takes recidivism to the highest (or lowest) plane! Something they might contemplate facing possible additional terms in prison--separated from each other, of course.

NOW WHAT?

The Shoe on the Other Foot

Remember way back when I first started in the Justice Department I described being viciously harassed by one of the supposedly experienced trial attorneys, I called Joe Murano? Well, as they say, "What goes around comes around."

Generally, as chief of the Great Lakes Office, I was the responsible authority for antitrust enforcement in my area of jurisdiction. An exception was when a staff from one of the many litigation sections in Washington brought a case in my area. The chief of that section in Washington would supervise that staff. Joe M headed up just such a staff conducting a grand jury investigation of a major industry in my geographic area of jurisdiction. It seemed that he was just as vicious with his witnesses before the grand jury as he was with me.

Following many complaints of abuse, the chief judge of the federal district called me into his chambers.

"What the hell is going on with that grand jury? Is that Joe Murano out of his mind? I won't stand for it!"

"With all due respect Your Honor, it is not my problem. He is supervised out of Washington."

"I don't give a damn. You are the top responsible antitrust enforcer in this district and I am holding you personally responsible for any more abuse that that guy commits. If he gets held in contempt, you get held in contempt. Do I make myself clear?"

"Well hell, Your Honor, you put me in an impossible position."

"That's your problem; mine is keeping abuse out of my grand juries. End of discussion!"

I made a simple ultimatum to my bosses: either replace the staff conducting the investigation or give me total supervision over the staff attorneys, especially Joe Murano. They chose the latter.

249

The next time Joe was in town, I called him into my office. "Remember me, Murano?"

"Sure, you're the chief of this office."

"Try ten years before that in the New York Office."

"Weren't you the one who worked with Mary Gardiner Jones?"

"You got it. Now the shoe's on the other foot, you S.O.B. I'll be all over you on this grand jury investigation like paint on a wall, and I promise you this, I'll ride your ass out of this district if there are any further complaints of abuse. Everything, and I mean *everything* you do, will be first cleared with me. Is that clear?"

I suppose it was petty of me to be so spiteful, but it felt so damn good!

NOW WHAT?

Autographs, Toilet Paper and Jesters

We had some real characters appear before the grand jury. One, a rather famous sports figure, was scheduled to testify. The judge supervising the grand jury called me into his chambers.

"Mr. Steinhouse, do me a favor, will you? Would you get the witness's autograph made out to Pete? That's my nephew."

"That's kind of sticky, judge. After all, I'm supposed to be subjecting this witness to a serious interrogation. How will I look if I, the prosecutor, go pandering up to him like a star-struck fan, asking for his autograph?"

"Come on, Carl, you can do it--as a favor to me."

I wasn't doing it for my son, Sam, so why should I do it for his damn nephew, Pete? But on the other hand, when a judge in your district puts it to you that way and you face the prospect of appearing before him many times in your career, it's hard to say no. It takes a brave and principled prosecutor to refuse. I wasn't that man.

I approached the witness during a break. "I'm sorry to bother you and this is something I do not normally do, but my judge insists that I ask you to sign autographs for his two nephews."

"No problem. To whom shall I address the autographs?"

"Sign one to Pete and the other to *Sam*."

Hell, as long as I had to embarrass myself, I might as well get something for my son.

During his testimony, there was a knock on the door. We halted the examination and the sergeant-at-arms opened the door and in walks the courthouse custodian with about ten rolls of toilet paper for the lavatories in the back of the grand jury room.

251

The witness took one look at the custodian passing him by and said, "Are you trying to tell me what you think of my testimony?"

The next sports figure came into the grand jury room wearing a full length, and I mean full-length, mink coat. It covered his shoes. I always knew these guys were overpaid. More startling was the outfit underneath-- a jump suit, of which the top half was bright red on the left side and midnight black on the other; the bottom half was reversed--midnight black on the left side, and bright red on the right. I thought we had called the court jester of King Henry VIII to the witness stand.

Whatever happened to showing up to testify in a suit and tie?

VI. MY DAYS ON THE OTHER SIDE--PRIVATE PRACTICE

Martinis and Stuffed Monkeys

When I let it be known that I was interested in making the move to private practice several of the top firms in Cleveland offered me jobs. What I considered the premier law firm in the city, if not in the nation, really interested me. That firm's offer was substantially above the others. Interviewing with the managing partners of one of the other firms was an experience.

"Carl," he said, "I want you to consider me like a Dutch uncle."

I looked at him suspiciously, since I'd met him for the first time only a few minutes before. "I'm listening, John."

He got up from his desk and came around behind me, putting his hand on my shoulder. "I know you were offered more money by that other firm, but take it from me; a partnership in my firm is much more valuable."

"I see," I replied. "So your advice, as my Dutch uncle, is for me to take one third less pay for the privilege of working here."

"That's about it."

"Well Dutch Uncle John, I can see why you'd be the black sheep in my family. Why should I work for a firm I consider inferior for less pay?"

The interview went downhill from there.

NOW WHAT?

Having accepted an offer from the firm I had my eye on, I managed to put my foot in my mouth before I ever worked a day in the office.

The senior partner who recruited me invited me to the annual firm function in June, being held at the Cleveland Museum of Natural History. The problem: on this same day, the staff at the Antitrust Division gave me a going-away party and by the time I reached the museum I was almost blotto. The great hors d'oeuvres served up by the firm did not make much of a dent in my condition.

In a serious discussion with my escorting senior partner about the museum, I suddenly threw in, "You know, I think it's a great mistake holding a party like this in the Museum of Natural History."

"Oh, why is that?" he inquired. "I had thought it was an excellent and interesting place for such an affair."

"Well, the problem is that if I imbibe too much, I could end up drinking a martini from a stuffed monkey's ass."

Diana grabbed my arm. "You'll have to excuse him, he's just come from a going-away party the Justice Department threw for him; he's really had too much to drink. I had to drive him here."

The senior partner nodded. "I can handle it."

From then on, he'd make introductions of me to other partners with a firm grip on my arm, forcefully steering me away before I could say much of anything.

Obviously, the firm wasn't as uptight as its reputation because it hired me anyway.

CARL L. STEINHOUSE

One of My First Clients, the Mamzer

If a nice Jewish boy joins an old-line WASP firm, what's he to expect? I only knew that as a government attorney, I never experienced any overt or disguised bias in dealing with this firm's attorneys in my investigations and cases. But I also knew it would have been pretty stupid to piss off the prosecutor in me by exhibiting such behavior. I did know that the firm had quite a few Jewish attorneys and partners, and it did, after having a dozen partners interview me, offer me a job. So how bad could it be?

In fact, I experienced no bias in the firm to myself or other Jewish attorneys. I moved up quickly in the firm and so did other Jewish lawyers who showed merit (not all did). Oh, I'm sure some old-line partners, congregating in their restricted golf clubs, may have expressed or harbored some anti-Semitic feelings, but they kept it well hidden from me. I think the firm appreciated my experience in the Justice Department--I was the first of many prosecutors it later hired. We tested the waters for a while with a wary eye--I and the firm both not being sure I could or would adapt to private practice and defense work. As it turned out, I did not find it difficult. I approached matters the same way I did in Justice, *i.e.,* identify my objectives, determine what the problems are, and solve them.

Early on, I had a Jewish client, I'll call him Mr. B, who manufactured expensive women's dress shoes; you know, the kind with spikes that could maim or kill. I defended a private antitrust suit for triple damages brought against him by one of his large customers, alleging an illegal boycott.

NOW WHAT?

Well, Mr. B was really worried, as well he should be, standing to lose millions of dollars in treble damages, plus costs, if he lost. Mr. B said, "You win this case without trial and I'll keep you wife in shoes for the rest of her life."

I said nothing, but knew I couldn't accept such gifts.

It took me three months, but I had the case tossed out on summary judgment. That was as quick a disposition of an antitrust case as one could hope for. Some of these cases drag on for years. Right proud of the result, I sent the client a final bill.

I received a call from our accounting department. The client had sent in exactly half the amount I had billed, so I called him. The client was pleasant enough. "Carl," he explained, "I know how accountants and lawyers overbill, so I make it a practice to pay only half of what I am invoiced. Don't feel bad, I do it to all of them."

"Is that so, Mr. B?"

"Facts of life, Mr. Steinhouse."

Then I salted some Yiddish into my response. "Don't think you can screw me with the facts of life, you *mamzer* [low life, SOB]. Don't you try to *handlen* [bargain down] me with that *dreck* [crap] you're handing me. I got you out of that treble damage case dirt cheap, and you know it. You think I am going into my managing partner and tell him that after all I achieved, my Jewish client is going to try to cheat him as he does all his lawyers? It's people like you that may spark a resurgence of anti-Semitism. I need clients like you like a *loch in kop* [a hole in the head]."

"And how's this for a fact of life, Mr. B, I'll sue your ass for the remainder of the fee and when I show the judge the result I achieved I wouldn't be surprised if he didn't award punitive damages and costs.

"You wouldn't."

"That's *my* policy, sorry." I hung up on him.

The check for the balance came in the mail the following week.

And he never offered my wife a single pair of shoes.

NOW WHAT?

Never Take a Witness' Answer For Granted

I wasn't above injecting, when the spirit moved me, some levity, or even an occasional practical joke, while defending serious antitrust suits.

A plaintiff supplier of airplane parts brought an antitrust action for three times damages, claiming that several manufacturers, my client included, conspired to drive the plaintiff company out of business. Sometimes plaintiffs' attorneys in private antitrust cases name a whole bunch of other defendants with no realistic connection to the acts being alleged. I'll call those unfortunate defendants the tangential parties. Plaintiffs' lawyers often include them as defendants because they have more leeway in discovery against parties to the action, in the hopes of turning up something--anything--that might be helpful during such discovery--basically a fishing expedition.

Plaintiff's attorney was taking the deposition of witnesses of several defendants who were tangential parties. Because these tangential parties knew there was no proof of any connection to the alleged acts of conspiracy and knew their employees would so testify, the law firms representing such parties often sent their young and somewhat inexperienced attorneys to these depositions to give them some exposure and seasoning. Not unlike in sports when a coach throws his little-used players in the game towards the end when the outcome is no longer in doubt.

We sat in the large conference room of the plaintiff's law firm in Kansas City and there was no space to spare, with all the counsel for the tangential parties added to the regular coterie of plaintiff and defense counsel. Lead plaintiff's counsel questioned the employees or officers of each of the tangential parties and as expected, got nothing of value. Then counsel for each

259

of the tangential party would ask a single question, carefully scripted beforehand by the defense team, "Are you aware of any agreement between the manufacturing defendants and your company to not to do business with the plaintiff company or to somehow engage in some other anti-competitive acts?"

Each witness would simply answer "no" and that would end that deposition. That is, until the very last deposition. This is what happened.

A significant part of a trial defense counsel's work is composed of discovery, which in some instances can be very, very boring. This was one of those times, because these tangential parties had nothing of value to say. The plaintiff's counsel knew it, the tangential parties counsel knew it, and we knew it. Not known as a patient man, I simply had to do something besides pick my teeth or clean my fingernails. We had taken a break for about ten minutes and the unseasoned young counsel, I'll call him Mr. Young Attorney, left the deposition for the restroom. His client had just testified to plaintiff's questions just as the others before him had, with no surprises on the witness stand and it was Mr. Young Attorney's turn to do the cross-examine. He might have been a little nervous.

I signaled the rest of the counsel to remain in the room. Mr. Young Attorney's witness was also in the room.

"I have a great idea," I began, "if you're all willing to cooperate." Since my reputation preceded me, the room was all ears.

"We'll keep this off the record. Mr. Court Reporter, when Mr. Young Attorney asks his one question, don't take down the witness's answer."

He nodded. The court reporter would go along.

"Mr. Witness, when your counsel asks you his one question, answer 'yes' instead of 'no.' You will have the opportunity to give the truthful answer afterwards, I promise you."

Mr. Witness was quick and immediately caught on. It's not often you have a chance to really tweak your attorney. He smiled and nodded his agreement, as did the rest of the attorneys in the room.

Mr. Young Attorney returned and took his seat. The witness was reminded he was still under oath. He responded he understood.

"On the record again," Mr. Young Attorney told the court reporter.

The court reporter nodded but kept his hands under the stenographer machine, instead of on the keys.

"Mr. Witness," began Mr. Young Attorney, "are you aware of any agreement between the manufacturing defendants and your company to not to do business with the plaintiff company or to somehow engage in some other anti-competitive acts?" The question was right according to the script.

The witness suppressed a smile. "Yes, I am so aware."

A moment of silence. Mr. Young Attorney sat there, wide-eyed and agape.

His next question came out in a high squeaky voice, "You are?'

The witness shook his head resolutely and finally the attorneys, no longer able to contain themselves, broke out in hysterical laugher.

Poor Mr. Young Attorney. I realized at that in that instant he must be seeing his career flushing away.

I needn't have worried. If anything, it prepared him for any courtroom surprises and years later, I am happy to report, he earned his partnership in that prestigious law firm.

CARL L. STEINHOUSE

Flying, Cruise Control, and Spiced Apples

My partner Joe and I traveled to Iowa, visiting the plant of our manufacturer client, to dispense antitrust advice. It was in dead of winter and not a good time to traipse to this area, but we made it to this small Iowa town.

Finishing our business in late morning, the client importuned us to visit his other plant in St. Cloud, Minnesota, several hundred miles to the north. We would meet the St. Cloud plant manager at his country club for dinner. The problem: there were no commercial flights between where we were and St. Cloud. Well, a client's a client, so we checked at the small local airport, actually a cleared-away cornfield. We found a pilot with a single engine Cessna willing to fly us to St. Cloud for a price.

Joe, substantially heftier than I, took the larger co-pilot's seat while I sat in back. About midway there Joe turned to the pilot. "Is it hard to fly one of these planes?"

"Not really."

Joe nodded. "In the navy, I captained a large LST and they were a bitch to control. I think I could handle this small airplane."

I did not like where this conversation was going.

"You want to try?" the pilot asked.

"Absolutely," Joe gushed.

"Now wait a damn minute," I protested but they ignored me. What could I do? I certainly couldn't open the door and get out.

The pilot gave Joe a brief instruction. It was: "Take over."

Joe grabbed the wheel and immediately the plane went into a dive that took several Gs of force to come out of.

"Handle the wheel lightly," the pilot admonished. "As you can see, the aircraft is very responsive."

NOW WHAT?

"The hell with lightly," I complained. "He should take his hands off the wheel completely and let you fly."

The pilot assured me we were perfectly safe. I wasn't so sure.

We continued up to St. Cloud with Joe at the controls, the plane bouncing up and down in Joe's own man-made turbulence. I am not one prone to travel sickness but I was sorely tested that day. Only the fact that we hadn't eaten lunch probably saved me from soiling the Cessna. We made it safely to St. Cloud, the pilot taking over as we approached the airport.

At the airport, I rented a car and we headed right out for the country club without grabbing a bite to eat because of the late hour. Now I was at the wheel and I noticed the car had cruise control. Back in those days, that device was a rarity and I had been dying to try one. The problem was the roads. They'd just had an ice storm and the roads were like skating rinks. But I had to try the cruise control.

"What the hell are you doing?" Joe cried out, "You can't use cruise control on icy road like this."

"Just watch me," I said, a devilish smile formed on my lips.

"You're getting back at me for flying that plane, aren't you?"

I shook my head. "Not me." Joe's smart and of course, he was absolutely right, but I steadfastly denied this was my little bit of revenge.

Notwithstanding the cruise control, we slid and skidded until we finally reached the country club, an hour late. And we were starving.

As we sat with the client having drinks at the dinner table, the waiter brought over a huge relish tray with fresh cut raw vegetables garnished around the perimeter of the tray with spiced apples. Within ten minutes we had almost finished off the entire tray, the only remaining food were those spiced apples, which neither one of us liked.

"You know," the client said, "I never saw any table finish off an entire relish tray. You guys should be in the Guinness Book of Records. He called over the waiter. "You'd better take this away before these two guys eat the damn tray." (Many years later, Joe got the last laugh when, for my sixtieth birthday party, my wife asked the guests to bring me sixty of anything. Joe brought me sixty spiced apples.)

The Education of Richard Doorknob

The Federal Trade Commission investigates and brings action against companies for consumer fraud and misrepresentation. Our firm had a large client, one of whose subsidiaries was a computer programming school that was under scrutiny by the FTC for taking money from students without giving them adequate training, the government claiming that the students who graduated the course were almost as ignorant of computers as when they began and were unable to find jobs in their field *for lack of training.* Other charges included falsified student enrollment records (such as taking names off of tombstones to glean more governmental monetary aid). If one believed the allegations, we were really representing the scum of the world in the trade school education business.

One of the schools, located in New Orleans, was claimed to be one of the big offenders. My partner Joe and I traveled down to this Deep South city to interview the staff. At our first interview of the top salesman in the school, one look at him and I had that bad feeling we were in trouble, even before he uttered a word. Dressed in white buck shoes, a bright yellow sports jacket and crimson red trousers, he greeted us with a "How y'all?" Still, it was those white buck shoes that troubled me the most.

He gave us the salesman's pitch. Oh, he was good--too good. No school could live up to his hype.

Joe suggested we set as one of our tasks, contacting by telephone, as many ex-students as possible to see how they fared on the job market. Obviously, notwithstanding Mr. White Buck Shoes, if a number of students actually received jobs in the computer-programming field, the defense of our client would be significantly bolstered.

We planned to work from a hotel room we'd taken just for this purpose. Our sleeping quarters were separate. I had come down to this Deep South city with my wife and when we checked in, we were told the hotel was overbooked, but not to worry, they'd put us up in the presidential suite at their normal room rate. To call the suite luxurious would be a gross understatement--four rooms stocked with every type of alcoholic beverage and its own private swimming pool just outside on the penthouse patio. The next day we were told that we'd be moved to a standard room. We could hardly quarrel with that. We went about our business as the hotel assured our belongings would be moved when the room became available later in the day. About nine in the evening we returned to the hotel and were given our new room key. Opening the door, we had to squeeze between the end of the bed and the television to get at our luggage. The room was the size of a small broom closet. No amount of complaining would change things. The hotel was full and besides, we were told, we had no basis to complain considering the suite we had last night. Obviously, the hotel was intent on averaging out our benefits.

That left me in a sour mood the next morning and when we met for breakfast in our swanky hotel, we asked for a table for three.

"I'm sorry monsieur, the dining room is filled," the maître'd advised.

I looked over his shoulder and saw at least half the tables were empty and set for dining. "There are plenty of empty tables," I said, a definite edge apparent in my voice.

The maître'd stuck his nose up in the air. "As I just advised you," he said in a haughty tone, "there is no room--end of discussion."

"Like hell it's the end of the discussion you fucking idiot."

That caught the attention of the diners who, as one, looked our way.

Joe, always proper and conservative, grabbed me by the arm. "Listen, Carl," he whispered earnestly, "you simply can't talk like that in a fancy place like this." He put a lot of pressure on my arm forcing me to back out of the vestibule of the restaurant.

I shook my arm loose. "Just watch me."

Diana stepped in front of me. "Don't you dare embarrass me like that again!"

Two against one. I conceded the point and we left the hotel to find some breakfast. Thinking to hell with my diet, I headed for Café Du Monde overlooking the Mississippi River.

I needed a relaxing breakfast, so I ordered chicory-based coffee and beignets with powdered sugar.

Meanwhile, Joe and Diana had a healthy breakfast somewhere else. That was okay because I wasn't good company anyway.

Getting back to our investigation, Joe decided that best way to reach the most students is to call them from the phone numbers on their student record cards maintained by the school. I have this thing about telephones. I hate talking on them, especially cold calls to strangers. That's why I'd never make a good salesman. I'll do anything to avoid it--and I did.

Joe kept making calls and I kept busy examining documents.

"How many people have you contacted," Joe asked after a while.

"I'm still working on the documents," I muttered, almost under my breath.

"You haven't made any calls? The hell with the documents, they can wait for later."

I didn't look up. "I'll be finished soon," burying my face in an enrollment form.

Joe shrugged and began making more calls.

An hour later, and then another hour later, we went through the same routine.

"You have no intention of making any calls, do you?" Joe accused, finally catching on.

I shrugged noncommittally.

He pointed his finger at me. "You have a phone phobia, don't you? I should have seen it sooner."

"Not really," I replied unconvincingly. "I just rather do the documents while you handle the phone calls."

* * *

That night, the phone rang in our broom closet hotel room. Diana picked it up. "It's for you." She handed me the phone.

"Carl Steinhouse here."

"Is this Mr. Steinhouse representing the computer school?" the voice said in a hoarse whisper.

"One and the same."

"Hello, Mr. Steinhouse, I am Richard Doorknob, a former student at the school."

I motioned to my wife to get me a pad and pencil.

"Yes, Mr. Doorknob, what can I do for you?"

"I have some information that will be of great interest to you."

"And what that might be?" I poised my pencil to write.

"That you're as gullible as they come," he said, his voice no longer hoarse and laughing like hell.

"Joe, is that you?"

NOW WHAT?

"I gotcha," he replied, still laughing and hung up the phone.

I owned Joe one.

Hostile Takeover Stories--Big Fish Little Fish

Story One: Paper Tigers and Other Obscenities

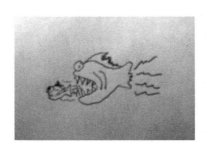

The call came in out of the blue. The managing partner of the firm called Joe and me in.

"A large oil company has just made a hostile tender for our client, a producer of energy through thermal steam--the big fish trying to swallow the little one. We have one week to put a case together and file in Los Angeles in federal district court for a preliminary injunction. Get right on it and put together a team to get it done."

First a brief explanation to put things in perspective. Hostile corporate takeovers are a bitch to defend against. Normally, antitrust cases can drag on for years with discovery, depositions, and interrogatories, not to mention the innumerable motions and pretrials before the judge. But everything is turned on its head with a hostile takeover. The corporate raider has had months, if not years, to prepare for the takeover, and if it was smart--and it usually is--the raider will do its nefarious work in absolute secrecy and strike suddenly and without warning. The victim corporation usually has about two weeks max, starting from scratch, to file for a preliminary injunction to try to stop the takeover until a court can decide the case on the merits. That's the theory. In real life, it works much differently.

NOW WHAT?

To win a preliminary injunction blocking the takeover, the victim corporation must show that there is a *probably* of success that it will prevail--not a possibly, but a probably. As a practical matter, the preliminary injunction action basically decides the matter because the victim corporation is like the egg that, once scrambled and integrated, cannot be put it back together again. If the target company loses that hearing, it will be absorbed and that is usually that. On the other hand, if the target corporation wins its preliminary injunction, the raider faces months, if not years of litigation. It will quickly lose its interest and desire and move on to easier prey. So using the preliminary injunction to preserve the *status quo* until a trial on the merits is a myth. Either way the preliminary injunction action is decided, unless the government is the plaintiff, it rarely ever gets to a trial on the merits. Thus, injunction hearing is not really preliminary; it's usually the whole ball of wax, the end game itself.

In this hostile takeover environment, we, the lawyers opposing the takeover, had to learn the industry and gather documentary and witness evidence, and had one week to put together a complicated antitrust action to show the acquisition would likely violate the antitrust laws.

The firm had an apartment in downtown Cleveland near its offices and that's where we slept every night that week when we could. With the evidence gathered and put together as best we could in the time allowed, a group of us boarded a plane for Los Angeles. I sat next to the managing partner while my partner Joe sat across the aisle as we drafted the final complaint and preliminary injunction motion in the six hours we had on the flight. On arrival, typists were standing by in our Los Angeles office to grind out the pleadings. We checked for typos and finally got to bed at four in the morning.

Since we arrived in Los Angeles three hours earlier than it was it Cleveland we had literally worked a twenty-seven hour day and I'm sure the client's eyes popped out when he saw his bill for twenty-seven hours in a single day.

The managing partner had scheduled a meeting for him and me with the adversary law firm the next morning, a firm that was one of the largest and well heeled on the West Coast. He sent Joe on another vital mission. As we went up the elevator in the downtown office building, the managing partner turned to me.

"Carl, let me do the talking, I've had a lot of experience in these situations."

My managing partner was not a trial attorney so I had my doubts about that approach. "Are you sure," I said, "because that's what you pay me for. It'll be a down and dirty scrap and I've been in many of them."

"No, let me take the lead. I know what I'm doing."

I nodded. He'd always been a brilliant planner and strategist, so who was I to rain on his parade?

We were shown to the conference room. Four attorneys for the other side and their client's general counsel sat on one side of the large table and we two sat on the other side.

I could see this would be a tough meeting because the opposition lead counsel, whom I'll call Rough and Tumble, had the reputation of a rough and tumble gutter fighter, and like me, he came from the Bronx.

"The ball is in your court," Rough and Tumble said gruffly.

"Um, yes." The managing partner pulled out the complaint and motion for a preliminary injunction and slid it over to his adversary. "If you persist in going ahead with the hostile takeover, we are prepared to file immediately these pleading to block your action."

Rough and Tumble grabbed the papers and quickly scanned through them. I didn't like that we had given him this opportunity to do so. He threw them on the table. "Well, I see you've been busy little beavers this week putting together this piece of garbage."

"Well I . . ." my managing partner started to say.

Rough and Tumble interrupted. "Listen, you fat fuck, we don't have to listen to your bullshit. You're nothing but a paper tiger and we'll wipe up the floor with you."

My managing partner, who, I admit, was on the fairly heavy side, struggled for a response. I doubt if, in his entire long and distinguished legal career, anyone ever had addressed him in that manner.

I put my hand on his shoulder. "Let me take over, this is right up my alley; I've been dealing with guys like this, these gutter snipes, all my life."

My managing partner nodded.

I turned to Rough and Tumble. "Listen, shithead, my managing partner may be a fat fuck, but one thing I promise you, he isn't any paper tiger." I grabbed the pleadings away from him. "Too bad you weren't a little more courteous. Now you'll have a chance to study these only after when we file them and serve your client, not before. I've cleaned the clock of foul-mouthed braggarts like you before. Trust me; you're getting more than you bargained for. This meeting is over."

I stood and began walking out. The managing partner took my lead and followed.

On the way down in the elevator, he looked at me for a while. Finally, before the elevator reached the lobby, he said, "Thank you for defending me--I think!"

Obviously, we were not paper tigers, and the efforts of Joe, me, and all our attorneys bore fruit because our opponents shortly thereafter withdrew their hostile offer to take over of our client. No sooner was I packing my bags that I received a call from a client in Chicago to come there immediately because it had been hit with a hostile tender offer and there was no time to spare. Here I go again!

Oh well, it still had been a good day. After all, how many days can you have where your side wins a great victory without filing a case and you get to call your boss a "fat fuck"?

Story Two: To the Mattresses! Taking a Leaf from the Godfather

I know people who hold lawyers in about the same regard as the Mafia. I resent being tarred with such a broad brush, but must admit secretly that we sometimes borrow from some of the gangland practices. But before you say "I told you so," read on.

One day, the head of the litigation section, called me into his office. "Carl, today our client, Oil Company, was hit with a hostile takeover attempt. Our client is not interested in being absorbed by the raider. We have two weeks to put together a case for preliminary injunction. Our best bet is to oppose this on antitrust grounds and you, one of our most experienced antitrust partners, will be responsible for gathering all the evidence necessary to prove the takeover will be anti-competitive under the federal antitrust laws. Our client is relying on you to preserve its independence; *I* am relying on you."

"Two weeks," I gasped.

"Two weeks," he reaffirmed.

Once again we were facing a hostile takeover situation where our opponents were well prepared and we were starting from scratch.

An antitrust associate, Tom D, a team of paralegals and secretaries, and I headed out to a small town in the Midwest, the headquarters of the Oil Company. We immediately set out to review documents, interview witnesses and experts, and obtain an intimate understanding of the U.S. oil industry and pipeline system that supplies gasoline to all parts of the country. It was a monumental task requiring some all-nighters and twenty-hour days.

We took a leaf from the *Godfather* movies where, during the gangland wars, the Corleone family and its

275

soldiers took to the mattresses, that is, they would hole up in a safe house, sleeping on mattresses on the floor until the current conflicts were resolved. We also took to the mattresses--literally. We did not have time for the niceties of a hotel so Tom and I commandeered an empty house owned by the Oil Company. Conveniently, the house was just across the street from its offices, and usually used by officers of the company, newly transferred to headquarters, as home for their family and furniture until they found a place to live. The house did not have a stick of furniture, so we scrounged up a few thin mattresses from the client, put them on the floor, and that's where Tom and I bedded down for our few hours of sleep, when we could.

Working closely with a team of the Oil Company employees, we began to put together our case. One night, well past midnight, when none of us had stopped for dinner, we descended on the Oil Company cafeteria and requested to be fed. The chef sent back word he does not cook past midnight. I sent back word that if we couldn't complete our work because we were not fed, the Oil Company would be taken over and he would lose his job. Needless to say, the CEO, in any event, would not take kindly to this refusal. Admittedly, I did not say it quite as politely as that. But a half hour later, a hot meal was served to all the workers.

It was heady, if difficult, times for us. Tom and I had the unfettered use of the Oil Company's fleet of jet planes and limos as we traveled far and wide interviewing witnesses, but always returning at night to the Oil Company and our mattresses.

Two days short of two weeks, I received a call from the head of litigation asking where the evidence was.

"You gave me two weeks," I growled. "I have two days left, and *then* I will be back with the evidence." Well, we returned in two days and in a highly contentious preliminary injunction hearing against the raider oil

276

company, represented by a highly capable Wall Street firm, the court granted our request for preliminary injunction, finding that we had established, by credible evidence, the probability of success that the takeover would violate the antitrust laws. As expected, raider was no longer interested and withdrew its takeover attempt.

During the course of our stay at the Oil Company, several tee shirts were produced, some by the Oil Company, others by our staff, extorting our troops on to victory; some were funny, some obscene. My contribution was a red sweatshirt, distributed to the team, switching around the first letters of the two-word phrase.

Many months later, at an American Bar Association Antitrust Section meeting at a resort in California, I wore my sweatshirt while lounging at the pool.

Author in his infamous sweatshirt

Later, my partner, then chairman of the Antitrust Section and much more conservative than I, pulled me aside, and told me that at the council meeting, one of its members, an old fuddy-duddy antitrust professor from out West, moved to expel me from the Section because his wife's sensibilities were affronted at the pool when she saw my sweatshirt. The council thought it was a big joke and voted down the motion. My partner, however, was not amused and though I pointed out there was not a single obscene word on that shirt, he strongly suggested that henceforth, I refrain from wearing it during the ABA meetings.

Story Three: Paper Bags and Computers

A large manufacturer began a hostile takeover bid for our client, another manufacturer in a related industry. We filed a suit under the Clayton Act to prevent the acquisition on the grounds that will likely harm competition. To preserve the independence of our client pending a trial on the merits, we moved for a preliminary injunction hearing to enjoin the acquisition.

We launched discovery against the raider and I had the occasion to take the oral deposition of the CEO who had the reputation as a hard-nosed gruff businessman with a foul mouth. During the course of the deposition, I asked, "What do you think of your counterpart in the company you are trying to acquire?"

The CEO looked straight at me and testified. "He's so stupid, he couldn't find shit in a paper bag."

Testimony as profane as this continued to the end of the deposition.

At the preliminary injunction hearing before the judge, the CEO was well prepared by his attorneys and on his best behavior and try as I might, I couldn't instigate him to use foul language. Oh, I could have used his deposition testimony at the preliminary injunction hearing to cross-examine him but it just didn't have the impact of live obscenities.

One of the issues in the injunction hearing was whether the CEO intended to control my client pending a trial on the merits. In other words, we would argue, you can't unscramble an egg--or companies--once the assets are scrambled, destroying our ability to get effective relief later. The other side argued that the acquired company would be kept independent pending the lawsuit and therefore, a preliminary injunction was unnecessary.

On direct examination the raiding company CEO testified he had absolutely no intent to influence the

279

company pending a trial on the merits. But during the course of our discovery, I had found out that this CEO hated computers, hated them with a passion, and he refused to permit any in his company.

I cross-examined the CEO. Midway through the examination and unable to incite him to profanity, I suddenly asked, "What do you intend to do with computer department at my client?"

He stiffened. Now his voice grew angry. "I'll throw the damn machines out pronto. There will no computer department anymore at the company."

The judge, at the conclusion of the hearing granted us a preliminary injunction, ruling from the bench. The raider ultimately withdrew its hostile tender offer.

That hostile CEO later hired our firm to represent his company.

Friday the Thirteenth

It was pretrial time in Phoenix, Arizona and Friday, the thirteenth--definitely not a good combination. I got up around six in the morning. While brushing my teeth, the telephone rang. My son Sam was on the line.

"We had a boy," he said. "His name is Justin Daniel."

"My Lord," I thought, "I'm a grandfather." I looked in the mirror. There was plenty of gray in my beard, though not much on top of my head. I guess I qualified for grandparenthood.

"Susan and the baby are doing fine," he said. I'm sure Susan must have had other ideas at that moment like, "Next one, Sam, you have!"

Sam was all excited, I was excited, and I'm sure Diana, in Cleveland, was excited. I know because I called her right after Sam hung up.

I had one tiny regret--I wished they'd named him Daniel Justin--after my stepfather, Dan Grossman--but the Daniel was there, in his name. I could always call him "Danny Boy."

Danny Boy

I finished dressing, had breakfast and headed for the courthouse. Judge R ran a tight courtroom and it wouldn't do to be late. Besides, we had a busy day ahead.

I was one of the attorneys defending the cement industry against many class actions, which were consolidated together for one trial. The industry was accused of price fixing and there were fifty attorneys suing us for two billion dollars on behalf of almost one million class members, their clients; add to that, an another sixty attorneys defending, making it very a crowded courtroom. Attorneys were hanging from the rafters.

I represented one of the major cement companies. I went up to my co-counsel, attorney Bill McC, an elder statesman, wizened and experienced, whom we appointed to lead the defense group--a calm and steadying influence representing one of the defendants.

Bill McC, a calm and steadying influence

"Bill," I said, "I need a few minutes of the court's time the first thing this morning."

McC shook his head. "The judge will go ballistic with any interruption--can't do it."

"It's important and I insist," I said.

McC sighed. "What's it about?"

"Can't tell you."

He looked at me, very annoyed. "You want me to tell the judge that you want to take up his valuable time, but you won't tell me what the subject is? Is that what you're asking me?"

"That's about it, Bill."

He shook his head again. Just then the bailiff banged the gavel down, yelling "Oyez, Oyez!" That told us the judge was entering the courtroom. It means, "Hear ye, hear ye." I don't know why they speak in Latin when our language is English--tradition, I guess, or the bailiff likes to show off.

We all stand for the judge. When he sits and bangs his gavel, we sit, like the automations we are. The bailiff then says in a most serious tone, "G-d save the United States of America and this Honorable Court."

He doesn't ask to save us--just the court. McC leaned over and whispered in my ear, "You'll really need saving after whatever stunt you're going to pull."

The judge looked down on us from his high position on the bench. He did not have a reputation for patience or tolerance. "Gentlemen and Ladies, we have a busy day so let's get started."

McC stood up and cleared his throat. "Your Honor, Mr. Steinhouse has requested some time now to address the court."

The judge glared at McC. "Heh? What's it about, Mr. McC? You know I don't want any interruptions today!"

McC spread his arms and shrugs. "Sorry, Your Honor, he wouldn't tell me and I take no responsibility for anything Mr. Steinhouse says." He sat down and wouldn't even look at the judge.

All eyes in the courtroom focused on me, including the burning stare of the judge. I wondered if I was being wise.

The judge didn't help. "Mr. Steinhouse? This had better be the most important thing you've ever said."

I stood up. I saw Bill McC bent over, his head in his hands. The plaintiffs' attorneys (my opponents) were smiling, figuring I was going to get myself and the rest of the defense counsel team in mucho trouble. Everyone in that courtroom knew it didn't take much to set off Judge R.

"I assure you, Your Honor, it is the most important thing I ever said. Since I have spent eight years on this case, and came to know everyone in this courtroom, well, I felt strongly that you all should be the first to know that I am a grandfather for the first time. It happened early this morning and his name is Justin Daniel Steinhouse." I sat down, holding my breath.

The judge glared at me and banged his gavel. "Mr. Steinhouse," he said in a low growl, "that is a most important thing." He broke into a big grin. "Congratulations! Now let's get to work."

I thumbed my nose at Friday, the thirteenth and flashed a big grin at elder statesman McC, who seemed shell-shocked.

NOW WHAT?

Stuck

Only one grandson story, I promise. Justin Daniel, now an engineer building bridges, was a precocious child. One evening, when he was about three-years-old, he and his parents, Sam and Susan, were over our house for dinner.

As we were clearing the dishes, Sam announced, "I think we'll go out on the town and leave Justin here to spend the night with you."

Justin did not take to that idea. "I have a very nice red-brick house (we lived in a wood-frame house), with a very nice bedroom where I have all my favorite toys. I want to go home and play with them. I don't want to stay here."

Sam put his hands on his hips and stared at his son. "Listen kid, we're going out and you're staying here. End of discussion."

I could see Justin's lips quivering with anger and frustration.

Sam and Susan picked up and exited our house with Justin looking out the window pane of the closed door as his parents pulled out of the driveway in their car. Justin started to cry pitifully.

Diana tried to comfort him, pointing out that since his parents had left, they couldn't hear him crying and it would have no effect on them. "So why bother?" she counseled. "On the other hand, if you stopped crying, we could sit down and play games and have a grand old time."

"Not fair," he sniffled.

I turned to Justin, shaking my head. "I don't know what you're crying about. We didn't expect to have to babysit you, when we would've gone out ourselves."

Justin straightened up and faced me, and taking a line right out of a Sesame Street song, he groused, "I guess I'm stuck with you and you're stuck with me!"

NOW WHAT?

Legal Vignettes of Private Practice

Story One: A Startling Legal Maneuver

When you think you've seen it all in court, an event happens to humble you.

I was one of the attorneys defending an antitrust civil class action case where one of the lawyers on the plaintiffs' side was an assistant attorney general for a state. I'll call him Steven.

Steven was homely, no doubt about it, and he had an aggravating, gravelly voice and a combative, surly nature that made every minor dispute, a major battle. I had the impression this disagreeable attorney was disliked by even his co-counsel on the plaintiffs' side.

But I'll give Steven credit for one thing--he came up with the most startling maneuver in this long and protracted civil proceeding stretching over years. Having missed several court sessions, we wondered what had happened to Steven. Then one day, a new attorney showed up on behalf of the state attorney general's office named Stephanie, at least we thought it was a new attorney. It wasn't. Steven had had a sex change operation--the reason he missed several court sessions-- and now represented his state as Stephanie. If he was homely as a male, you can imagine how he, excuse me, she, came off as a female--with the same looks, same voice and the same surly deposition. If he/she intended the operation to be a distracting presence in court, he/she certainly succeeded. But it didn't help. Plaintiffs still lost the case.

CARL L. STEINHOUSE

Story Two: Object, You S.O.B.!

Ever know a guy that was nice enough, but had idiosyncrasies that could drive you to distraction? Well, read on.

Sometimes clients get fed up with their attorneys. It works the other way too, but attorneys are less likely to express their discontent to the hand that feeds them. I'm thinking of personal little quirks of a client that bugged the hell out of me.

I was defending a client in a civil treble damage antitrust lawsuit against an entire industry. My client's in-house lawyer was one such person that frequently set my teeth on edge. First of all, he was extremely indecisive in two areas, parking spaces and menus. When driving, we dreaded entering a half-empty parking lot. He'd drive around and around for ten minutes trying to decide which parking space to pull into. We'd grumble, "Just pull into any damn space," but he'd just ignore us, pandering to his compulsion.

No less trying was a dinner in a restaurant. Like the parking spaces, he simply couldn't decide for the longest time, what to eat. After he'd finally ordered, like clockwork, he'd disappear for, I'd estimate, over forty-five minutes. This happened at every dinner meal. What he did during that time, I have no idea. When he returned, if his food had sat too long and was cold, he'd send it back. It was embarrassing. A meal with him took three hours, if we were lucky--usually time we could ill afford to spend, having to prepare for the next day's trial. When the president of his company, scheduled to testify, stayed over at our hotel and called me for dinner, I said fine, but I really didn't have the time for a three-hour extravaganza. He caught on right away.

"It's my in-house counsel, isn't it? You don't have to answer because *I* dread having dinner with him."

288

NOW WHAT?

I picked up the president at his hotel room. "Come on in, I'll just be a second," he said. Then he dialed the room of his in-house counsel, letting it ring once and hanging up. He smiled. "I guess he's not in his room. We'd better go eat without him."

He got no argument from me.

In court, the in-house counsel could be just as unsettling. He'd sit right behind his trial team, of which I was the lead attorney. He'd constantly whisper orders to object to this or to that--a very poor strategy when the testimony is harmless. Multiple meaningless objections can lead the jury to believe you want to hide something bad to your case. During the testimony of a rather famous icon of the industry, the judge and the jury sat in rapt attention while he testified to the history of his illustrious family. The in-house counsel kept whispering in my ear, "Object, it's irrelevant" or "Object, it's hearsay." Well, I shook my head and refused. The testimony may well have been irrelevant or hearsay, but it was rather favorable to our side and I was loath to anger the judge and the jury, who were hanging onto the witness' every word.

He finally whispered into my ear, "If you don't object, I'll call your managing partner and have you replaced."

Well that did it. I turned around and whispered back, "If you don't shut up and let me try this case, my managing partner will have to replace me because I'll pull the entire trial team out of this court and explain to your president why."

That shut him up for the duration.

Story Three: What Not To Say to a Judge--Most of the Time

    Sometimes you have to put your foot in your mouth to accomplish your objective.

    I represented an individual client, the general sales manager of a defendant corporation, in a price fixing criminal action brought by my old outfit, the Department of Justice. Now I'm well versed in grand jury practice, having spent fifteen years as a prosecutor. I knew what these Justice attorneys were pulling because they tried it out on my client, that is, they offered to give him immunity if he would testify to *specific* facts A and B, and implicate C, or *anyone* in an executive vice president position or higher. Can you see what that does? The individual client suddenly sees a way to avoid jail by agreeing to the Department's version of the facts, *whether true or not*. It's a damn good inducement to perjury, so I got the full story out of my client *before* I presented Justice's deal. Those facts were not true and being a moral man, he did not go for the offer.

    But just think. There were maybe sixty witnesses, all offered that deal. I guarantee that if the prosecutors called them before the grand jury and gave them immunity, it was because they accepted that deal with the devil and would testify to facts they way the prosecutors wanted, not the facts they knew to be true.

    My client and many others in the industry were indicted for price fixing based on such testimony. During the pretrial motion phase I moved to dismiss the indictment on the basis of grand jury abuse by the prosecutors, arguing that the grand jury had no way of ascertaining the truth with the sixty witness pressured by the Department to testify a certain way.

    In the argument before the judge I accused the prosecutor of gross abuse. The judge looked at me.

    "I don't see what I can do," the jurist said.

"Sure you do, Your Honor. If you dismiss the indictment the prosecutor will learn, he's a smart man, not to abuse the witnesses if he wants his indictments to survive."

At that the chief prosecutor, a burly man, flew out of his seat and charged me, yelling, "How dare you?"

Fortunately, his co-counsel restrained him.

The judge waited for the room to calm down.

"I don't have any power over the Justice Department," he insisted.

I shook my head. "You know Your Honor, I come from the Northern District of Ohio and I never heard our Chief Judge whine he had no power over the Justice Department."

My co-counsel sat there frozen. I think some sidled away from me.

The judge absorbed what I had just said and then sprang out of his chair on the bench. He leaned forward, an angry scowl on his face. "If you said what I thought you just said, I'll whine you right into the hoosegow, Mr. Steinhouse."

In the end, he didn't throw me in jail nor did he dismiss the indictment. Well, at least it was nice to know he learned my name.

But I accomplished my purpose. The prosecutor's boss, the chief of his office was in the courtroom. He knew I, a former chief, was right; he also knew any conviction would be vulnerable to any appeal I promised to initiate. We had a meeting of minds. My client pleaded out for a small fine and no jail time. Many of the other individual defendants were not so fortunate.

CARL L. STEINHOUSE

Story Four: Hit 'Em with the Bottom Line

German businessmen are very meticulous, leaving no stone unturned when making a decision, and the prospective client, CEO of a German manufacturer with a subsidiary in the United States, was no exception. He had a carefully worked-out plan to hire the best lawyer in Cleveland to defend him. He did this by conducting many interviews of lawyers and law firms. It seems he and his American subsidiary were under criminal grand jury investigation for price fixing.

When he visited me, he was quite blunt.

"I am very impressed with one of the attorneys in Cleveland that I interviewed and I'll probably hire him, but because you have a fine German name, I decided to see you. This other attorney, I must tell you, graduated first in his law school class, has had a lot of trial experience, and became the youngest partner ever in his law firm. Can you match that?"

I could have matched that and then some by pointing out that in addition, I prosecuted cases like that for fifteen years in the Justice Department and, as their former supervisor, I'm on a friendly basis with all the prosecutors in the Great Lakes Office, including those conducting this investigation. But I didn't mention any of that. I had only one clarification and a question to ask this German CEO.

"Notwithstanding my 'fine German name' my ancestors have nothing but Russian blood in their veins. That out of the way, let me ask you this. I have defended dozens of individuals indicted for price fixing and none has ever gone to jail. Can the attorney you were so impressed with match that?"

He hired me. Nothing succeeds like success.

NOW WHAT?

Story Five: You Can't Get More Dramatic Than That

I did a lot of antitrust compliance lectures for my clients, trying to teach company officers and salesmen how to avoid violating the antitrust laws, particularly price fixing. The clients liked my lectures because they felt I made an impression on my audience who generally ignored dry and boring legal lectures. I was successful because I was graphic--very graphic. I'll give you an example.

I posed this question to my audiences: "Let's assume you've had a full day at your trade association meeting and congregated at the bar with counterparts from your competitors. You are relaxing. Now suppose one of your competitors, over friendly drinks, proposes to stabilize the price of product X, in other words to fix its price, and eliminate all the vicious and loss-producing price-cutting. Others around the bar, sipping their martinis or scotch neat, seemed to murmur approval of the idea. What would you do, based on what you heard today? Would you get up and leave immediately?"

The officers and salesmen all voiced their approval with that action as the best way to avoid getting themselves into legal trouble.

"Wrong!" I would shout, pounding the table. "In criminal law, you often get convicted not so much what you have actually done as what you have *appeared* to have done. Three years from now, when the grand jury is questioning the witnesses about this gathering at the bar and some squealer who was given immunity tells about the price fixing conversations and identified who was present, do you really think he'll remember that you quietly slipped out of the room?"

I saw several heads shake no.

293

"Of course he won't! The government will nail your ass to the wall along with everyone else."

"So what do we do?" a voice shouted out.

"I'll tell you. You leave in a manner that no one in that room will ever forget."

"How?" someone else in the audience asked.

"Simple. Be dramatic. One sure way is to hop onto the bar and take a leak, yelling, 'I'm not staying for this discussion. Goodbye!' I guarantee you nobody will ever forget you left."

And I guarantee you, dear reader, that no one in that audience ever forgot that example.

Story Six: Bring Your Toothbrush

A Japanese manufacturer acquired our client, an American manufacturer in the same line of commerce. This occasioned a frantic visit from the general manager of the American company.

"Mr. Steinhouse, I'm at my wits' end. My new boss in Japan has spoken to our competitors and insists that I adhere to a price schedule they all agreed on. I told my Japanese boss that I did not want to go to jail for price fixing and he just waved away my concerns as meaningless. I'm not about to do anything that will land me in jail; but on the other hand, I don't want to lose my job either. What am I going to do?"

"Is your Japanese boss scheduled to visit your company anytime soon?"

He nodded. "As a matter of fact, yes. He's due in next week."

"Okay, here's what to do. Put off any action on prices for a week and arrange a meeting between your Japanese boss and me. I think I can change his mind."

The next week, in the client's main conference room, I met with two Japanese gentlemen and my American client. The man was who clearly the boss was a very old, wizened, diminutive gentleman. The younger Japanese turned out to be his translator.

I don't remember the boss's name. I'll just call him Mr. Saito.

I tried to explain the American antitrust laws to Mr. Saito and how his American employee could not agree to prices with his competitors because there was the risk of going to jail.

The translator repeated my remarks in Japanese. The old man nodded. I was wary. My experience in Hawaii with the Japanese was that they always seemed to be agreeing with you by nodding their heads and smiling but in fact they were merely signaling that they understood what you said.

I pressed on. "Does Mr. Saito understand why his American employee can't do what was requested?"

The translator conferred with Mr. Saito in whispers. I don't know why because neither of us Americans understood a word of Japanese.

"He understands but Mr. Saito says that ending price competition is important to profitability and his American employee must take risks for the good of the company."

"I don't think Mr. Saito quite understands what I just said. Tell him the next time he comes to the United States, he should bring his toothbrush."

"Excuse me, Steinhouse-san; I'm not sure I understand."

"Just translate verbatim for Mr. Saito."

He did.

"Mr. Saito says he always takes a toothbrush when he travels, but what does that have to do with anything?"

"It would be nice for Mr. Saito to have his own toothbrush when he gets thrown in jail on his next visit. When I said there was a risk of going to jail, I meant Mr. Saito was at risk. You see, if the American employee is caught fixing prices, the Department of Justice will go after the boss who ordered it. As soon as Mr. Saito comes into the United States, they'll have jurisdiction and snatch him."

The translator spoke to Mr. Saito. Both got up, bowed, thanked us, and left.

Later that day the order was rescinded.

NOW WHAT?

Story Seven: Water? What Water?

Major law firms go out of their way to woo
talented law school graduates to their offices. Our firm
was no exception. One way is to get them a year or two
before they graduate and give them a summer internship
at the firm at a very generous stipend. We'd wine and
dine them during their stay and try to demonstrate what a
great place Cleveland was to live and work.

I'd look forward to getting into a deep
conversations with the interns and then suddenly tell
them, "Enjoy this while you can; when you're hired to a
permanent position here you'll work your ass off and be
treated like dirt." You may think that's
counterproductive to all the effort the firm is putting into
these interns. Not really, because the law students,
especially the ones we go after, are not dummies and the
word quickly gets around the law schools as to the actual
working conditions at the law firms. They know what's
going on--for example, a magazine cartoon circulating
around the law schools at that time showed a sprightly
intern passing the office of a clearly frazzled associate
who sticks his head out and whispers, "Don't work here."
Since the interns already have a good idea of what's
going on, it's much more impressive to be honest. They
appreciate it and have much more confidence in what you
have to say thereafter.

Part of the intern program is to hold a round of
parties throughout the summer at various homes so they
can see how the firm's attorneys live--and be duly
impressed. It became a tradition to hold a lobster bake at
my home every summer. I had a tennis court and plenty
of acreage for volleyball, badminton, Frisbee, etc. It
actually became a selling point to obtain interns. The
firm catered the party, which was held *al fresco* on my

lawn, until one year, it poured, forcing all the guests into my junk-filled garage next to my garbage cans. Thereafter, the firm sprung for a tent, which of course guaranteed it would not rain.

Serving the clam chowder at the lobster bake

But they didn't anticipate water from within. The night before the lobster bake this one year, we had heavy winds and rain. I woke up the next morning and heard a drip, drip, drip sound. I don't know about you but I hate to be surprised with a drip, drip, drip sound because you know it's never good news. I got out of bed--so far, so good. Then I entered the hallway leading to the living room. A new sound emerged--worse that the drip, drip, drip--squish, squish, squish. I took off my slippers. Sure enough, my feet felt the soaking wet hall carpet. I squished into the living room--again, soaking wet. Where the hell was the water coming from? I could find no obvious leaks in the house. I finally went outside around to the back of house.

I was an amateur carpenter--very amateur. I had built a wood plant stand, about six-feet tall, and it stood against the house next to the outdoor spigot. The stand wasn't quite as sturdy as I thought. The wind had collapsed it, smashing the stand and the flower pots against the spigot, breaking the pipe off *inside* the wall and dumping water there all night until it eventually flooded the living room and hall. Now while it is true that the lobster bake is held outside, we didn't get away that easy because the guests do come into the house to use the facilities, schmooze, or enjoy our artwork. I wasn't about to rent a Porta-John, so we got one of those carpet-cleaning companies to come out and soak up the water. A few hours after they left the water, still remaining in the carpet lining, percolated up to the carpet surface returning us to squish condition red.

The lobster bake went ahead without much of a hitch. We roped off the living room and hall telling the guests it was under renovation. I threw a few ladders and tools in there for effect and let the guests go through the family room and kitchen to reach the facilities. Nobody complained. They were too busy filling their faces with clam chowder, Maine lobster, steamed cherrystone clams, buttered corn, roast chicken (there are always a few allergic to seafood) and all the beer and wine they could drink.

Besides, one of my partners kept them entertained with his annual rendition of poem, *The Shooting of Dan McGraw*.

CARL L. STEINHOUSE

Story Eight: My Last Defense: Prosecuting the Prosecutors

There are times when an indicted client may, technically at least, be guilty, but the circumstances surrounding the act or acts makes it highly unfair and inequitable to prosecute, thus requiring innovative defenses. In my last month in practice before I retired I had just such a client, who, along with his company, were indicted for price fixing, with a maximum penalty, at that time, of three years in prison.

Our client, the owner of a manufacturing company, found out that his general manager had violated the anti-nepotism rules of the firm by hiring and paying his daughter and showing her preference over other employees in the office, creating a morale problem. The client reprimanded the general manager and forced him to fire his daughter. In a fit of anger, the general manager contacted the Antitrust Division of the Justice Department and accused his own company, his boss, and the rest of the industry of conspiring to fix prices. His evidence was very thin, so the Feds urged him to encourage his competitors to arrange an agreement on prices for various products in that industry. The Feds set up a recording device on his phone.

The general manager called each of his competitors and, in recorded phone calls, induced some of them to agree on a fixed price. It was obvious that, with a little encouragement, some in the industry were not above such activities. Based in significant part on the recordings of the telephone calls placed by the general manager, the Antitrust Division indicted several companies in the industry along with some of their officers, including my client and his company.

My partner and I felt strongly that this was a clear case of entrapment instigated by the Justice Department. We knew, however, that such a defense rarely succeeds, so we looked for an alternative tactic to show the unfairness of this prosecution of our client. We came up with an unusual one. We knew it was a long shot but perhaps one with which we could make our point.

Since the Justice Department attorneys urged the general manager to try to entice industry members into an illegal arrangement and set up the recording device on the general manager's phone, we sued Justice under the Sherman Act, alleging it was a coconspirator in the price fixing scheme and asked the court to enjoin such conduct. As far as I knew, it was the first such action of its kind.

It came before Federal Judge M, a fair but no-nonsense judge, and one very tough on lawyers. The Justice Department moved to dismiss the case; the judge refused and we went to a hearing on the injunction. My partner and I had the opportunity to cross-examine the chief of the Great Lakes Antitrust Office and the staff members involved in investigating our client (actually we called them as our witnesses but because they were hostile parties, the court permitted us to conduct our examination as if it were a cross-examination). We watched the Justice attorneys squirm on the stand just a little, trying to first, put the best face on their instructions to our general manager and second, to explain why, after their investigation, they still ignored proof that the general manager had an ulterior motive to lie in order to get back at his boss and the company. Some of the Justice staff called as witnesses I had supervised earlier when I had been in the Justice Department and chief of that office, and they were not amused. But you do what you have to do to represent your client.

It was not a surprise when the judge dismissed our action after the hearing. But we accomplished our purpose. We were able to get the unfairness of Justice's action before the court, which let my partner (I had since retired) negotiate a favorable plea agreement that got our client off with a small fine and no jail time, a deal that was immediately approved by Judge M.

VII. TRAVEL ADVENTURES

CARL L. STEINHOUSE

Asia--They Come In Threes

Ever hear the old canard, disastrous air plane crashes occur in series of threes? Well, I think the same thing is true of close calls on airplanes, as well. At least that is what happened to us on a single trip to the Orient while we were still living in Hawaii.

Diana and I decided as long as we were this close to Asia (well, it is only 3900 miles to Tokyo from Honolulu and that is close, relatively speaking, compared to our prior home in Yonkers, New York), we'd take a two-week holiday to some countries in Asia. It was a good deal. The babysitting was free (well, it was for us-- of course, it did cost my parents a few thousand dollars to fly to Hawaii from the East Coast) and we hooked up on a tour with about forty local Hawaiians.

Don't worry; this is not going to be a travelogue, so I'll get right to the airplanes. Our first flight, on Pan American, left Honolulu bound for Tokyo. It seems we encountered unexpectedly strong and persistent head winds, so much so that the pilot decided we'd never make it to Japan. Running low on fuel, he decided to make an emergency landing on Wake Island, which had only one runway. As we approached, the pilot ordered us to assume the crash position because there was a dangerous cross wind and, notwithstanding the peril, he had no choice but to land the plane. I removed my glasses and assumed a modified fetal position. The Boeing 707 jet came in hard, bounced up in the air and came down, again hard. The plane tipped precipitously, causing the right wing tip briefly to scrape along the runway. By the time the plane was brought to a halt, trailed by dozens of emergency vehicles, it had blown all its tires. It seems Pan Am could repair the wing tip easily enough but we had to wait a day in Wake Island for the airline to fly in a new set of tires. We reached Tokyo a day late, but without further incident on that flight.

Flying from Tokyo to Hong Kong on our second flight, we took a Taiwanese plane of China Airlines, a Lockheed Electra. Let me explain to those of you who are too young to know. Lockheed Electras became notorious when several of them, for no apparent reason, lost wings in flight, with calamitous results. I swore I would never fly on an Electra but what was I to do? I was on a tour and did not want to be left behind in Tokyo. So when I boarded the plane and confirmed it was an Electra, I took a deep breath and settled into my seat. I almost regretted it. We stopped off in Taiwan briefly and then taxied to take off again. The pilot revved the engines and we started down the runway and we kept rolling down the runway and rolling down the runway. You get a sense of when a plane should be in the air and clearly, this plane wasn't going up. I stiffened. As we approached the end of the runway I heard the plane's engines suddenly reverse and off the runway we bounced onto a grassy field before finally coming to a stop. I looked out the window, expecting to see an Electra wing left back on the runway. No, both of them were still attached. The pilot came on the intercom and apologized. He had to abort the landing, he explained, because of a malfunctioning lavatory. Now I have heard lame excuses from airlines before but this one receives the award for the most chutzpah, blaming the almost-crash on the crapper.

Number three flight was about to occur. We were leaving Hong Kong for Thailand on Japan Airlines. All the stewardesses paraded up and down the aisle in stunning kimonos. Indeed, it was a momentous occasion for JAL--it was the inaugural flight introducing the brand new Convair 880 jet liner into service. Flying in first class were high-level JAL and Convair executives.

I don't know if you've ever flown out of Kai Tak Airport, but in the best of times, it's a hair-raising experience. The airport, abutting downtown, is surrounded by high-rise apartment buildings and on takeoff, the aircraft must ascend rapidly and turn sharply to avoid clipping those structures. As our brand-new Convair 880 took off, it seemed to clear the buildings by only a few feet and I could clearly see laundry hanging out to dry on the roofs.

A half hour into the flight, I looked out the window and there seemed to be oil streaming out of one of the four engines, blackening part of the wing. I pointed this out to the stewardess.

"Ah so. Not to worry," she assured, "it is a new plane and has to be broken in. The pilot is well aware of everything."

Nothing she said alleviated my concerns and I insisted she inform the pilot. Now she looked annoyed but before she could dismiss me as a nuisance, the pilot came on the intercom. "We are having a problem with one of the port engines, and since we are not yet halfway into the flight, we will return to Hong Kong. Drinks will be with our compliments."

I looked out the window again--I was on the port, or left side of the plane--and this time I saw smoke billowing from that same engine. Eventually (that can be a relatively long time when you're 30,000 feet up), the pilot managed to get the fire under control and we limped back on three engines. I did not look forward to landing over the apartment buildings and into Kai Tak on three engines so I took up JAL on its offer and had several martinis, which seemed to resolve my anxieties. Since I am writing about this, you can assume we landed without incident, although for the second time on this trip, I had to assume the fetal position during a landing.

Just some asides on the trip because they are human-interest material. Hawaii has no railroads or subways and, unless a native-born Hawaiian had traveled

outside the state, he or she would never have the
opportunity to ride on a train

In Japan, our tour included a ride on one of the
trains connecting Tokyo and Nara. The Hawaiians
stepped onto the high speed train with great trepidation,
like they were taking the same risks as the astronauts on
the first manned flight to the moon. The train swayed
slightly along the tracks, totally petrifying the Hawaiians
who hung on for dear life.

"How are we going to get off," one of the
quivering Hawaiians asked me.

"Don't worry; they slow the train down enough so
you can jump off." The worried look on his face told me
not to kid him. The train will come to a complete stop
and you can get off just like you do on the local busses."
Now that he got the picture, he could smile--until the
train lurched again.

The very same people that went through the crash
landing on Wake Island with total aplomb were
completely cowed by this uneventful railroad trip.

One other thing most Hawaiians have never
experienced is snow. It was late March and when we
went up to a resort in the mountains near Nara, it snowed
overnight.

"What is *that*?" one Hawaiian woman exclaimed
the next morning as she exited the lobby doors to the
outside.

Standing outside at the time, I educated her.
"That's snow," I said.

"Oh my gosh, I'd never thought I would see snow
in my lifetime." She bent down and picked some up and
looked at me, perplexed. "It's cold."

"Yes," I explained with just a hint of sarcasm in
my tone, "it generally is; that's what causes it to become
snow."

CARL L. STEINHOUSE

After a few snowball fights and some rolling in the slush, the Hawaiian group had enough and made a beeline for the warmth of the resort dining room. While it was a rather balmy (for snow) 40 degrees, these protected Hawaiian souls had never experienced temperatures below seventy. For them, this weather was like an Arctic blast and a few minutes of exposure was all they could take. But now they had stories some day to tell their grandchildren of how they braved the wild ride on the passenger train and withstood the bone-chilling cold to play in the frigid snow.

NOW WHAT?

Scotland--Circa 1974

Story One: I Slept with Her but it's not What It Looks Like

During his teens, we sent our son Sam to a wonderful adventure camp where the boys learned to fend for themselves. No camp songs of undying loyalty, no color wars, just exciting adventure, be it rock climbing, hiking the glaciers, or bicycling in Europe. Chris, the camp owner, had a great relationship with "his boys." Forty years later, Sam and Chris are still friends, periodically exchanging visits.

The trip in question took the adventure camp to the British Isles where the adventurers would bicycle through England, Ireland, and Scotland. After Sam left for camp--and the British Isles--Diana and I were trying to decide what we would do for vacation. I hit on the bright idea of camping and bed and breakfasting in Scotland. (Then it was a bright idea, today you couldn't get either one of us into a tent.) The fact that we'd be in the same general area as the adventure camp was never a consideration since we had no idea where in the British Isles our son would be on any given day.

Driving up to Scotland in our rented car, we picked up a hitchhiker, a pre-med student named Andrew. He was a pleasant young man and we had no objections to his tagging along with us for a while. He was perfectly willing to sleep in the car.

One evening, Diana announced that she had no intention of sleeping in the tent that night. It was that time of the month and she simply did not feel up to it. We found her accommodations at a bed and breakfast, a neat sheep farm in the Highlands. Satisfied she'd be well taken care of, I invited Andrew to share my pup tent.

""I've always had a thing about heather. The name alone impresses me," I told Andrew. "Can we find some heather to set up the tent in?"

"I think I know just the place, about a mile down the road."

A few minutes later, there was the hill, covered with a riot of purple of beautiful heather. We pulled off the road and bounced up the hill with the tent. Bounced, because the heather turned out to be quite cushiony and an ideal place to bed down. After wolfing down sandwiches graciously supplied by the sheepherders, we chatted for a while and decided to turn in early.

It was about six in the morning when daylight began filtering into the tent. As soon as I awoke, I knew something was wrong. The stench was unbelievable.

"Jesus, Andrew, what the hell did you do? You stink like hell!"

Andrew grunted, but clearly, he was still asleep.

I turned over to face Andrew and inadvertently jabbed a dirty, wooly apparition, sprawled out between Andrew and me. The thing awoke with a bleat and in a panic, stood up in the tent, bringing it down around the heads of Andrew and me in what turned out to be a full grown female sheep that had slipped into the tent while we were sleeping and snuggled between us. It took quite a while to untangle ourselves while that ewe was bleating, kicking, and thrashing around. Believe me, if I'd had a knife handy, I would have cut open the tent to affect a rapid exit.

Bruised and now smelly, we finally extricated the ewe and ourselves from our intimate sleeping arrangements. I looked sternly at Andrew. He denied inviting the ewe in the tent for immoral or any other purpose.

I smiled benignly and assured Andrew his proclivities and preferences were of no concern to me.

NOW WHAT?

When we picked up Diana at the sheep farm, the sheep herder smiled and asked, "Did ye enjoy the bonnie sandwiches we provided?"

"They were very good," I replied, "but I did not appreciate the extra ewe that you threw in."

CARL L. STEINHOUSE

Story Two: Oh, Ye Take The High Road And I'll Take The Low Road

After our close encounter with the P-ewe, we headed down the road to Edinburgh. Serendipity set in.

"Look, Carl," Diana said excitedly, "I think I recognize one of Sam's camping buddies on that bike."

Sure enough we came across several more familiar bikers.

I rolled down my window. ""Do you know where Sam is?" I yelled.

"About a mile ahead of us," came the response.

I speeded up and pulled in behind the familiar figure on the bike, waiting at a traffic signal.

I walked up beside him. "Sam, if you're late for dinner again you'll be grounded for two weeks!" I bellowed.

A space alien might just as well have materialized out of the sky. He was speechless.

I stood there, with my hands on my hips, smiling.

Finally he got his voice back. "Dad! Mom! Where did you come from? How did you get here?"

"If you must know, I came here from lying with sheep and Mom from lying with sheep herders."

He looked at me, totally confused.

"Never mind, I'll explain it to you later. Now, just give me a hug."

NOW WHAT?

Israel--Past Life in Palestine?

We visited Israel in 1973 and joined in celebrating its 25th anniversary as a nation. It had been a traumatic year for me. First, I was in the process of changing jobs, harboring a lot of self doubts about the wisdom of the moving from something I was comfortable doing to the unknown; going from the Justice Department over into private practice with a leading Midwest law firm. Second, my mother was dying of cancer.

Until I visited India, many years later, I was sure that the roads in Israel were the most dangerous in the world--no, not from terrorism but from the Israeli drivers themselves. I noticed that the horn, not the brakes, is the main instrument of accident avoidance (I can tell you that it is not a particularly effective approach to safety); that the right way goes to the driver with the most chutzpah, and finally, that crosswalks are considered pedestrian target areas.

What struck me as most strange were all the Mercedes Benz automobiles clogging the roads. Virtually all the taxis were Mercedes. Here, I spent my adult years distaining to purchase automobiles manufactured by one of the companies that had served the Nazi cause, often by working slave labor, mostly Jews, to death. Yet the country I would expect to find most sensitive to this issue was awash in German cars. Of course there's an answer; there always is. The Mercedes shipped to Israel were part of the reparations package from Germany so that these luxury cars were damn good deals in that Middle East nation. Well, at least they were wrecking German cars on the Israeli roads.

We visited Jerusalem as the Sabbath approached. The Fourth Commandment says "Remember the Sabbath day, to keep it holy" and "On the seventh day, . . . thou

313

shalt not do any work . . ." The people of the ultra-religious neighborhood of Mea Shearim take Ten Commandments, particularly that one, very seriously and we were warned not to drive through that area on pain of having our automobile stoned by those orthodox Jews who consider it a sin to do any work on the Sabbath, menial or otherwise, including riding in automobiles, cooking, or turning on lights or electrical appliances. Sabbath or not, inappropriate dress could also subject the wearer to the wrath of the inhabitants. And you thought the Old City's Arab section was dangerous!

We in fact did stroll in the Old City, passing through the Arab quarter, in order to get to the site of the holy Western Wall. The British, when they had the Palestine mandate, named it the "Wailing Wall." When Rome destroyed the Second Temple in 70 C.E., only the outer wall remained standing. And that's the Western Wall. It became a holy site to the Jews well before the emergence of the State of Israel, a place to pray for the return of the Jewish homeland.

The Western Wall with the Temple Mount in the background

The wall became imbued with a mystic quality where religious Jews regularly hold Sabbath services and chant prayers while visitors come simply to pray to Almighty--or gawk. Eventually, a custom developed where beseechers to the Lord slipped into the cracks in the Western Wall, pieces of paper containing handwritten prayers. Well, that's what I did, slipping into one of those openings my written prayer for my mother's recovery.

Author depositing written prayer at the Western Wall

While in Tel Aviv, shopping for a gift for my mother in the lobby of the King David Hotel, a woman came up behind Diana and said, "Hello, Joann."

Diana turned around. "Excuse me? My name is Diana."

The woman had a sheepish look. "Of course. Sorry, from behind you looked just like Joann. She's a good friend of mine."

Diana nodded. "Were you expecting her?"

"Not really. She lives in the United States and I have no information that she's coming, but I had a strong premonition she'd show up in Tel Aviv."

Diana frowned. "A premonition?"

The woman smiled. "I'm what you call a 'sensitive.' Supposedly I can sense things beyond the ordinary. Well, I sensed that Joann would be here in Tel Aviv. Obviously, I'm wrong. Do you mind if I relate something I sense about you, Diana?"

"Sure, go ahead."

This woman, I'll call her Ms. Sensitive, continued. "I sense that you're an old soul from around these parts."

315

"But I've never been to Israel before."

She shrugged. "As I said, it's simply what I sense. I can't give you anything more definitive than that."

We ordered a watch for my mother, to be picked up in a few days. We bid Ms. Sensitive goodbye and headed for Haifa, a delightful Israeli port city on the Mediterranean. Well, delightful until we entered the old section of the city. When we reached in a neighborhood with a street going down a long hill to the harbor, I noticed Diana getting very antsy.

"What's the matter?"

"I'm not sure but I want to leave. I have the feeling I know this place and that something terrible happened to me down there." She pointed down the hill.

"But you've never been here before!"

"I know, but the feeling of despair is very strong. Please, let's leave this place."

We made a beeline out of Haifa and several days later found ourselves back in the lobby of the King David Hotel in Tel Aviv to pick up the gift we had purchased earlier.

Sure enough, we ran into the Ms. Sensitive again in the hotel lobby.

"Diana, I want you to meet Joann," placing her hand on her companion's shoulder.

Diana's eyes widened. "You mean Joann actually showed up in Tel Aviv after all?"

"Yes, I told you I sensed her presence and she showed up right after you left."

Diana nodded. "You know, I had one of the sensitive moments myself in Haifa. I had the feeling I knew a particular neighborhood and street and that something terrible happened to me there. I couldn't wait to leave."

Ms. Sensitive frowned. "Can you describe where in Haifa you had this feeling?"

"In the old city, on a street with a long hill leading down to the harbor."

She looked at Diana. "That's where Jews were massacred several centuries ago during the period of the Crusades."

Diana discussing her premonitions in Tel Aviv's King David Hotel

Diana nodded. "I could almost picture it happening. I felt as though I had been transported back in time to that horrible street."

Ms. Sensitive smiled. "I told you, you were an old soul, now I'm sure of it. I have a feeling though, that you won't want to remember that part of your past life."

Diana shook her head. "Certainly not if it was in Haifa."

CARL L. STEINHOUSE

Alaska--I Prefer My Moose to Be a Dessert

Diana and I explored Alaska one summer--well, sort of--partly by cruise ship, partly by tour bus. Coming face-to-face with a grizzly by backpacking in Denali State Park was not my idea of a vacation and certainly not Diana's.

Exploring the Alaska tundra sounds exotic and adventurous. The tundra--just the name conjures up a wild, frigid frontier. What excites the imagination about Alaska more than the tundra? Well, forget about it. Our bus tour through the tundra consisted of miles and miles of what looked like mounds of the stuff you strive mightily to keep out of your garden--moss. That's it! We saw no polar bears or other animals from the bus window. The only animals I did see were not while I was safely ensconced on the tour bus.

Here's what happened. We stayed at some inn in the tundra, east of Fairbanks. Sleeping was not easy since the summer night hours were dark for only an hour or two before bright daylight greeted us. So, tossing and turning one night--or day--I arose at about three in the morning, looked out and, seeing a bright, sunny day, decided I needed exercise. I dressed and went out onto the highway for a slow jog, the only type of jogging I would tolerate--jogging had the same excitement and attraction for me as fishing--in other words, zilch.

I got out onto the road in my NYU tee shirt, lavender shorts (school colors), and Reeboks, custom-made for slow running. A half a mile down the road, which was totally devoid of automobile traffic, I saw the bushes rustle and stopped to investigate (any excuse to stop jogging is good enough for me). Out strolled the smallest, cutest moose calf I ever saw--well, maybe an exaggeration, since I don't think I ever saw a moose calf before. I kind of cooed to it, you know, like you would

318

talk to a four-month-old baby. It looked at me non-committally. While I was enjoying this moment of communing with nature and its creatures, the bushes rustled again, this time accompanied by a very loud and very disconcerting bellowing. Out charged mama moose, much taller than I and some 500 pounds heavier. She didn't seem impressed by my alma mater, NYU. Killing my sense of communing, I didn't wait to ascertain big mama's intentions. I did a crisp and smart about-face, and took off about ten times as fast as I came. My slow jog outing turned into a 100-yard dash that would do an Olympian proud. Did big mama chase me? I have no idea because I didn't turn around until I reached the inn.

When I did, big mama and baby had disappeared back into the brush and the road was once again quite empty.

When I returned to the room, Diana propped herself up in bed. "Where have you been? I was worried."

I shrugged. "You needn't have been. I simply decided this was an opportune time to be one with Mother Nature."

She looked at me suspiciously. "And was looking at the tundra close up, more exciting than from the tour bus?"

I smiled. "You might say so. It took my breath away."

CARL L. STEINHOUSE

Africa

Story One: Alitalia Screws up Coming and Going--the Coming Phase

Our trip to Africa did not start out auspiciously. Our mistake was flying on *Alitalia*. We arrived in Rome to connect with a flight to Nairobi, Kenya. We were checked into our connecting flight in Rome's Leonardo DaVinci Airport and advised it would be delayed. We sat in the boarding area with the rest of the passengers. At nine in the evening the crew finally arrived. The plane's lights came on. We still sat. No *Alitalia* agents advised us of anything--anything at all. Ten o'clock came. I noticed the plane was now dark. The crew must have sneaked off. We looked for an *Alitalia* agent. The desk was deserted. Now it was eleven o'clock and the only activity in Leonardo DaVinci were the restiveness of the stranded passengers and the Italian soldiers patrolling the corridors with their Uzi submachine guns.

Several of us took matters into our own hands. We left the boarding area and confronted the Uzi-wielding guards. One does not ordinarily become aggressive facing the business end of a submachine gun that can spit out 600 rounds a minute, but desperate people resort to desperate measures. Of course, the guards only spoke Italian and we set upon them screaming in English. Shouting, "*Alitalia, Alitalia,*" they finally got the message and got on their portable radio. A half-hour later an *Alitalia* agent showed up, no explanations, no apologies, and herded us on buses to a nearby Holiday Inn. Undoubtedly, if we hadn't taken matters into our own hands, we would have spent the night in the airport boarding area.

NOW WHAT?

We finally arrived in Kenya the following afternoon. But with *Alitalia*, the worst was yet to come.

CARL L. STEINHOUSE

Story Two: A Bull in a Kenya Stop

Racing across the Serengeti in Kenya in a Range Rover-like vehicle driven by our guide, Moses, and believe me, there were several times on this trip where all six of us tourists felt we needed deliverance. The first incident occurred on a narrow dirt road. As we rounded a bend, Moses slammed on his brakes, propelling us all to the front of the vehicle in hasty fashion (there were no seat belts). In front of us, a huge bull elephant blocked the road.

Moses, our intrepid driver and guide

"What do we do now, Moses?" I asked.

He smiled (he always smiled. I'm sure if an earthquake swallowed him whole he'd go down grinning). "I will first institute Plan A," he reassured.

"Which is???"

He answered by blowing the horn. The bull didn't take kindly to that and answered with ferocious trumpeting, much, much louder than Moses' horn. Then he charged with the obvious intent of crushing the vehicle and all the annoying insects within.

"What's Plan B?" I implored in a near state of panic.

Moses answered with a grinding of the gears as he jammed the transmission into reverse and started backing up with the pedal to the metal, as they say.

The elephant chased us for a few hundred feet then stopped. So Moses stopped.

"Why are we stopping?" One of the tourists piped up.

Moses turned around. I would have rather he kept his eyes on the bull elephant. He still had that damn smile. "Once we backed away," Moses explained, "the elephant was satisfied that it had successfully asserted its dominance and therefore had no need to pursue us any further."

"So Plan A was a mistake?"

Moses smiled. "With that bull, it certainly was. We will wait here until he leaves the road."

Sure enough, several minutes later the bull elephant disappeared into the brush, and Moses started to move forward.

"Wait a minute," someone protested. "What if he's laying in wait for us?"

Moses laughed. "He's too big to lay in wait; besides, elephants just don't do that. They're not like tribesmen with spears."

"You mean we could be attacked by spear-bearing tribesmen?"

Moses shrugged. "It's not likely."

To tell you the truth, I would have been far more comforted if he'd said, "Absolutely not!"

Story Three: Setting a Table for the King of the Beasts

The next day, Moses found us a pride of lions. He explained to us that the lions would ignore us because they can't smell the humans *inside* a running vehicle over the stench of the exhaust from the engine. So, with the canvas roof of the vehicle pulled back, we bravely stood up and started photographing the beasts, which were mostly lying around in the sun, except for two that were having a grand time copulating. Moses explained they could continue that way for hours on end. It gave new meaning to titles like Richard the Lionhearted.

We started to move away when he suddenly stopped the car. "Ladies and gentlemen," Moses announced, "I'm afraid we have a flat tire on the right rear."

"So what do we do?" I asked.

Moses smiled. "We change the tire, of course."

"What do you mean 'we'?"

"Well, since we have no jacks in these vehicles, it will be necessary for all the men to lift the right rear end while I change the tire."

"Wait just a cotton pickin' minute," I protested. "Once we leave the vehicle, won't the lions will catch our scent?"

He smiled. "You are, of course, absolutely correct."

"I don't know about the rest of the passengers but I'm not going to be part of the dining table for those lions."

Murmurs of assent rose from the rest of the passengers.

"Oh, I wouldn't worry," he said soothingly, "I will radio the park rangers who will come out here and protect us while we change the tire."

NOW WHAT?

Well, that certainly made me feel better as I waited for half an hour for some heavily armed rangers to move in and surround the vehicle.

We saw the dust rising in the distance.

"There he is!" Moses exclaimed excitedly.

He? I wondered. Not they??

Sure enough, a single ranger pulled up in a Range Rover, hopped out and took a position between the pride of lions and our vehicle. His weapon? A riding crop held smartly under his right arm, his hand gripping the leather handle.

Viewing the unimpressed lion from the roof deck of our vehicle while awaiting the park ranger

CARL L. STEINHOUSE

Park Ranger to the rescue while we fix the flat tire. Note Diana eying his "weapon"

"That's our protection?" we said rebelliously.

Moses smiled. "Not to worry, he knows what he is doing."

"Where's his gun?" someone cried out.

Moses shook his head. "Oh, they're only allowed to carry them when they are pursuing poachers."

The lions viewed the ranger with idle curiosity, all that is, except the two having sex; they just continued, oblivious of the drama unfolding. (At least we saw it as drama.)

We finally filed out of the vehicle and we lifted the right rear (with three men, it was much easier than I ever imagined) holding it up while Moses changed the tire. All of us had our eyes glued on the pride. If any of those lions made the slightest move toward us, I'm sure as one, we'd have dropped the vehicle on Moses and scrambled back inside.

The tire changed, we thanked the ranger and went on our way to our next stop, the Mount Kenya Safari Club, nestled in the shadow of Mount Kilimanjaro. Once checked into our very luxurious room, we immediately left to engage in Diana's favorite activity, shopping. We found the club's gift shop and while we eying with

326

interest an acrylic painting by local Kenyan artist named Heidi Lange, the proprietor, a good looking man, listened indulgently and chain-smoked as we excitedly related our adventures of the past few days.

To get the price down on the Lange painting, I tried buttering the shopkeeper up a little. "Did anyone ever tell you look just like the American actor, William Holden?"

He smiled and nodded. "As a matter of fact, get that all the time because I am William Holden and I own this whole place."

I paid the asking price for the Heidi Lange.

CARL L. STEINHOUSE

Story Four: Most Unforgettable Character

My most unforgettable character was not human--but I am getting ahead of myself.

Diana and I arrived at the lodge at the base of the Virunga Volcano Mountains in Rwanda, the country often called the Switzerland of Africa, with its mountains and lush greenery.

At seven the next morning we were transported to the national park. Three guides, one armed with an automatic rifle, the others with machetes, met us. Seven of us, with three porters, were led past the farms at the base of the mountain. Knowing we would be hiking up mountainous terrain, we had trained in Cleveland--well, sort of--by walking up long hills. There were no mountains to speak of in northern Ohio. Believe me; we were unprepared for climbing through dense forest and jungle. We found out what the machetes were for--to hack through the dense underbrush and thick bamboo. That accounted for the use of the machetes but not the rifle. Finally I worked up the nerve to ask the guide why he was carrying a rife. "To protect us from the vicious gorillas?" I naively asked.

"Oh, no, Sir, to shoot poachers, if we come across them--they are usually armed too, you know."

Oh great, I thought; now they tell me about the ongoing war with the poachers and a potential firefight. The poachers, the guides explained, kill the magnificent gorillas for their hands--it seems they make great ashtrays. I looked at my own hands. Nah, I thought, no would be interested in mine to extinguish their butts. Besides, I had dirt under my fingernails--not an appetizing ashtray. I did wonder that whether from a distance, with my full beard, I might be mistaken for a gorilla--granted, a puny one, but a gorilla nevertheless.

Halfway up the mountain the lead guide suddenly disappeared up in the air. I looked up. There he was dangling upside down, his left leg caught in a noose hanging from the top of a tree. It was a poachers' game snare. The other guides cut down the sheepish leader, who, it turns out was unhurt except for his dignity. So there really were poachers out there. Great.

Along the way the guides destroyed several gorilla traps they had found. There was never a guarantee that we would find a gorilla family. We certainly wouldn't have on our own. But the guides were very adept at discovering the signs of recent gorilla presence--spoors (you know, the like the dog stuff we try to avoid stepping into on sidewalks) and nests (yes, gorillas have nests--not to lay and hatch eggs but to sleep in, usually low in the trees).

Diana, the guides, and porters in search of the mountain gorillas

We were exhausted, climbing the mountain for two hours--and a little discouraged, because sometimes it took up to four hours to find them. Suddenly, the lead guide stopped and put up his hand for silence. He took out his field glasses and pointed. "They're up there," he whispered.

We were given instructions. No loud noises and no sudden movements. If a gorilla charges you, they advised, drop to the ground in a groveling position and that usually satisfied them. I focused on the word *usually*. No mention was made of that in the travel brochure!

Slowly we ascended. I spotted the dominant male in the group, a huge silverback probably weighing 500 or 600 pounds. Then I saw three adult females, two juveniles and one infant gorilla. Forget all my earlier bitches. This was worth all the trials, tribulations, and money it took to get here.

Silverback gorilla we encountered, the alpha male

I watched the big silverback swing through the tree. The branch broke under his weight and he tumbled out of the tree onto the ground, flat on his back. He looked at me and sat up, running his arm across his eyes. I swear, the big lummox was embarrassed.

Well, the cameras clicked and the VCRs whirred. The animals more or less ignored us until--there I go again, getting ahead of myself.

I was like a pig in mud, as the saying goes, taking snapshots and videos. I walked down this path, apparently made by the gorillas. There on the side of the path was a juvenile, about a quarter the size of an adult, and really cute, enjoying the inside of a bamboo stalk, a gorilla delicacy. I slowly brought up my camcorder and began shooting. Damn! My wife also was so anxious to see that she pushed against me shaking my camera.

NOW WHAT?

Without taking my eye off the juvenile, I hissed, "Stop pushing, you're ruining my shot."

Twenty feet behind me, I heard Diana say, "I'm nowhere near you, dear. You'd better turn around."

I did and right in my face was this 600-pound silverback, already very impatient to get around me on the path. As my mouth dropped, he grabbed me by the waist with one of his large hands, tossed me off the path, and busily continued on his way. He didn't hurt me, but I did fly about a few feet in the air. Normally, my wife would get hysterical. I asked how come she was so calm with this 600-pound behemoth on top of me. She responded that she just knew he would be gentle.

We left the gorillas after our time limit of one hour in their vicinity. Halfway down, Diana was exhausted. She couldn't take another step. Her porter took the backpack and gave it to her. That was strange; she needed help not a greater load. Then it was all clear. He hefted Diana on his back and carried her the rest of the way down the mountain.

CARL L. STEINHOUSE

Story Five: Mamba Mambo and Dashing Hippos

After we visited the mountain gorillas of Rwanda, we made a beeline down to the game preserve in Botswana. On arrival, we were assigned to our own cabin, about one hundred yards from the main building which housed the dining room. Notwithstanding the existence of the camp, we were told that this was considered a wild area with no protective enclosures, so whenever we left our cabin, we were advised to be on the lookout for elephants (head for the closest building for protection), monkeys (watch your handbags and cameras--they'll snatch them away), and mambas, the deadly snake in those parts (if you hear a hissing, head quickly in the other direction).

It was close to eight o'clock and starting to get dark when we left our cabin to walk down the path to the dining room. Ten steps down the path, I heard the dreaded hissing. Scared witless, I pushed Diana back where we came from, and with shaking hands, finally managed to get the key in the lock, get into our cabin and slam the door behind us.

Ten minutes later, we tried again and again we were greeted with hissing. Again, we retreated to our cabin. (This time I had not locked the door!) My God, there must have been deadly mambas all over this place and it looked like dinner (included in our tour) was no longer an option.

"Damn it, I'm hungry," I groused to Diana.

Grabbing my flashlight (it was pitch black by now), I opened the door once again.

"Are you crazy, Carl? What are you doing?" Diana was never noted for outstanding bravery in the face of danger.

"I'm going out to investigate", I said. "Perhaps the bright light will chase the mamba away." Of course, I

332

had no scientific evidence or the background to support such a theory, which Diana pointed out in no uncertain terms. Shrugging, I stepped outside--gingerly.

I went the same ten feet and there it was again! The hissing. Gulping, I whipped my flashlight in the direction of the sound. I smiled and went back and fetched Diana.

We finally arrived at the dining room where the others were already halfway through the meal.

"Where have you been?" the tour guide inquired.

"Dodging those intrepid hissers. After all we didn't want to be soaked by your damn sprinkler system!"

The dreaded mamba? Or just sprinklers?

* * *

The hippos of Botswana appear to be a very serene and peaceful. They languished a lot, floating lazily in the middle of the river; only their young ones cavorted around.

Several of us hired a guide and what was essentially his rowboat with a small outboard motor, to take us up river to see these gentle-appearing creatures.

As we approached within a few hundred yards of a group of hippos--they turned out to be a lot larger in person than we imagined--the guide turned off the engine.

I looked quizzically at him. He caught the look. "Noise upsets them," he explained. "It's safer to just float for a while as we observe them."

I nodded tentatively. I wasn't entirely convinced this was the safest course of action. But the strategy seemed to be working, that is, until another, bigger, louder boat roared up next to us.

That pissed off the hippos. Now a hippo doesn't look designed for speed, but believe me, looks are deceiving. Two or three male hippos began to roar and let me tell you that Little Red Riding Hood would have been far more impressed with the size of the mouth and teeth of those hippos than any old big bad wolf in grandma's clothing. And fast--they began covering the few hundred yards between us with amazing grace and speed.

Big daddy hippo heading for us

The big boat that started all this, of course, had its engine running, so it had no problem reversing course and scampering off. We, on the other hand, were sitting quietly and dead in the water, as our guide frantically jerked on the starter cord, trying to get his engine to catch. Three hundred yards became two hundred yards and the hippos were gaining rapidly. We could almost smell their bad breath. Yank, curse, yank, curse (it was a tribal language so I can only assume he was cursing as I certainly would have been). At twenty-five yards the outboard motor finally roared to life, and the guide twisted the accelerator handle with great force while jamming the boat into a violent u-turn, sending all tumbling to the bottom of the boat.

Once a safe distance away from the no longer threatening hippos, our guide smiled and announced he

would now set out to show us a herd of elephants. We
assured him we'd pay his full fee, if today, at least, he
just took us directly back to camp without the privilege of
encountering those magnificent beasts in his boat.

CARL L. STEINHOUSE

Story Six: Ad-libbing in Zimbabwe—1990

The day of vacation started innocently enough. It was, after all, only an overnight stop in Harare, Zimbabwe--formerly known as Salisbury, Rhodesia--to catch the once-a-week plane to Nairobi. How did I know I'd be arrested as an agent provocateur?

It was Christmas morning and Diana and I had a few hours to kill. Our flight wasn't until noon. We got up early to explore. I read my trusty Fodor's guidebook on Zimbabwe and off we went to hit the streets. Harare presented an unusual scene--a large, all-black city, decorated with white Santa Clauses--a vestige of the Rhodesian days of white rule.

Walking through downtown, I indiscriminately recorded video impressions of the city. A photographer once told me: in order to get one outstanding scene, you must take 100. I used up a lot of tape. In the end, it was self-defeating. I had so much footage that I never edited it. The tapes ended up in my "will do" drawer, behind the Amazon, Alaskan, Australian tapes--well, you get the picture.

Anyway, two black men in business suits, one quite tall and the other of medium height, came up to us from behind. The tall one said to me, "Excuse me, we would like to speak to you."

My wife gets nervous when approached by strangers in foreign lands. Once, in the Paris Metro, a man tried to grab the pocket computer in my fanny pack; another time in Barcelona, a boy on a motor scooter snatched the purse of one of our traveling companions.

Sensing my wife's discomfort, I said to these two gentlemen, "Look, I don't want to buy anything and I don't want to discuss politics or America; we just want to be left alone."

We walked away and they followed us. We went through this routine several times. Diana was frightened.

NOW WHAT?

I had had enough. Pointing to a traffic cop, I warned, "If you don't stop bothering us, we'll go to the police."

The tall one smiled. "We are the police."

Uh, oh, I thought. "Are we under arrest?"

"Not yet, we just want to talk to you."

My finely-tuned lawyer's ear caught the "not yet". It was not encouraging.

"And if refuse to talk to you?" I asked, knowing the answer.

He smiled, pulling back his jacket lapel far enough to show me his holstered revolver. I decided not to ask if the gun was loaded. "Just follow us, please."

We crossed the street and entered a four-story office building. Walking up to the second floor, we were ushered into the one room office of a police officer, I'll call him Inspector Magumbe. I don't really remember his name but it makes it easier to tell the story.

"We are sorry for the inconvenience but we want to ask you some questions. Please be seated."

"We are inconvenienced," I said. "We must be on the once-a-week flight to Nairobi. *We* are outraged by your conduct."

Diana whispered under her breath, "Speak for yourself!"

Harare police were very touchy about this building

I can tell you that bravery cuts no ice in a situation like this. Inspector Magumbe made a phone

337

call, smiled, and remained quiet. We sat that way for five minutes.

"Well, ask your questions already," I complained peevishly.

"A detective from Central Police Headquarters will be here soon to pick you up. They'll question you there," Magumbe said.

"What are we supposed to have done?"

"You, not her." He smiled, as if that explained everything.

Finally, for what seemed like hours--actually, 15 minutes--two more detectives arrived. Diana was told that she was free to go, but declined. They shrugged and bundled us into the unroomy back seat of their small Fiat.

We drove for a long time. I thought this might be an elaborate ruse to kidnap us--for what reason, I hadn't the foggiest idea. I was wrong. We finally arrived at Central Police Headquarters and were led into the Chief Inspector's office.

"Sit down, please," the Chief Inspector said. There were two hard chairs in front of his desk. We sat. He stared at us for a few minutes. The two detectives remained in the room.

He asked our names, addresses, and occupations. I was a lawyer, I told him.

"In what law firm?" he inquired. I didn't trust him.

"Jones, Day, Reavis & Pogue."

"Hmm, I never heard of it."

"It's only the second largest law firm in the world," I said, adding, "with offices all over the globe, except, of course, here in Harare."

The smile left his face. "Why are *you* in Harare?"

"I'm a tourist on vacation."

"Then why were you taking videos, 'Mr. Tourist'?"

"I told you, I'm on vacation. That's what tourists do. It's illegal to take videos?"

"Don't be smart, I'm the one asking the questions here."

I tried flattery. "I was simply recording all the sights and sounds of this beautiful city."

That didn't work either.

The Chief Inspector bored in. "You're really a journalist for South Africa, aren't you? And up to no good in Zimbabwe!"

"Of course not," I said, "I'm just a lawyer on vacation. I've never even been to South Africa." That was the truth.

He swiveled his chair so that his back was to me. Suddenly, he stood up, wheeled around, and pointed his finger two inches from my face. "You're an agent provocateur, aren't you? Admit it!"

I wasn't even sure what an agent provocateur was. I read it in a few spy novels, but never dwelt on it. *Boy, has this guy one overactive imagination!* I thought.

"Me, an agent provocateur? Why, when Zimbabwe freed itself from the yoke of racist Rhodesia, we celebrated."

I could see Diana's eye roll. I am a criminal lawyer. She's frequently heard me wax eloquent about clients who failed to follow the cardinal rule of never, but never, ad-libbing when questioned by the police. You can meet yourself coming back.

He pounced. "How did you celebrate?" He was up to something.

"We went out to dinner and ordered a fine wine for a toast."

Diana closed her eyes.

"Aha," he said, thinking he found an opening. "If that is so, then precisely when did we obtain our independence, Mr. Wise guy?"

Diana slunk down in her chair.

"April 1980."

339

He lifted his eyebrows. "What day, precisely?"

"The eighteenth."

Amazed, he exclaimed, "That's right!"

"I told you."

After a few more questions, he told us we could go. After I complained that I had no idea where I was in Harare and had a plane to catch, he told Spike--that was his name, I swear it--to drive us to our hotel.

On leaving, Diana whispered, "How did you know the date?"

"Read Fodor's guide book, this morning," I whispered back.

On the way to the hotel, Spike said that South African guerrillas had earlier blown up one of the buildings I had videoed.

"The government just restored it and we thought you might be scoping it out for another try," he explained.

We arrived at the hotel. Our guide, Solomon, was angry.

"Damn Americans--no consideration. You are late and we have a plane to catch. Now, I must rush and put myself in danger."

It's tough to dress down someone named Solomon, but I tried. "Look, Solomon, I just about had enough from you people. It just so happens I was arrested and tortured by the Harare police at Central Police Headquarters. Isn't that right, Spike?"

He smiled. "Oh, absolutely, Mr. Steinhouse. But we were careful not to leave any marks, now weren't we?"

I nodded. Solomon turned ashen, put our bags in the car, and didn't utter another word during the rush trip to the airport.

I gave Solomon a good tip and as we boarded the Nairobi flight, I waved good-bye to him.

NOW WHAT?

Story Seven: Alitalia Screws Up Again--The Going Phase

Returning home, *Alitalia* outdid their incompetence in getting us to Africa. Once again, we had to make connections in Rome on the way home. We arrived around eleven o'clock in the morning. The airport was a madhouse and once again the passengers on our flight were herded into a boarding area similar to the one in which we nearly spent the night. The airline announced the boarding of our flight, but not from the boarding area where we were sequestered. The plane took off without us!

Now we met others who had been waiting over a day for the same flight. It seems that *Alitalia* was two days behind in flying their passengers back to New York. A few of us raised hell with the agent, to no avail. This situation required an innovative approach. I took out my business card and carefully printed in black ink, PRACTICING ATTORNEY BEFORE THE FEDERAL AVIATION ADMINISTRATION OF THE UNITED STATES.

I handed the card to the agent and demanded to see an officer of *Alitalia* immediately, or I was going to call Washington concerning the airline's landing rights at Kennedy Airport. That brought an official of *Alitalia* to our boarding area. I threatened that all sorts of dire consequences would be visited on *Alitalia* if our connection wasn't met within the next two hours. I don't think he believed me--I wouldn't have--but he obviously decided to not to take the chance and we found ourselves on the next flight out to Kennedy, much to the consternation of passengers who had been waiting for a flight longer than we had.

Now, I turn down any tours that involve a flight on *Alitalia* for any leg of the trip regardless of how short.

CARL L. STEINHOUSE

Hospitality--Soviet Style

The National Conference on Soviet Jewry ("NCSJ") dedicated itself to pressuring the Soviet Union to permit Jews, desiring to leave the country, to emigrate to destinations of their choice. But the Soviets couldn't admit that their society was anything less than a workers' paradise and that people would actually want to depart that utopia; hence, the Kremlin resisted letting Soviet Jews emigrate. Merely to apply for an exit visa was to visit upon the applicant all sorts of discrimination by the state. But most of the Jews refused to withdraw their exit visa applications. Those trapped Jews were called "Refusniks."

NCSJ worked on many fronts to assist the Refusniks. Members of NCSJ, usually couples, visiting the Soviet Union on "vacation" would bring in requested medications and supplies and take out requests for the next couple to bring in. In the early 80's, we had scheduled a trip to the Soviet Union and agreed to bring in medications and supplies. Among the supplies were many pairs of American jeans because at that time, the Refusniks could sell those at high prices in Moscow to help support themselves.

On arriving at the airport in Moscow, our luggage was searched thoroughly and while the many pairs of jeans elicited some interest, they were left alone. What was confiscated was a James Bond 007 novel by Ian Fleming and my wife's MS Magazine.

On Friday evening, Sabbath eve, we knew that the Refusniks gathered at the main synagogue in Moscow and there is where I would contact them. Sure enough, we found a large crowd milling about in front of the synagogue and we managed to hook up with an English-speaking Refusnik who relieved us of our supplies and promised to direct them to the intended recipients.

342

"Who is in need of anything?" I said. "We can bring that information back for the couple who will be visiting next time."

"Keep your voice down," the Refusnik remonstrated. He nodded his head in the direction of two men standing off to the side. "There are KGB agents all over the place," he whispered. "You should see Professor Soyfer. He desperately needs your help. He's standing over there, pointing to a man of medium height in his early forties."

"Does he speak English?"

The Refusnik nodded. "Go over and speak to him before he leaves."

Street in front of the Moscow Synagogue

We introduced ourselves to Professor Soyfer who told us he could really use our help. He invited us to his apartment for tea. Valery Soyfer owned a small flat in a large apartment complex. He lived there with his wife and daughter.

He explained that he had been head of the Molecular Genetics Institute of Moscow when the board of the institute suddenly fired him because he was a Jew who had applied to emigrate. Soyfer was sure the government had leaned on the board to take that action. His wife, a public school teacher was fired from her job, also for the same reason. Now, this noted molecular geneticist, in order to put food on the family table, worked as a janitor in the apartment house where he lived.

"What's even worse," Soyfer offered, "is that the doctors at the hospital won't treat my daughter who has a kidney disease. They insist nothing is wrong with her. She must get treatment soon or she will be in real trouble."

"Can you withdraw your exit visa application?" I asked.

He shrugged. "It wouldn't matter. Once you've applied you're tarred permanently. Besides I don't want to withdraw it. I have several offers for employment in research in America, but the Soviet bureaucrats block all my attempts to respond by mail, cable, or telephone. For all those people in American know, I am not interested in their positions. Some of these noted geneticists could put pressure on my government, if they only knew I was a prisoner in my own country."

"Tell me what can I do?" I asked.

He nodded. "I can give you the names, addresses, and phone numbers of several people in the United States. If you could contact them and tell them I am interested in their positions but am not allowed to communicate. If they, and the Israeli ambassador, could raise loud protests, it would help immensely."

Soyfer gave me all his contact information, which I jotted down in my small notebook.

His face darkened. "The KGB probably knows that you visited me. Don't let them find that information on you. It could spell trouble for both of us. You'd better memorize your notes and get rid of them."

"How" I asked.

"By the time-honored Soviet way. Tear them up and flush them down the toilet."

I knew I couldn't trust my memory for such an important subject. I would have to figure out another way.

NOW WHAT?

I always carry a spare camera on my trips. I asked him if he could use one of them.

"That would be very nice. I could get a good price for a fine camera. It could feed us for a month."

I gladly handed the camera over to him.

* * *

Back at the hotel, I photographed all the notes I had taken and then ripped them up and in Soviet fashion, flushed them down the toilet. It was a good thing I did.

The next morning, we had a Moscow tour scheduled. Walking toward the bus, I realized I had left my camera up in the room.

I ran up to the room, waited for the floor matron to let me in (guests were never supplied with keys--the matron on each floor let you in). She hesitated.

"I'm in a hurry, can you move faster?" I'm not sure the matron understood English, but she could not miss the impatience in my voice.

She fumbled for the key for a while then knocked. I wondered why.

When she saw my impatience was at its limit, she finally opened the door and I barged in on two men in suits, going through my belongings.

"What's going on here?" I demanded.

"Maintenance men," one of them stammered in broken English. "Excuse please."

"Maintenance men in business suits? Come on!"

Shrugging, they both left the room closing the door behind them. Soyfer was right; the KGB agents were looking for anything the geneticist might have given me. What he had given me now existed as negatives in my camera.

At our departure from Moscow, I was only worried that the KGB would find an excuse to detain us. It knew we contacted Refusniks in front of the synagogue

345

in Moscow; and it knew I visited Valery Soyfer in the dead of night.

As our passports were being checked, I was asked to follow a police officer into what I guessed was an interrogation room. The policeman rummaged through a box and found the envelope he was looking for. He ripped it open, discarding the envelope.

"Is this yours?" he asked, handing me a book and a magazine.

I looked at them. It was my James Bond 007 novel they had taken from me when I had arrived and the MS Magazine taken from my wife. I nodded.

"Take them with you," he ordered.

I'll tell you one thing; the Soviet filing system is a hell of a lot better than ours.

On our return to the United States, I contacted all the people on Soyfer's list, including the Israeli ambassador, explaining the geneticist's predicament and asking for their help in approaching the American government and the Soviet embassy to raise a hue and cry.

I don't know if my calls made a difference, but two years later, while visiting Israel, I was advised by a government official that Valery Soyfer and his family had successfully immigrated to Israel.

Amazon

Story One: Hey, There's a Crocodile and Boa Constrictor in My Zodiac

We floated down the Amazon in Brazil from Manaus to the Atlantic Ocean. Well, that's a little misleading. We actually floated on a small cruise ship (about 40 passengers) and since it was an adventure tour, we spent a great deal of time in zodiacs (powered rubber rafts) exploring the byways of the Amazon. We were warned at the start to keep our hands and feet inside the boat at all times to avoid feeding the piranha and their ferocious appetites.

Zodiacs

Our leader landing a piranha. Note those teeth

347

The wilds of the Amazon were interesting, but once again, you're not here to read a travelogue, so I'll go right to the time several of the tour staff (a naturalist, a zoologist, and a biologist) decided one midnight to go out in a zodiac to capture a caiman, which is the name they give the man-eating crocodiles down here. To be sure, they only intended to trap a small one and bring it back to the boat for display, and then release it the next day. Why late at night? It gives us the ability to spot the bright red eyes of the caiman in the water with the help of a powerful searchlight mounted on the zodiac. The staff invited passengers to go along but only a few were interested in sharing a raft with a crocodile. I, of course, volunteered to accompany them. I was not one of those weak-kneed passengers--weak-brained perhaps, but not weak-kneed. Three other unwise passengers joined me.

Barely trolling along in an Amazon side stream, our searchlight sweeping the water ahead of us, we spotted two red eyes moving slowly in our direction. The eyes were close together, so the zoologist concluded it was probably a small caiman and one that we could handle. We slowly drifted up to it and the zoologist suddenly leaned over and grabbed the caiman by the neck before the reptile could take off his hand.

As we turned around to head back, one of the staff yelled out, "Look in that tree, there's a boa constrictor! Maneuver the boat under its branches and let's see if we can also bring us back that snake."

Now things were getting sticky. It is one thing to bring in a small caiman, but totally another to try to load into the boat, a boa constrictor. Besides, I wondered how in hell we would get that boa out of the tree. It was up about at least ten feet. I looked up at the tree and couldn't even spot the boa.

The zoologist had it all figured out and you're not going to believe this. But first, he had to have his hands free so, without asking, he simply shoved the caiman into my hands and I had no choice but to grab that thrashing caiman's neck and hold it at arm's length. Well, I didn't come on this trip to miss out on photographic opportunities like this, so I whirled around and slapped that caiman into the startled hands of passenger sitting next to me.

Surprised, he accepted the caiman in good humor

My hands free, I whipped my camera out of its waterproof sack and was ready for anything--or so I thought until I saw exactly how the zoologist intended to capture the boa--by shaking it out of the tree.

Boa in tree. Tough to spot

"Um, we won't know where it will land, will we?" I asked my voice clearly showing trepidation.
"True, but at least I can get it in the zodiac, I think."
"But we're in the zodiac too."

"Good, then it can't get away."

That was not the answer I was looking for. There had to be a better plan than that.

There wasn't. The zoologist shook the branches violently while I held my breath and took pictures.

Suddenly there was a thump in the boat.

"The son of a gun bit me!" the zoologist yelled out.

"That's bad," I said.

"No, that's good," he responded. "It shows we have a healthy and rambunctious snake."

I was about to issue a sarcastic observation on who needed rambunctiousness when I felt something wrap around my leg.

"Anyone locate snake yet?" the zoologist shouted.

"I have, he's wrapped around my leg," I yelled, perhaps a little frantically.

"That's good; at least we know where he is. Just sit quietly and I'll put it in this plastic bag. Don't worry; it's more afraid of you that you are of it."

That, I doubted very much.

He knew what he was doing and soon had unwrapped that boa from around my leg and expertly inserted it into a specially designed baggie with holes for breathing.

The boa bagged

The passengers were in for a treat. They could see creatures of the wild close up. Me, I already had hands-on experience--close up.

NOW WHAT?

Boa on display on board ship

Story Two: The Excitement of Sloth Watching

When we were in Manaus, we explored the outdoor market alongside the harbor, wandering among the vendors selling every imaginable item. A big business was done in captured wildlife. We came upon a sloth in a small cage, looking miserable and forlorn. (I learned later they always look miserable and forlorn,) I caucused with the other travelers. If it were possible to release the sloth in the wild, later in our trip, we would chip in and buy it. We consulted with our staff zoologist who confirmed we certainly could release it in the jungle. That did it. We purchased the sloth and dragged its box back to our ship.

The sloth was right at home on the ship

That sloth hung from the rafters of the ship or from a specially erected pole, moving nary a muscle for hours at a time. It was cute looking but watching a sloth in action is like watching paint dry. Anyway, he sailed with us for the better part of the week just hanging around--literally. The zoologist finally found an appropriate spot on the river and we piled into the zodiacs with the sloth and headed for shore.

The zoologist put him on a tree. He clung there. We waited three hours for it to climb a quarter of the way up the tree. When we were sure it was high enough up to

be safe from predators on the ground, we lit out. While
that sloth had no schedule to keep, our ship sure did.

I plan to retire to the life of a sloth; it's just that I
won't spend it hanging from a tree--maybe instead I'll be
ensconced in a Lazy-Boy. Wait a damn minute--I am
retired! What am I doing tiring myself writing these
memoirs?

India and Thailand

Story One: Mother Knows Best

Jai was not your ordinary Asian Indian. He obtained a law degree at Oxford and masters of law at the University of Virginia Law School. Hired by the Jones Day law firm in Cleveland, he became an esteemed partner of mine; his specialty was corporate acquisitions and mergers. He had it all: urbane, handsome, and quite the sophisticate--except when it came to do his mother's bidding. Momma, in New Delhi, India, selected the brides for all her sons, and Jai was no exception. Summoned by his mother, Jai flew home to India to meet his new prospective bride. I got the impression that mother's selection made it a done deal but she was willing to let her son at least meet his fiancé before the wedding. I don't know whether the match was really etched in stone, but the question became moot when a smitten Jai met his intelligent and beautiful prospective bride.

We were invited to the wedding in New Delhi. Who could turn down such an opportunity? His family was prominent in Indian society, his father a top Indian jurist, and we expected the wedding to be quite an extravaganza. We were not disappointed.

First things first. On arrival in New Delhi and after a good night's sleep, Jai's mother and aunts took Diana and several other American women guests to a sari house. Western style dresses, regardless how fancy and expensive, were out of the question; saris were the order of the day. At the sari shop, hundreds of fabrics, one more beautiful than the other, were laid out in dramatic fashion by the proprietor. Even Diana became embarrassed at all the fabric the owner had to pull out and exhibit--and that takes some doing because she is far

354

from a shy shopper at pulling out potential selections. It even bothered me but the owner assured me he was completely unperturbed; the indecision of his customers was expected, he explained, as he continually pulled bolts of silk material off the shelves and snapped the fabrics sharply to roll and spread them out in expert fashion to present the best display. A consensus finally reached, Diana had picked out two fabrics to be made into saris-- one sari for the less formal ladies day affair and one sari for the highly formal wedding itself. When I saw the finished product on Diana, I developed a much greater respect for the ladies' consensus--the wedding sari looked sensational on her.

Indian weddings are typically a three-day affair. On the first day there was a ladies' reception; on the second day, we attended a religious ceremony in the morning followed by the wedding itself that evening; and finally, on the last day, his parents threw a big catered bash.

At the ladies' reception in the home of Jai's parents, all the men, including Jai's father, a prominent jurist in India, were relegated to the lawn in the back of the house. We could hear the women laughing, screaming, dancing, and carrying on. I thought I was eavesdropping on a bachelors' party! We were lucky that someone thought to bring some food out to us exiles. While lawns typically do not hold my interest for very long, if at all, and this lawn was nothing but your standard grass plot, albeit large in size, there was one feature that sparked my curiosity.

"What are those oxen doing eating the grass on your lawn? How come you permit it?" I asked Jai's father.

He laughed. "I can see you have not been in India very long. That's the Indian lawnmower. I hired these gardeners to trim the lawn and they bring their own equipment, those oxen. And the fertilizer is free!"

The big day had arrived. The religious ceremony is quite impressive visually, but don't ask me to explain it. These rites take up the entire morning. Several Indian holy men, sitting cross-legged in a circle, light what appears to be incense and candles, chanting prayers in a language not known to me, and involving, each in his or her turn, Jai, his brothers, his parents, and relatives.

Holy men preparing for the ceremony

Mid afternoon and we were told to come to Jai's parents home. I wondered why. The wedding wasn't to take place until the evening. I discovered and was surprised by the preparation of dress required for the men. Each male guest was assigned, for want of the proper term, a turban master, whose job it was to wrap a turban around the head of the guest. This is no mean feat and requires a great deal of dexterity to get the turban to stand up and not collapse. My turban master sat me on a webbed chair on the lawn behind the house. I was but one of many male guests being attended to. My turban master picked up a large roll of a muslin-appearing material and started to unroll it around my head. Unroll is perhaps a simplistic term for the procedure because building a turban requires a special talent to keep the material from collapsing around the eyes, ears, and nose. It took him the greater part of an hour to get that turban just right. The result was a headpiece that added close to a foot to my height. We all received bright red turbans. That color, I learned, had been assigned to the groom's family and guests. The men in the bride's family and male guests showed up at the wedding all wearing white turbans.

Author being turbanized

Dressed for the wedding

Diana and I arrived at the hotel, she in her gorgeous formal sari and me in my tall turban, feeling like, well, a Sikh warrior. As we got out of the cab, I started ascending the steps to the lobby when the doorman--who really did look like a Sikh warrior--literally tackled me and held me in a bear hug.

For a minute, I thought I was being taken away for interrogation.

"Don't move a muscle," he said into my ear.

"Terrorists?" I whispered hoarsely, sure the end was near.

"No," he whispered back. "Your turban is caught in the taxi door and if you move your head one more inch or take another step forward it will totally unravel."

Another Sikh rushed past me to the cab. I heard the cab door open but couldn't turn to look because the doorman still had me in a head vise. According to Diana, who was able to witness the entire debacle, about six feet of my turban ran like a thick ribbon from inside the cab to my head.

Once the material was released from the taxicab, the doorman, still holding my head, carefully sat me down on the steps and meticulously repaired the unwound portion of the turban. Apparently Indian men, especially Sikhs, are experts at, for want of a better term, turban raveling.

It's the custom, when the family can afford it, for the groom to ride to the wedding ceremony on a white horse, followed by a large marching band. Jai was no exception. The sophisticated corporate lawyer in high stakes mergers and acquisitions had shed his blue serge suit for gleaming white robes with a red sash, a bejeweled turban, and sported a long, curved sword.

The Groom

In this outfit, he intended to ride up on a huge white stallion and then canter up the marble stairs and into the hotel lobby. Security concerns for his prominent Indian family caused the guards to nix that idea. Thus, he arrived in an Indian automobile--a somewhat garishly decorated Ambassador--and walked up the stairs like most normal grooms do.

The groom's "white stallion"

The next night was devoted to gluttony--well, gluttony if you like chicken. In a large tent set up in Jai's parent's back yard, the huge quantities of every type of Indian fare graced the huge buffet tables. I can tell you that in India--and on these buffet tables--there are more ways to prepare chicken than I ever dreamed existed. If you didn't like chicken in India, you could end up looking like a modern version of Mahatma Gandhi.

Server sitting on one of the many buffet tables helping the guests

359

CARL L. STEINHOUSE

Story Two: Autos in India: It's Safer Wrestling Crocodiles

After the wedding days, Diana and I had an opportunity to tour some parts of India and I won't bore except to make some observations about Indian travel. We hired a driver/guide to take us to Agra to see--what else?--the Taj Mahal. Indian highway traffic is downright dangerous. I can say that categorically and without doubt, or as lawyers impressed with themselves would say in briefs, "beyond cavil." Let's put it this way: If I wanted to commit suicide, I'd hire a cab to drive me on India's highways. It would take a week, at most.

Let me give you an example. Our driver stopped at a railroad crossing with the gate down and warning lights flashing, waiting for the passing train to clear the crossing. Our auto was the lead car at the gate--waiting. As the train began passing, I noticed a strange thing. Other cars on our side of the crossing had begun jockeying up to the gate by going around the line of waiting cars and filling up the lanes for traffic going in the opposite direction!

"Serma," I queried my driver, "why are the cars lined up in the oncoming lanes?"

Serma shrugged. "They always do it. Indian drivers can be very impatient, you know."

I looked at the passing train and wondered with concern what was happening on the other side. "Serma, are they doing the same thing on the other side of the crossing?"

He smiled. "Of course."

"Isn't it dangerous?"

He shrugged.

The shrug was not in the least reassuring. The last railroad car finally disappeared from view and auto engines were revving up, waiting for the gates to rise. Sure enough, facing us in our lane was a line of cars from

360

the oncoming traffic. I gripped the seat tightly we and the rest of the autos did a dance macabre, weaving, avoiding, and cutting, tires squealing, and horns blaring. Amazingly, we made it through that grab-ass traffic madhouse with nary a scratch, though I can't speak for the other cars.

Diana and Serma--more calmer times outside the car

Speaking of trains, India has among the highest rate of fatalities, not only on its road, but also its railroads. And I can see why. The railroad cars are so packed that space even on the roofs of the passenger trains is at a premium. The train that passed us had hundreds of people hanging on for dear life to something on the roof with one hand and onto their luggage with the other, at the same time fending off hot cinders flowing from the smoke stack of the locomotive. I hope the Long Island Railroad commuters don't get any ideas reading this.

Story Three: Mahouts, Elephants, and Tigers, Oh My!

Part of our India tour took us into a game preserve with the tongue-twisting name of Bandavgarh. A highlight of the experience was an elephant ride through the tiger-infested jungle. We sat atop the elephant in a box-like compartment strapped to the animal. The driver, called a mahout, controlled the elephant with a long metal pole sporting a vicious-looking hook on its end, the hook held close to the elephant's eye, I assume as a warning to the beast to behave. It did not instill a lot of confidence in us bumping up and down high on the elephant.

Author and wife riding elephant in Bandavgarh

But, as it turns out, it was not high enough for me. We came upon a family of Bengal tigers sunning on a large rock. One very large male got up and stretched, clearly looking us over. I suddenly felt very exposed on top of that elephant, after all, isn't India known as the home of the man-eating tigers? All I know is that I saw the movie, *Jungle Book*, when I was a kid. And I do remember.

"Can that tiger jump up and reach us on top of the elephant?" I asked the driver.

"Undoubtedly, if it had a mind to."

"Then isn't it dangerous to approach them?"

Again, like the taxi driver, he shrugged, "They don't usually attack elephants, Sahib."

Tiger looking us over

And once again, I was not reassured. I didn't reply but focused on the operative word, "usually." I looked at the hook next to the elephant's eye and wondered why the pachyderm was not pissed off enough to swipe us off his back with his trunk and then stomp us, or alternatively, leave us on the ground as a gourmet meal for the Bengal tigers. Since I'm writing this, needless to say, none of those imagined scenarios occurred.

Story Four: Assaulted In Chiangmai

On our way home from India, we stopped off for a few days in Thailand. We took a trip up to the northern country, Chiangmai, to see the training school for elephants. Finishing our tour, we had several hours until our flight back to Bangkok and asked our driver-guide for suggestions on how to kill the time.

"I have an excellent idea. We have in Chiangmai, world-famous massage parlors. People from all over the world visit our parlors. I can get you a discount."

Diana and I looked at each other. There was always the chance we could be robbed or kidnapped. Burmese rebels were active in the area close to Chiangmai. We shrugged. What the hell, we'll never pass through here again.

There were no robberies or kidnapping. Only the roughest massage I've ever endured. We entered this room and stripped down to our underwear. Two women scantily dressed and hefty enough to be mistaken for sumo wrestlers came in and motioned us to two sheet-covered massage tables. I settled on the table, face down, and Miss Sumo Wrestler immediately pounced on me, sitting on my back straddling me. She also had the power of a sumo wrestler, pounding every inch of my body with a fury worthy of a Tasmanian devil. I heard Diana scream out but I was too engrossed in my own torture.

Once again we survived and surprisingly, none the worse for wear. But we promised ourselves to swear off these exotic vacations and perhaps try instead two weeks in the Catskills or a Princess Caribbean cruise to the Saint Thomas.

NOW WHAT?

Story Five: Mommy Dearest, Daddy's Gone!

Going to India without your spouse can be deleterious to your marriage. One of the women in our group did just that, leaving Cleveland happily married. On her return to Cleveland a tearful daughter met her. "Where's your stepfather?" the traveler asked.

"He's gone," she choked out.

"You mean on a business trip, don't you?"

"No, just gone."

"My heavens, did he die?"

The daughter shook her head. "No, he has moved out and told me to tell you he wants a divorce."

The trip to India, it turns out, was a wash: one marriage consummated, one destroyed.

CARL L. STEINHOUSE

Grand Canyon--River Run, River Fun, A Lot of Fact, and Some Fable in 2001

Eighteen years before, I had so much fun rafting down the Colorado, I decided I had to take my entire family on such a trip--well, almost my entire family. Daughter Jane and her husband Max, daughter Lani and her boyfriend Hyatt, and son Sam and his sons and my grandsons, Justin and Nick, joined me for the rafting trip. Diana said one rafting trip was enough for her and elected to stay home. Sam's wife, Susan, stayed home to tend to her ailing mother.

The raft glided smoothly through the currents of the river, under Megan's sure guidance. So far the water was low and the rapids not particularly challenging. But this one morning the Army Corps of Engineers apparently released water from the upstream dam at Lake Powell and the river was high with twice as much water volume. This made Megan nervous--it was her first as trip leader (we would've been nervous too if we had known that then)--and the ferocious Hermit Rapids was coming up. Even worse, Mike was at the helm and she knew what a cowboy he was with his 360 wheelies through the worst part of the rapids--if he turned the raft over during HER trip, she'd kill him. And her assistant, Amy was just as nervous. They weren't' the only ones. Eighteen years earlier, on a similar rafting trip with Diana, I was riding on the outboard pontoon of the raft imitating a bronco-riding cowboy when the rope broke torquing the pontoon and flipping me into the Hermit Rapids, which I had to ride down on my butt with Diana screaming to the leader to turn the raft around, *go up the rapids* and get me. Of course they had to wait for me to reach the bottom of the rapids to fish me out.

"Everyone down on the raft," Megan shouted, "and get good hand holds front and back; Hermit Rapids coming up!" Inexplicably, third guide Amy, began to do the "That's what it's all about" dance on one of the outboard pontoons and Megan, who never met a dance she could resist, forgot her concerns and matched Amy's steps, putting her right foot out. She never got the left foot out. A huge swell stood the raft on end and pitched Megan out of the raft. She tried to grab the Kool-Aid container--too late. Then Megan grasped Amy's life jacket for support and they both pitched into the Hermit Rapids.

Amy and Megan could dance anywhere, anytime

I, having been through this once before, hunkered down and gripped tight, damned if I was going to ride Hermit on my butt again. John and Lynn, the only sock-wearing rafters in the history of the Canyoneers (they would never reveal their deep dark secret of the need to wear wet, dirty socks all day), stood up. "Ole," John shouted, waving his arms and shaking his hips in glee, "this looks like more fun that assisted-living; let's jump in, too!" Lynn, who seemed otherwise intelligent, went along with John's hare-brained idea and both jumped in. Lynn's blood-curdling screams on hitting the cold river water could clean the wax out of your ears. Jesse yelled, "Cool," and started to stand up. Matt restrained him. "Sit down little bro, wouldn't you rather be an orphan than dead and departed?"

Meanwhile, Lani and boyfriend Hyatt, hanging on in the front seat of the raft went on smooching into the rapids without missing a beat, tuning out everything else. Justin, seeing his chance, tried to pitch his pesky brother, into the river. Dad Sam, oblivious, was too busy clapping in time with the dance until Nick complained to him that his brother had almost pitched him out of the raft. Justin gave his aggrieved, unjustly accused angel look, while Sam, annoyed having his concentration on the dancers broken, told Nicky to stop making up stories to get his brother in trouble. Nicky sputtered his protest but one fisheye look from Sam shut him up.

Jenn, braiding Juli's hair, admonished her to sit still. Jenn and Juli were the rather attractive college-age daughters of George who insisted on taking them on this trip. "I hope Dad falls in the rapids for making me go on this trip," Juli muttered. George didn't hear comment because he was crouched down low, under his enormous straw hat to keep from getting wet. Just because he was a civilian worker for the U.S. Marines didn't mean he had to act like one.

Juli and Jenn

The meantime, my daughter Jane, the mistress of embellishment, in a high-pitched voice, was recalling the time she allegedly almost drowned in a canoe going down rapids in Ohio. Max didn't believe a word of it and had he been listening, he would have said "fantastic." He learned early in his marriage that "bullshit" was not an appropriate response. It was all moot because Professor Max was preoccupied with the radio tower he'd spotted on the rim of the canyon and was busily framing a future lecture for his college class on the subject of radio communications in the Grand Canyon and the future of heavy metal DJs on the floor of the canyon.

Max and Jane

Mike, seeing Megan and Amy struggling to reach the vessel, accelerated the raft, keeping it out of their reach. "Good training for the girls," he said to no one in particular. A sly smile formed on his face.

As it turned out, there were no casualties. John and Lynn were pulled back into the raft by their socks-- I guess that's why they wore them--of course! But did Lynn learn her lesson? No! Two days later she would jump off a cliff into the Colorado, at John's instigation, naturally, arm in arm with him.

Megan and Amy, sputtering, were finally pulled back in the raft, whereupon they immediately continued their dance. "You put your left foot in, you put your left foot out, you put your left foot in and you wiggle it all about, you do the hokey pokey and that's what it's all about."

Daughter Lani

Juli complained that Jenn braided her hair all crooked. Taking umbrage, Jenn tried to throw Juli overboard but the martial arts training both received from Dad resulted in a wrestling standoff. George kept out of it because he knew the two of them, if provoked, could easily take him and he wasn't anxious to take a 45-degree dunking in the Colorado. Jesse, frowning, turned to Matt after his sock-wearing parents were hauled into the raft, and sighed. "Well, I suppose this means that we'll have to take this trip again next year."

Jane faced Max, who was still transfixed by the radio tower on the rim of the canyon. "Max, did I tell you how I just nearly lost my life on the Colorado?" Max maintained his gaze on the rim. "Fantastic, dear, now shut up and let me contemplate upper band signals on the lower canyon." Jane turned to me but I acted like I didn't hear her.

Up front, Amy and Megan were finally completing their dance. They had just put their whole bodies in and shaken them all about--and nearly fell in again.

Mike, still at the helm, spotted some mud flats and leering at Nick, Jesse, Matt, and Justin, said, "I have a great idea." Then he looked at Juli with a glint in his eye. She glared back at him. "Don't even think about getting that mud on me or you'll end up with a broken arm or your head in The Duke." The staff had named the army ammo can painted white with red trim topped with a toilet seat resting on top of it, "The Duke."

Author and the Duke

The group later surprised me with a 70th birthday party, but they weren't kind--inserting candles that re-ignited themselves after being blown out, turning the birthday boy blue. Megan and Amy treated me to a simulated version of their concept of "Sweet n' Low." I don't dare reveal how they described it.

Amy and Megan celebrating author's 70th birthday

But it wasn't the party that made me feel old; it was a fellow rafter's comment, "I hope I'm as spry as you when I reach your age." Until then, I did not think I was that much older than everyone else. Anyway, when I go down the Colorado again at age eighty, I look to do better than Canyon legend Bert Loper, who at that age, died shooting the rapids of the Colorado in a wooden dinghy.

L to R back row: Author, Jane, Justin, Nick, Max, Sam.
Down low in the water, Hyatt and Lani

Burgundy—Locks and Docks, Oui, Oui

It sounded like a wonderful idea. What a great way for me to reconnect with a dear childhood friend, Mike. Our careers had us going down different paths, he ending up in California, a noted medical researcher in infectious diseases, and me in the Midwest pursuing a career as a criminal and civil trial attorney. So when Mike called and suggested we rent a houseboat and, with our wives, cruise down a river in Burgundy, France, I jumped at the idea.

Never mind that none of us had any experience in boating (oh, I sailed an eight-foot Sunfish years ago, hardly qualifying me to pilot a forty-foot power vessel). We plunged head first into our adventure--Mike, Betsy, Diana and me, the four of us and our large houseboat (two bedrooms, a sitting room, a bathroom, and a kitchen), cruising down the river and through the locks. Locks? Wait just a cotton-pickin' minute! Take a forty-foot houseboat through over forty locks? This wasn't the Panama Canal, you know; and some of these river locks were barely wider than our houseboat!

The boat company had our concerns well in hand with a training program that lasted all of twenty minutes, half of which time was taken up with instructions on how to start the boat and how to use the kitchen and head (bathroom for you landlubbers) facilities. The owner gave us a map of the Yonne River and the Canal Du

Nivernais, and showed us where to turn in the boat, and we were on our way.

We discovered pretty quickly that a houseboat is not a car. Turning the steering wheel or applying the brakes (or more accurately, putting the engine into reverse) does not bring instant results or satisfaction. Depending on your speed and the direction and power of the current, it could take you a quarter of a mile to come to a complete stop or to finish executing a turn. This came into stark relief as we approached the first lock. Things had been going swimmingly, so to speak, until that lock came into view. We were going down river, which meant we would enter the lock high up, the water would empty out of the lock, and we would exit on the lower part of the river.

The gates to the lock were closed which meant we had to stop and wait. Mike, piloting the boat, kept inching closer to the lock and finally, put the engines in reverse but the boat did not stop--slow, yes, but not stop. To avoid crashing into the gate, Mike headed for the shoreline and ultimately did a wheelie heading us in the opposite direction.

Mike at the wheel

By the time he turned the boat around again, the lock gates were open and we headed in very, very slowly. We bounced off the side of the lock as I managed to throw a line around the stanchion on the top side of the lock and tied the boat very securely to it--a big mistake. While it halted the boat in the lock sure enough, I did not take in account the laws of gravity and physics. As the water emptied out of the lock, the boat, of course, began lowering in the lock, tightening the rope. When I realized what I had done the rope was so taut I could not release it. Slowly, the houseboat began tilting downward on one side of the lock, hanging by its line. I grabbed the axe at the boat's fire station and with two chops, severed the rope. Whomp, the boat went as it flopped back into the water in the lock.

Waiting as the lock empties

In my three years of high school French, my vocabulary memorization assignments never included French profanity, and it's a good thing, too. Otherwise I might have been highly insulted by what the lock keeper yelled at me as he shook his fist. After that, we learned that one of us had to get out of the boat stand on the lock pathway, and slowly release the line, letting it slide down around the stanchion.

Mike, letting the rope play out the proper way

The lock keepers, in happier times

I had similar problems to Mike the first time I piloted the boat into a lock. It just takes time to hone your judgment and instinct as to what the boat can and cannot do. By about the fourth lock we were seasoned veterans, and it was a good thing too, because we had close to forty locks still ahead of us. Some locks were DIY; there were no lock keepers and we had to operate the lock ourselves, having first to figure out the instructions, posted only in French.

Mike and Betsy working a do-it-yourself lock

We also learned things went a lot easier if you tipped the lock keeper on the way in. The boat company taught us none of that in our twenty-minute course. At the beginning there was some grumbling from my female shipmates that this was too much hard work for a vacation. I can understand that after taking some escorted boat tours where we sit, eat, sit, eat, tour, sit, eat and sleep. But after we got the hang of things, it became easier but still required physical labor.

NOW WHAT?

Diana tying up the boat at the shore of the river in the company of sheep

Make no mistake, despite our little traumas, we had a marvelous time. The four bicycles on the boat enabled us to ride into small towns along the river and explore, shop, sightsee, and sample the cuisine and wine. We'd buy provisions and cook our evening meals on the boat, sometimes eating them on the shore alongside of our tied-up houseboat.

Shopping

Cooking

One evening we docked at the city of Auxerre and treated ourselves to dinner at a five-star restaurant (with five-star prices!). Poor Betsy. Mike's wife watched in horror as Mike, Diana, and I reverted back to the ways of our old Bronx neighborhood where we would share meals from each other's plates, like family meals in a Chinese restaurant, thereby widening our experience of tasting the local cuisine. Betsy, a Baltimorean, would have none of it. She'd eat everything on her plate and not a morsel from anybody else's.

Five-star dining

Country dining-- The only photographic proof author was on trip

Picnicking by the boat

Before we turned the boat in we spent several hours cleaning it. In our eyes, at least, it was spick and span, and we fully expected to get the full return of our deposit. "The boat, she is dirty," the owner pronounced.

"I will keep the deposit and apply it to cleaning the houseboat." I guess I could have lived with this little scam, but not Mike. Well over six feet, when he stands up straight, he towered over this five and a half foot con man and let him have a verbal pasting. The Frenchman quickly backed off and returned our deposit.

When we reached Paris, I learned just how much of a renowned medical researcher my friend Mike was when he invited us to the Louis Pasteur Institute where he was honored and then delivered a talk on infectious diseases to the distinguished scientists at the Institute.

Betsy following the boat on a bicycle

Diana and Mike

Auschwitz and Josef Levi of Stuttgart

Although these memoirs are written in a light and humorous vein, one not-funny-at-all thing is worth telling here--my trip to Auschwitz, or in Polish, Oswiecim, the former site of the infamous Nazi extermination camp of World War II.

You've heard tales about my friend Fred Schwartz, the humorous practical joker. Well, he had a serious side, being a highly successful entrepreneur in the fur business in New York as Fred The Furrier of the Fur Vault and, on retirement, engaging in a variety of philanthropic activities, the most notable of which was the creation and founding of the Auschwitz Jewish Center, located in Oswiecim, where students of all persuasions come to learn about the Holocaust and Jewish culture, and memorialize the victims of the Nazis. Involved in the Auschwitz Jewish Center as a contributor, I was invited to go to Poland for the dedication of the Center and the synagogue in Oswiecim restored by the Center, and help facilitate an educational program on genocide for the benefit of mid-level leaders in developing countries. This was the first of what would be many such conferences to help recognize the signs of incipient threats of genocide and the steps to prevent it.

A tour of the concentration camp, including Birkenau, the killing center, needless to say, was heart rendering and gut wrenching. But with the exception of some survivors of the Holocaust who accompanied us on the trip, it was more traumatic for me. I'll tell you why.

As I related earlier, after the death of my father, my mother remarried when I was thirteen. We moved in with my stepfather, who had a full-time housekeeper, Martha Levi. She really wasn't a nanny to me but did look after me when my parents went on vacation. Over the years, we became fast friends. My oldest child, Sam, and Martha were very close. She was like an aunt to him.

Martha's father, Josef Levi, lived in Stuttgart (a city in southern Germany). Martha alone was fortunate to escape to America in 1938. When her parents and brother attempted to leave a few years later they were not so lucky--the Nazis closed the door on emigration and Martha's family found itself trapped in Germany. For a while, Martha was able to maintain contact with her family through the mails. Then she stopped hearing from them and her letters were returned unopened. She feared the worst and my family and I suffered along with her. When the war ended in 1945, I was fourteen and recall vividly when Martha got the news that the Josef Levi family of Stuttgart--her mother, father, and brother--had been gassed at Auschwitz. Needless to say it was very traumatic for her, and vicariously, for me and the rest of my family. I can tell you, it's something that will stay with me for the rest of my life.

We entered the Auschwitz Concentration Camp through a gate with the hypocritical sign, "*Arbeit macht frei*", a German phrase meaning "work shall set you free." At Auschwitz II, called Birkenau, we saw what was left of the gas chambers and crematoria where millions of Jews suffered horrible deaths. Later, a tour of the museum in Auschwitz exposed us to the grisly sight of what was left over from the victims: mounds of human hair (some of which was used to make soft slippers for the U-boat sailors), prosthetic arms, legs, and crutches; and thousands of shoes, combs, and other possessions. But what ultimately undid me was an exhibit of the luggage of the victims. Picture bags jammed floor to ceiling in the exhibit; of the thousands of pieces of luggage, one close to the front immediately caught my eye--a bag stenciled along its side with "Josef Levi, Stuttgart." Just like someone hammered me between the eyes with a club, I broke down and began crying for the family of my friend, a family I could never meet or get to know. It took me several minutes to compose myself so I could continue the tour. Having written a book on heroes of the Holocaust, it steeled my determination to continue writing on that subject and I published many more books, six at this writing.

VIII. ODDS AND ENDS

CARL L. STEINHOUSE

WHAT GOES AROUND . . .

Bringing up children is not easy. I am sure you have said to your children, as I have, "Just wait until you have your own children." I really shouldn't have wished that upon them, but truthfully, I do get some perverse pleasure from the same frustrations they now have in dealing with their children, my grandchildren.

Hair raising

My children, all three of them, at least as far as their hair is concerned, inherited my wife's curly locks (what I call, when my wife is not around, "brillo hair"). Left unattended, their hair could grow into wild, hugely round, afros. It bugged the hell out of me when my first child, son Sam, in high school, let his hair grow out into this huge billowing ball on the top of his head. No amount of cajoling could get him to go to the barber for at least a trim (he may have been getting back at me for the enforced short haircuts I gave him in his younger days in elementary school). Well guess what! His younger son, Nick, in high school and then college, with the same hair as his father, is fiercely resisting his old man's admonitions to trim back his afro, just as outstanding as his father's had been thirty-five years before. Ah, sweet justice.

384

NOW WHAT?

Grandson Nick, 2006

Son Sam, 1973

CARL L. STEINHOUSE

Declaration of Independence

Our second child, daughter Jane, was the most fiercely independent and headstrong, with virtually every discussion becoming a knock-down, drag-out fight.

In 2003, she and husband Max adopted an eight-month-old girl in China, travelling there to pick her up. And so we acquired our third grandchild, the beautiful and wonderfully delicious Sophia.

Author and Granddaughter Sophia, 2003

Sophia grew from that adorable baby into a beautiful girl, as headstrong with Jane as Jane had been with her mother. In pre-school, despite Jane's pleading, Sophia dug her heels in and eschewed the company of her mother anywhere in the vicinity of the school. She insisted Jane drop her off outside and leave--pronto. Ah, sweet justice. Oh yes, one other thing. Sophia loves to do what Jane would never have thought of doing: helping her mother by doing the dishes, and earlier in her life, folding her own diapers and sheets.

NOW WHAT?

Sophia, 2006

Sophia, 2013

Double Trouble

Cooper   *Jesse*

Our third and last child, daughter Lani, added two grandsons to our repertoire by delivering non-identical twin boys, Cooper and Jesse, in 2003. Beyond being hyperactive boys, it's too early to tell what form of justice the boys will be visiting on Lani, who, in her younger years, while managing to get into considerable trouble, was able, most of the time, skillfully to keep that knowledge from us, her parents.

Jesse and Cooper with halos? Yeah, sure. 2011

IX. RETIREMENT

CARL L. STEINHOUSE

I am Retired, so what Do I Do with the Rest of My Life?

When I announced to Diana, in 1993, at age 62, that I planned to retire because I suffered burnout from the pressure of trial work, and the firm would let me retire on a substantial retirement, her reaction was, "What? A type A personality like you? What are you going to do with yourself?

Without waiting for answers, her psychologist experience kicked in. She grabbed a pad and a ballpoint pen, handed it to me and said, "Make a list of the ten things you plan to do on retirement." She shoved all this into my unwilling hands.

Well, I managed to squeeze out ten things, such as metal sculpturing, woodworking, taking liberal arts courses that I studiously avoided in college, reading the classics . . . you get the picture. Result? I did none of those things (at least for the first 15 years of retirement). I did the one thing not on the list. I wrote.

It was discouraging. I wrote about what I knew: criminal legal work, in the form of two legal thrillers. Here's where I discovered a dirty little secret in the world of publishing. Agents and publishers are not interested in unpublished authors. It's a chicken and egg thing. Since I am not a published author, I cannot get an agent, much less a publisher, to even read my work, regardless of how good it is, and I firmly believe my writing is good. Submit it and it goes into the slush pile, to be shredded or returned unread.

Then I went on a trip to Eastern Europe and while in Budapest, Hungary, I discovered the heroic tale of Raoul Wallenberg, the Swede who saved a hundred thousand Jews in Hungary during World War Two. It inspired me to write the first of my heroes of the Holocaust.

390

On the same trip we were in Czechoslovakia, on a bus heading for the Theresienstadt concentration camp. One of my co-travelers told the story of one trip where the husband died and the wife refused to give up her vacation, so she had him boxed up and took him along as baggage. She challenged me to write a short story based on those facts--before we reach Theresienstadt! I had a hand-held computer, one of the first back then, and with my thumbs, batted out *The Boxing of Sean,* my first of many short stories--and one of my favorites.

Anyway, with my Wallenberg manuscript in hand, I discovered the world of self-publishing and the Print-on-Demand (POD) publishers. These POD publishers would print your book, and get it in the hands of wholesale distributors so that it could be ordered through most of the book sellers like Barnes & Noble and the late Borders Book Stores. But the snobbery of the publishing world extended right down to the sellers, who turned their noses up at POD books. Oh, they'd order them quick enough for customers, but stock them on their shelves? Rarely. So, for awhile, I ran around to the book stores begging and pleading with them to carry my books. Occasionally, they would deign to permit me to have a book signing in one of their stores, so they'd carry a few of my books to sell during the signing. But even that dried up after awhile and I sold most of my book through speaking engagements and through my website. Even when I received excellent reviews, no one in the publishing world was interested.

So I decided that I would not give up my day job (just an expression, I had no such job) but would continue to write for enjoyment. I authored five additional Heroes of the Holocaust books, all POD published. And then I discovered the world of digital books. Remember those two legal thrillers early in my retirement? Well, I updated and rewrote them (I learned a lot since my first writings) and I forsook POD publishing, which is not inexpensive. Instead, for virtually no cost, I could upload those books, *Harassment* and *Extreme Malice* and sell them on Amazon (Kindle), Barnes & Noble (Nook), and Apple, and keep 75% of the selling price. So that's what I did, but it did not end there. I also uploaded all my Heroes of the Holocaust books, and now get quarterly royalty checks, which I can't live on, but it's nice nevertheless.

What Is This Thing Called Golf?—2001

Everybody hates to hear golfers relive in excruciating detail, their last round on the golf course. Who gives a damn if he--or she--hooks the stupid little white (or yellow, or pink) ball into the lake and, hitting a turtle shell, miraculously rebounds back onto the fairway? Big deal.

Having said all that, I will nevertheless continue with the unusual event of one of my rounds of golf. First, you must understand that I am a lousy golfer who has not improved in three years. I shoot between 98 and 105 come hell or high water. I may start off with a bang but inevitably I self-destruct--usually after indulging myself in some fantasy that I have now finally, finally, figured out this masochistic game.

Let's face it--I'm miserable on the golf course. So why do I play? Because just maybe, the next round will be my breakthrough, that's why. Of course, I'm kidding myself. Let's face it--I plunked down a bundle of money to join this club and I paid a bundle in annual dues--so, by God, I was determined to get my money's worth and enjoy this game, whether I liked it or not.

I used to be a tennis buff, and unlike my golf game, I was a pretty good club player. I used to kid my golfing buddies that I would take up that sport (and I use that term loosely) after my first heart attack. Well, I didn't have a heart attack, but I did have a minor stroke, which affected my ability to make contact with a tennis ball on my racket, especially at the net. So what the hell, I took up golf. And it was fun at first, because I was taking lessons and hadn't actually played on a golf course. I soon learned that hitting the ball off an artificial mat at a driving range was a lot different than hitting the ball out of tall grass, pine needles, mud, and sand. Golf is such a stupid game that in areas where there is no sand for thousands of miles, they import it and surround the holes so even if you should be fortunate to get the little ball anywhere near the green, you are assured a fine time trying to blast it out of the trap of soft sand with an implement particularly unsuited for the task.

Anyway, I'm getting off the subject. Recently, I shot my usual game on the front nine--missed putts, shanked irons, and sliced drives, but struggled for a 48, not bad for me. Was I happy? Of course not. I cursed my way through the first nine holes--not that something unusually bad occurred; I always curse my way through the first nine holes. It gives me good practice for the second nine holes. I stepped up to the tee on the tenth hole and drove the ball about 220 yards down the middle. That's very good for me--for two reasons: If I drive the ball 150 yards, I'm lucky, and I almost never hit it down the middle of the fairway. Now you see why I curse.

"Good shot, Steinhouse," the chorus of my partners rang out in unison. I took the compliment with a grain of salt because I knew what they meant. For most proficient golfers it would be an average shot, but for a duffer.... Well, you understand.

"Don't worry, guys, I'll screw up the second shot." Now you have a good idea of my attitude--and it's not an unfounded one for it seems that every time I hit a good drive off the tee, I flub the second shot. It's almost axiomatic.

Anyway, there I was, just 70 yards from the pin, which was surrounded in the most literal sense of the term by high sand traps. If you hit the shot just a smidgen short, you could bury your ball in the sand; and if you gave it a little extra to clear the traps, you could roll down the green, which were slanted downward from the traps and toward the lake. If you were lucky, you didn't roll into the water.

I took my wedge. With no confidence whatsoever, took a mighty swing. Wonder of wonders! I actually hit down into the ball like you are supposed to, clearing the traps and landing on the green. Because of the height of the traps and the green, I could not see what happened to my ball once it reached the green. "You hit the green," my partner yelled, "let's hope it didn't roll off into the water." In case I wasn't already pessimistic enough!

I drove the cart around the traps and looked on the green hopefully. There were two balls on the green and one in the sand trap. With great expectation, I checked the closest ball to the hole. Not mine--shit. I checked the other ball on the green. Not mine--crap. The ball in the sand trap was another player's. I sighed. I took out my ball retriever and went to the pond where, obviously, my ball had rolled in. There was too much algae and I did not have the patience to spend time mucking around for a 75-cent used golf ball, so I dropped another down in the grass beside the bank and chipped it too hard. It rolled off the other end of the green and into the sand trap. I let out a string of obscenities that would embarrass even my children.

While I walked around to green to the trap, one of the other players putted his ball into the cup. "Hey," he yelled, "there's a ball in here already. A number 2 Pinnacle."

It was mine. On that par four hole, I had shot a two--an eagle, the first of my life. My ball had hit the green and rolled square into the hole. And nobody saw it. I couldn't even enjoy the spectacle of my first eagle. That's golf for you.

I got a three on the next hole, which was par. So here I was, with an eagle and a par on the first two holes of the back nine--a total of five strokes where I normally have ten strokes--if I'm lucky. I'm on my way to my best score ever!

Brimming with unwarranted confidence and convinced that I finally had this game figured out, I stepped up to the tee on the next hole and drove the ball far--into the lake. I managed to flub my way through the rest of the back nine ending up with a 49, one more than I had on the front nine, where I had neither pars nor eagles.

Screw golf.

NOW WHAT?

Concession to Age

We bit the bullet, forsook our life in the golfing country club community, sold our home there, and bought into an old age home. Not really--a retirement community of independent living for seniors. That's a mouthful, but all it means is that we continue to live the same way we did before--independently--until one or both of us cannot do so, in which case the community has "assisted living" (on the premises). No searching wildly for such a facility because it is part and parcel of our community. After all, we have reached our eighth decade and things are more likely to happen than not. But don't feel sorry for us. We live in a large, beautiful high rise apartment with spectacular views of the Gulf of Mexico, with east and west lanais to enjoy both the sunrises and sunsets. And so far, knock on wood, we don't need assistance.

Oh yes, guess what? I took up golf again with my neighbor and buddy John Francis Dill. We discovered "don't-give-a-damn golf". We found an inexpensive golf club with an easy 18-hole course; we play with no rules, no out of bounds, unlimited mulligans, and we cheat like hell on the score. And best of all, neither of us gives a tinker's damn. We have a good time, ending our golf game with hot salted pretzels and iced tea at the Subway in Wal-Mart's, hovered over by our attentive, always-on-the-job server, MaryAnn.

John is truly a man after my own heart. And why shouldn't he be? We both were in the army during the period of the Korean War and, as it turns out, we were both fellow veterans of the Counter Intelligence Corps, and proud of it.

The only fly in the ointment is that he was an officer and I, a lowly NCO. And while he doesn't throw

397

it up to me, he does occasionally don his full-dress lieutenant's uniform, obviously to impress me. I have no answer because my Ike jacket doesn't even come close to fitting me!

John Francis Dill, easy-going golf partner and mulligan and gimme grantor. Also, neighbor, fellow CIC man, great tenor, superb dresser, and good friend.

NOW WHAT?

Reflections on My Memoirs-Or, at Each Stage of My Life, Why Was the Grass Always Greener Elsewhere?

Oh, I'd love to be finished with NYU and out into the world--even if it's the army--I'll make my mark as a financial officer, after all, I am an accountant!

Well, I went summers and graduated a year early. I'm drafted into the army! Real life at last! Wait a minute. It's 1952 and I'm a grunt in the infantry--basic training, KP, obstacle courses, crawling through barbed wire and under fire of live ammunition and I am facing lord knows what in the Korean War. The army doesn't give a damn that I'm an accountant. If only I was in another branch of the service.

Good news! In my last week of basic training, I receive orders to report to Counter Intelligence Corps School. I become a secret agent. Wow! However, reality sets in. I am only an intelligence analyst. The job is 95% boring paperwork and 5% sheer terror, confronting Red agents coming across the Iron Curtain border. If only I could go back to civilian life and start my calm accounting career.

At last! Discharged from the army, I start my career as a CPA. As a junior account I do all the miserable work. I'm being used as a bookkeeper, not an accountant! Boring, boring, and boring. Is this my career, the one I studied for four years in college? I must escape! On to law school at night. Speaking of drudgery--work all day (six days a week during tax season) and go to school at night, come home and prepare the lessons for the next night. Ah, to be finished with law school, out of accounting and into the practice of law as a litigator.

Graduation at last! In my new job as a prosecutor--gonna put them all in jail and make a name for myself. Wait a second! Law is 97% dreary preparation, discovery, and brief writing and 3% courtroom trial work and that 3% comes with the utter fear of making a fool of myself. My Lord, I have to constantly think on my feet in court. If I am to endure this pressure why shouldn't I be paid like those attorneys in private practice? Oh, to be in private practice!

A prestigious law firm hires me at double my government salary! Wait a minute--why can't you simply let me practice law? I have to get clients; be a rainmaker? Where the hell am I going to get clients? Oh, that's my problem, is it? I also have to bill clients and make sure I collect the fees from them? Hell, that's no fun. It'll be great when I can retire and write the great American novel.

I'm retired with my gold watch, at last! Now I can write fiction and non-fiction--and I do. Is the grass really greener? Well--it would be if I could only get a real publisher for these Memoirs. . .